Theory of Structured Parallel Programming

Theory of Structured Parallel Programming

Yong Wang
Department of Computer Science and Technology
Faculty of Information Technology
Beijing University of Technology
Beijing, China

MK
MORGAN KAUFMANN PUBLISHERS
ELSEVIER AN IMPRINT OF ELSEVIER

Morgan Kaufmann is an imprint of Elsevier
50 Hampshire Street, 5th Floor, Cambridge, MA 02139, United States

ISBN: 978-0-443-24814-6

For information on all Morgan Kaufmann publications
visit our website at https://www.elsevier.com/books-and-journals

Publisher: Mara Conner
Acquisitions Editor: Chris Katsaropoulos
Editorial Project Manager: Sangeeta Gaur
Production Project Manager: Gomathi Sugumar
Cover Designer: Victoria Pearson Esser

Typeset by VTeX

Contents

1 Introduction

Parallel computing [1] [2] is becoming more and more important. Traditional parallelism often existed in distributed computing, since distributed systems are usually autonomous and local computer is single-core and single-processor and timed (Timed computing is serial in nature). Today, due to the progress of hardware, multi-cores, multi-processors, and GPUs make the local computer truly parallel.

Parallel programming language has a relatively long research history. There have been always two ways: one is the structured way, and the other is the graph-based (true concurrent) way. The structured way is often based on the interleaving semantics, such as process algebra CCS. Since the parallelism in interleaving semantics is not a fundamental computational pattern (the parallel operator can be replaced by alternative composition and sequential composition), the parallel operator often does not occur as an explicit operator, such as the mainstream programming languages C, C++, Java, etc.

The graph-based way is also called true concurrency [3] [4] [5]. There also have been some ways to structure the graph [6] [7], but these work only considered the causal relation in the graph, and neglected the confliction and even the communication. And there are also industrial efforts to adopt the graph-based way, such as the workflow description language WSFL. The later workflow description language BPEL adopts both the structured way and the graph-based way. Why does BPEL not adopt the structured way only? It is because that the expressive power of the structured way is limited. Then why does BPEL not adopt the graph-based way only? It is just because that the graph could not be structured at that time and the structured way is the basis on implementing a compiler.

We have done some work on truly concurrent process algebra [8], which proved that truly concurrent process algebra is a generalization of traditional process algebra and had a side effect on the structuring true concurrency.

Now, it is the time to do some work on structured parallel programming under the background of programming language and parallel software engineering. On one side, traditional structured programming got great successes in sequential computation [9] [10]; on the other side, current structured parallel programming focused on parallel patterns (also known as parallel skeletons, templates, archetypes) [11] [12] [13] [14] [15], with comparison to structured sequential programming, the corresponding structured parallel programming with solid foundation still is missing.

In this book, we try to clarify structured parallel programming corresponding to traditional structured sequential programming. This book is organized as follows. In Chapter 2, we introduce the backgrounds of structured and unstructured parallelism. We introduce truly concurrent process algebra APTC in Chapter 3, guarded APTC in Chapter 4, and distributed APTC in Chapter 5. The so-called building blocks based structured parallel programming is introduced in Chapter 6. We introduce the modeling and verification of

Theory of Structured Parallel Programming. https://doi.org/10.1016/B978-0-44-324814-6.00005-8

parallel programming language in Chapter 7, of parallel programming patterns in Chapter 8, and of distributed systems in Chapter 9. Finally, in Appendix A, we introduce a parallel programming language.

2 Parallelism and concurrency

In this chapter, we analyze the concepts of parallelism and concurrency, unstructured parallelism, and structured parallelism.

We introduce unstructured parallelism in Section 2.1, structured parallelism in Section 2.2, and the way from unstructured parallelism to structured parallelism in Section 2.3. In Section 2.4, we give the foundation of unstructured and structured parallel computation.

2.1 Unstructured parallelism – true concurrency

True concurrency is usually defined by a graph-like structure [4] [5], such as DAG (Directed Acyclic Graph), Petri net, and event structure. As follows, we give the definition of Prime Event Structure.

Definition 2.1 (Prime event structure). Let Λ be a fixed set of labels, ranged over $a, \cdots$. A (Λ-labeled) prime event structure is a tuple $\mathcal{E} = \langle \mathbb{E}, \leq, \sharp, \lambda \rangle$, where $\mathbb{E}$ is a denumerable set of events. Let $\lambda : \mathbb{E} \to \Lambda$ be a labeling function. And $\leq$, $\sharp$ are binary relations on $\mathbb{E}$, called causality and conflict respectively, such that:

1. $\leq$ is a partial order and $\lceil e \rceil = \{e' \in \mathbb{E} | e' \leq e\}$ is finite for all $e \in \mathbb{E}$.
2. $\sharp$ is irreflexive, symmetric, and hereditary with respect to $\leq$, that is, for all $e, e', e'' \in \mathbb{E}$, if $e \sharp e' \leq e''$, then $e \sharp e''$.

Then, the concepts of consistency and concurrency can be drawn from the above definition:

1. $e, e' \in \mathbb{E}$ are consistent, denoted as $e \frown e'$, if $\neg(e \sharp e')$. A subset $X \subseteq \mathbb{E}$ is called consistent, if $e \frown e'$ for all $e, e' \in X$.
2. $e, e' \in \mathbb{E}$ are concurrent, denoted as $e \parallel e'$, if $\neg(e \leq e')$, $\neg(e' \leq e)$, and $\neg(e \sharp e')$.

In the Prime Event Structure defined true concurrency, we can see that there exist two kinds of unstructured relations: causality and confliction. Fig. 2.1 and Fig. 2.2 illustrates these two kinds of concurrency (for the simplicity, we separate the causal relation and the conflict relation).

Fig. 2.1 illustrates an example of primitives (atomic actions, events) with causal relations. Note that, primitives, atomic actions, and events are almost the same concepts under different backgrounds of computer science, and we will use them with no differences.

Fig. 2.2 illustrates an example of atomic actions with causal relations and conflict relations. There exists a conflict relation between the second action in the left parallel branch

Theory of Structured Parallel Programming. https://doi.org/10.1016/B978-0-44-324814-6.00006-X

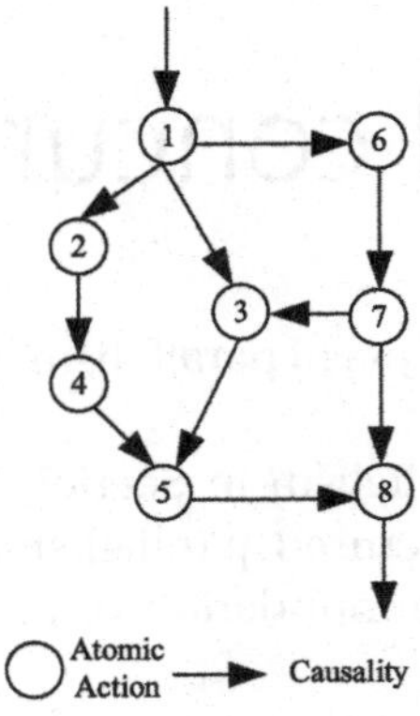

FIGURE 2.1 An example of unstructured parallelism.

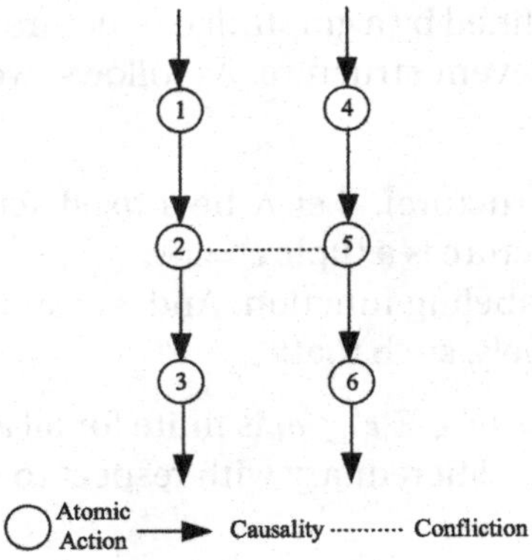

FIGURE 2.2 Another example of unstructured parallelism.

and the second action in the right parallel branch, if the condition *b* is **true**, then the second action and its subsequent actions in the left branch can execute, else the second action and its subsequent actions in the right branch will execute.

2.2 Structured parallelism

Comparing to structured programming in sequential computation [9] [10], we can intuitionally add a structured parallelism to the existed three basic programming structures (sequence, choice, and iteration) of structured sequential programming, to form four basic programming structures of structured parallel programming: sequence, choice, iteration, and parallelism. The intuitions and flow charts of the four basic structures are as follows.

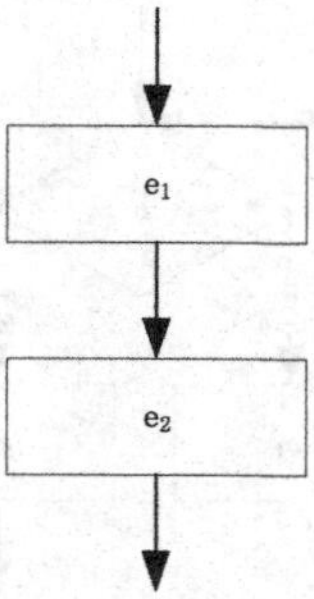

FIGURE 2.3 Sequence structure.

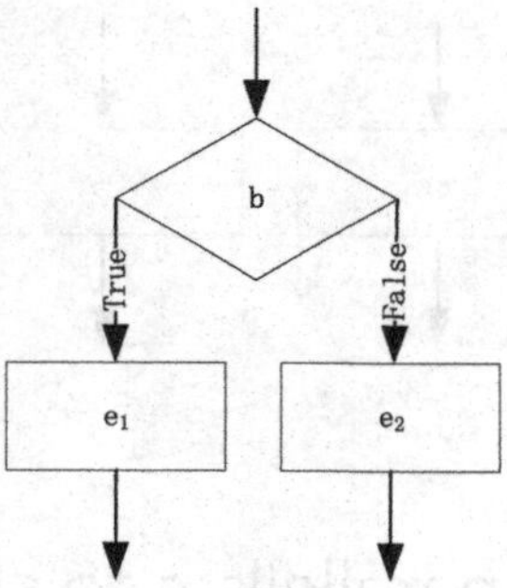

FIGURE 2.4 Choice structure.

The intuition of sequence (;) of two clauses $e_1; e_2$ is that after the successful execution of e_1, e_2 executes. The corresponding flow chat is shown in Fig. 2.3.

The intuition of choice if (b) then e_1 else e_2 is that if the condition b is **true**, then e_1 executes, else e_2 executes. The corresponding flow chat is shown in Fig. 2.4.

The intuition of iteration while (b) do e_1 is that while the condition b is **true**, then e_1 executes many times. The corresponding flow chat is shown in Fig. 2.5.

The intuition of parallelism ($\|$) of two clauses $e_1 \parallel e_2$ is that e_1 and e_2 execute simultaneously. The corresponding flow chat is shown in Fig. 2.6.

The programming of atomic actions, mixed by the above four structures is called structured parallel programming. We define Structured Parallel Program inductively as follows.

Definition 2.2 (Structured parallel program). Let the set of all primitives denote $\mathbb{P}$. A Structured Parallel Program SPP is inductively defined as follows:

1. $\mathbb{P} \subset SPP$;
2. If $e_1 \in SPP$ and $e_2 \in SPP$, then $e_1; e_2 \in SPP$;
3. If b is a condition, $e_1 \in SPP$, and $e_2 \in SPP$, then if (b) then e_1 else $e_2 \in SPP$;
4. If b is a condition, $e \in SPP$, then while (b) do $e \in SPP$;
5. If $e_1 \in SPP$ and $e_2 \in SPP$, then $e_1 \parallel e_2 \in SPP$.

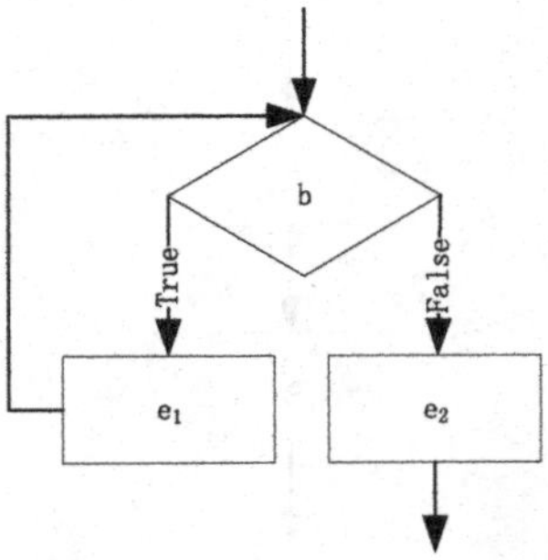

FIGURE 2.5 Iteration structure.

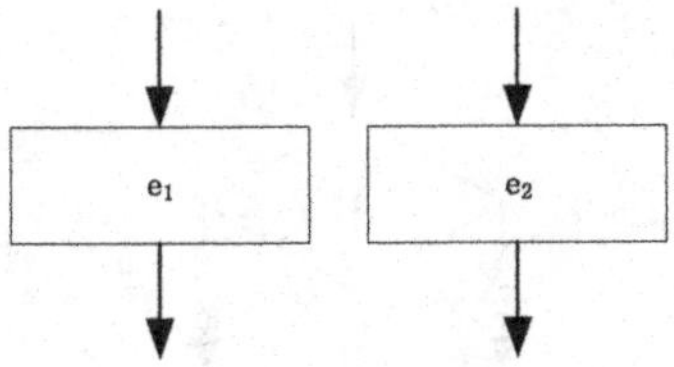

FIGURE 2.6 Parallelism structure.

2.3 From unstructured parallelism to structured parallelism

The examples in Fig. 2.1 and 2.2 are two kinds of typical unstructured parallelism. In this section, we try to structure these unstructured parallelisms.

Firstly, the unstructured causalities in the same parallel branch can be structured by the famous conclusion that Goto statement is harmful [9] and also the similarly well-known structured (sequential) programming [10]; and for unstructured causalities, we find the example in Fig. 2.1 can not be structured, and the proof is stated in the following conclusions.

Proposition 2.3. *The example in Fig. 2.1 can not be structured.*

Proof. The actions 3 and 6 have the same causal pioneer 1, they should be in different parallel branches. But, the action 6 is the causal pioneer of the action 3 through the action 7, so, they should be in the same parallel branch. These cause contradictions. □

How can we deal this situation? Yes, we can classify the causal relations into two kinds: one is traditional sequential causality, and the other is the communication between different parallel branches, since the causality between parallel branches being communication is reasonable. Fig. 2.7 is the causality-classified one originated from Fig. 2.1. This classification should be clarified during modeling time, that is, the programmer should draw Fig. 2.7 directly, instead of drawing Fig. 2.1 and then transforming it to Fig. 2.7, in the modeling

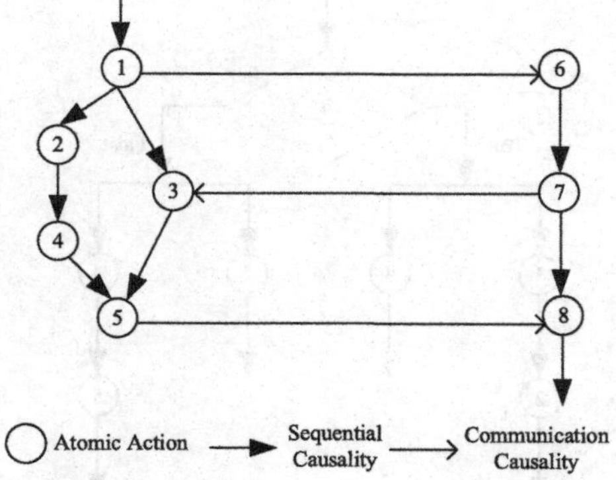

FIGURE 2.7 An example of structuring unstructured parallelism.

phase. Note that, multi-parties communications can be steadied by a series of two-parties communications without any loss.

Then the causality-classified parallelism can be structured, we show the structuring way of synchronous and asynchronous communications.

For synchronous communication, the program corresponding to Fig. 2.1 can be written as follows:

$$(1; ((2; 4) \parallel 3); 5) \parallel (6; 7; 8)$$

with three unstructured communications $sc_{1,6}$, $sc_{7,3}$, and $sc_{5,8}$.

The above program can be structured and equivalent to the following program:

$$sc_{1,6}; ((2; 4) \parallel sc_{7,3}); sc_{5,8}$$

We can see that the above program is structured, though the equivalence of the above two programs is not obvious. We will explain it through an rigorous way in the following chapters.

For asynchronous communication, the program corresponding to Fig. 2.1 can be written as follows:

$$(1; ((2; 4) \parallel 3); 5) \parallel (6; 7; 8)$$

with three unstructured constraints $1 \leq 6$, $7 \leq 3$, and $5 \leq 8$. Note that, $\leq$ is the causal relation.

The above program can be structured and equivalent to the following program:

$$(1; ((2; 4) \parallel \text{if } (7 \leq 3) \text{ then } 3 \text{ else } \textbf{skip}); 5) \parallel (\text{if } (1 \leq 6) \text{ then } 6 \text{ else } \textbf{skip}; 7; \text{if } (5 \leq 8) \text{ then } 8 \text{ else } \textbf{skip}).$$

Note that **skip** is a voidness primitive.

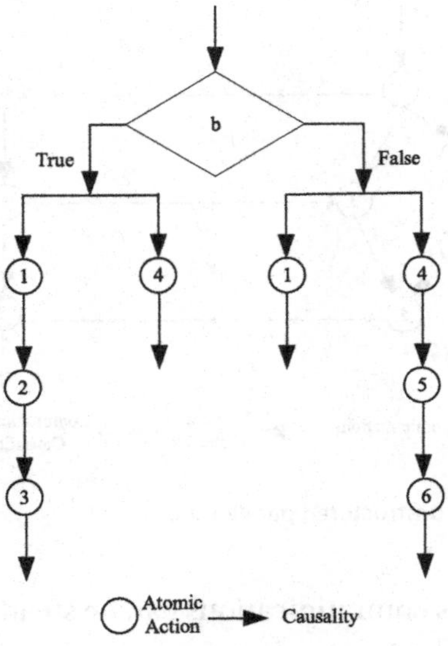

FIGURE 2.8 Another example of structuring unstructured parallelism.

The above conditions, like $1 \leq 6$, $7 \leq 3$, and $5 \leq 8$, are not based on the traditional results of data manipulation. Asynchronous communications are usually implemented by inserting an intermediate data structure, like mailbox or queue, between the two communicating partners, so, the above conditions can be the results of checking the data structure if the data are received in the data structure by the receiver. If the receiver has the ability to be blocked until the data are received, then the above conditions can be removed, and the structured program is the original one:

$$(1; ((2; 4) \parallel 3); 5) \parallel (6; 7; 8)$$

without any constraint.

Then, it is turn to consider the unstructured conflictions between different parallel branches, since it is already proven that conflictions in the same parallel branch can be structured [10], as the choice structure is a kind of structured confliction. Fig. 2.2 illustrates this kind of unstructured conflictions and can be expressed by the following program:

$$(1; 2; 3) \parallel (4; 5; 6)$$

with an unstructured confliction $2 \sharp 5$, and a condition b, if b is **true** then the primitive 2 and its successors execute, else the primitive 5 and its successors execute.

Fig. 2.2 can be structured by Fig. 2.8. The structured program corresponding to Fig. 2.8 is:

$$\text{if } (b) \text{ then } (1; 2; 3) \parallel 4 \text{ else } 1 \parallel (4; 5; 6)$$

2.4 Foundation of unstructured and structured parallelism

There existed several parallel machines [17] [18] to provide the foundation for unstructured and structured parallelism since quite long time ago. Among them, the one (or multi)-tapes multi-heads Turing machine called PTM (Parallel Turing Machine) [17] provides an intuitive foundation. The unstructured causalities and conflicts can be modeled as communications among the tape heads.

Prather [19] built the so-called structured Turing machines with the four basic structures (sequence, choice, iteration, and parallelism), which can realize every partial recursive function by a structured connection of simple machines.

3 Truly concurrent process algebra

In this chapter, we introduce the preliminaries on truly concurrent process algebra [8], which is based on truly concurrent operational semantics.

APTC eliminates the differences of structures of transition system, event structure, etc., and discusses their behavioral equivalences. It considers that there are two kinds of causality relations: the chronological order modeled by the sequential composition and the causal order between different parallel branches modeled by the communication merge. It also considers that there exist two kinds of confliction relations: the structural confliction modeled by the alternative composition and the conflictions in different parallel branches which should be eliminated. Based on conservative extension, there are four modules in APTC: BATC (Basic Algebra for True Concurrency), APTC (Algebra for Parallelism in True Concurrency), recursion, and abstraction.

3.1 Operational semantics

The semantics of ACP is based on bisimulation/rooted branching bisimulation equivalences, and the modularity of ACP relies on the concept of conservative extension, for the conveniences, we introduce some concepts and conclusions on them.

Definition 3.1 (Bisimulation). A bisimulation relation R is a binary relation on processes such that: (1) if pRq and $p \xrightarrow{a} p'$ then $q \xrightarrow{a} q'$ with $p'Rq'$; (2) if pRq and $q \xrightarrow{a} q'$ then $p \xrightarrow{a} p'$ with $p'Rq'$; (3) if pRq and pP, then qP; (4) if pRq and qP, then pP. Two processes p and q are bisimilar, denoted by $p \sim_{HM} q$, if there is a bisimulation relation R such that pRq.

Definition 3.2 (Congruence). Let Σ be a signature. An equivalence relation R on $\mathcal{T}(\Sigma)$ is a congruence if for each $f \in \Sigma$, if $s_i R t_i$ for $i \in \{1, \cdots, ar(f)\}$, then $f(s_1, \cdots, s_{ar(f)}) R f(t_1, \cdots, t_{ar(f)})$.

Definition 3.3 (Branching bisimulation). A branching bisimulation relation R is a binary relation on the collection of processes such that: (1) if pRq and $p \xrightarrow{a} p'$ then either $a \equiv \tau$ and $p'Rq$ or there is a sequence of (zero or more) τ-transitions $q \xrightarrow{\tau} \cdots \xrightarrow{\tau} q_0$ such that pRq_0 and $q_0 \xrightarrow{a} q'$ with $p'Rq'$; (2) if pRq and $q \xrightarrow{a} q'$ then either $a \equiv \tau$ and pRq' or there is a sequence of (zero or more) τ-transitions $p \xrightarrow{\tau} \cdots \xrightarrow{\tau} p_0$ such that p_0Rq and $p_0 \xrightarrow{a} p'$ with $p'Rq'$; (3) if pRq and pP, then there is a sequence of (zero or more) τ-transitions $q \xrightarrow{\tau} \cdots \xrightarrow{\tau} q_0$ such that pRq_0 and q_0P; (4) if pRq and qP, then there is a sequence of (zero or more) τ-transitions $p \xrightarrow{\tau} \cdots \xrightarrow{\tau} p_0$ such that p_0Rq and p_0P. Two processes p and q are branching bisimilar, denoted by $p \approx_{bHM} q$, if there is a branching bisimulation relation R such that pRq.

Definition 3.4 (Rooted branching bisimulation). A rooted branching bisimulation relation R is a binary relation on processes such that: (1) if pRq and $p \xrightarrow{a} p'$ then $q \xrightarrow{a} q'$ with

Theory of Structured Parallel Programming. https://doi.org/10.1016/B978-0-44-324814-6.00007-1

$p' \approx_{bHM} q'$; (2) if pRq and $q \xrightarrow{a} q'$ then $p \xrightarrow{a} p'$ with $p' \approx_{bHM} q'$; (3) if pRq and pP, then qP; (4) if pRq and qP, then pP. Two processes p and q are rooted branching bisimilar, denoted by $p \approx_{rbHM} q$, if there is a rooted branching bisimulation relation R such that pRq.

Definition 3.5 (Conservative extension). Let T_0 and T_1 be TSSs (transition system specifications) over signatures Σ_0 and Σ_1, respectively. The TSS $T_0 \oplus T_1$ is a conservative extension of T_0 if the LTSs (labeled transition systems) generated by T_0 and $T_0 \oplus T_1$ contain exactly the same transitions $t \xrightarrow{a} t'$ and tP with $t \in \mathcal{T}(\Sigma_0)$.

Definition 3.6 (Source-dependency). The source-dependent variables in a transition rule of ρ are defined inductively as follows: (1) all variables in the source of ρ are source-dependent; (2) if $t \xrightarrow{a} t'$ is a premise of ρ and all variables in t are source-dependent, then all variables in t' are source-dependent. A transition rule is source-dependent if all its variables are. A TSS is source-dependent if all its rules are.

Definition 3.7 (Freshness). Let T_0 and T_1 be TSSs over signatures Σ_0 and Σ_1, respectively. A term in $\mathbb{T}(T_0 \oplus T_1)$ is said to be fresh if it contains a function symbol from $\Sigma_1 \setminus \Sigma_0$. Similarly, a transition label or predicate symbol in T_1 is fresh if it does not occur in T_0.

Theorem 3.8 (Conservative extension). *Let T_0 and T_1 be TSSs over signatures Σ_0 and Σ_1, respectively, where T_0 and $T_0 \oplus T_1$ are positive after reduction. Under the following conditions, $T_0 \oplus T_1$ is a conservative extension of T_0. (1) T_0 is source-dependent. (2) For each $\rho \in T_1$, either the source of ρ is fresh, or ρ has a premise of the form $t \xrightarrow{a} t'$ or tP, where $t \in \mathbb{T}(\Sigma_0)$, all variables in t occur in the source of ρ and t', a or P is fresh.*

3.2 Proof techniques

In this subsection, we introduce the concepts and conclusions about elimination, which is very important in the proof of completeness theorem.

Definition 3.9 (Elimination property). Let a process algebra with a defined set of basic terms as a subset of the set of closed terms over the process algebra. Then the process algebra has the elimination to basic terms property if for every closed term s of the algebra, there exists a basic term t of the algebra such that the algebra $\vdash s = t$.

Definition 3.10 (Strongly normalizing). A term s_0 is called strongly normalizing if does not have an infinite series of reductions beginning in s_0.

Definition 3.11. We write $s >_{lpo} t$ if $s \rightarrow^+ t$ where $\rightarrow^+$ is the transitive closure of the reduction relation defined by the transition rules of an algebra.

Theorem 3.12 (Strong normalization). *Let a term rewriting system (TRS) with finitely many rewriting rules and let $>$ be a well-founded ordering on the signature of the corresponding algebra. If $s >_{lpo} t$ for each rewriting rule $s \rightarrow t$ in the TRS, then the term rewriting system is strongly normalizing.*

3.3 Basic algebra for true concurrency

BATC has sequential composition $\cdot$ and alternative composition $+$ to capture the chronological ordered causality and the structural confliction. The constants are ranged over A, the set of atomic actions. The algebraic laws on $\cdot$ and $+$ are sound and complete modulo truly concurrent bisimulation equivalences (including pomset bisimulation, step bisimulation, hp-bisimulation, and hhp-bisimulation).

Definition 3.13 (Prime event structure with silent event). Let Λ be a fixed set of labels, ranged over $a, b, c, \cdots$ and τ. A (Λ-labeled) prime event structure with silent event τ is a tuple $\mathcal{E} = \langle \mathbb{E}, \leq, \sharp, \lambda \rangle$, where $\mathbb{E}$ is a denumerable set of events, including the silent event τ. Let $\hat{\mathbb{E}} = \mathbb{E} \backslash \{\tau\}$, exactly excluding τ, it is obvious that $\hat{\tau^*} = \epsilon$, where ϵ is the empty event. Let $\lambda : \mathbb{E} \to \Lambda$ be a labeling function and let $\lambda(\tau) = \tau$. And $\leq$, $\sharp$ are binary relations on $\mathbb{E}$, called causality and conflict respectively, such that:

1. $\leq$ is a partial order and $\lceil e \rceil = \{e' \in \mathbb{E} | e' \leq e\}$ is finite for all $e \in \mathbb{E}$. It is easy to see that $e \leq \tau^* \leq e' = e \leq \tau \leq \cdots \leq \tau \leq e'$, then $e \leq e'$.
2. $\sharp$ is irreflexive, symmetric and hereditary with respect to $\leq$, that is, for all $e, e', e'' \in \mathbb{E}$, if $e \sharp e' \leq e''$, then $e \sharp e''$.

Then, the concepts of consistency and concurrency can be drawn from the above definition:

1. $e, e' \in \mathbb{E}$ are consistent, denoted as $e \frown e'$, if $\neg(e \sharp e')$. A subset $X \subseteq \mathbb{E}$ is called consistent, if $e \frown e'$ for all $e, e' \in X$.
2. $e, e' \in \mathbb{E}$ are concurrent, denoted as $e \parallel e'$, if $\neg(e \leq e')$, $\neg(e' \leq e)$, and $\neg(e \sharp e')$.

Definition 3.14 (Configuration). Let $\mathcal{E}$ be a PES. A (finite) configuration in $\mathcal{E}$ is a (finite) consistent subset of events $C \subseteq \mathcal{E}$, closed with respect to causality (i.e. $\lceil C \rceil = C$). The set of finite configurations of $\mathcal{E}$ is denoted by $\mathcal{C}(\mathcal{E})$. We let $\hat{C} = C \backslash \{\tau\}$.

A consistent subset of $X \subseteq \mathbb{E}$ of events can be seen as a pomset. Given $X, Y \subseteq \mathbb{E}$, $\hat{X} \sim \hat{Y}$ if $\hat{X}$ and $\hat{Y}$ are isomorphic as pomsets. In the following of the paper, we say $C_1 \sim C_2$, we mean $\hat{C_1} \sim \hat{C_2}$.

Definition 3.15 (Pomset transitions and step). Let $\mathcal{E}$ be a PES and let $C \in \mathcal{C}(\mathcal{E})$, and $\emptyset \neq X \subseteq \mathbb{E}$, if $C \cap X = \emptyset$ and $C' = C \cup X \in \mathcal{C}(\mathcal{E})$, then $C \xrightarrow{X} C'$ is called a pomset transition from C to C'. When the events in X are pairwise concurrent, we say that $C \xrightarrow{X} C'$ is a step.

Definition 3.16 (Pomset, step bisimulation). Let $\mathcal{E}_1$, $\mathcal{E}_2$ be PESs. A pomset bisimulation is a relation $R \subseteq \mathcal{C}(\mathcal{E}_1) \times \mathcal{C}(\mathcal{E}_2)$, such that if $(C_1, C_2) \in R$, and $C_1 \xrightarrow{X_1} C_1'$ then $C_2 \xrightarrow{X_2} C_2'$, with $X_1 \subseteq \mathbb{E}_1$, $X_2 \subseteq \mathbb{E}_2$, $X_1 \sim X_2$ and $(C_1', C_2') \in R$, and vice-versa. We say that $\mathcal{E}_1$, $\mathcal{E}_2$ are pomset bisimilar, written $\mathcal{E}_1 \sim_p \mathcal{E}_2$, if there exists a pomset bisimulation R, such that $(\emptyset, \emptyset) \in R$. By replacing pomset transitions with steps, we can get the definition of step bisimulation. When PESs $\mathcal{E}_1$ and $\mathcal{E}_2$ are step bisimilar, we write $\mathcal{E}_1 \sim_s \mathcal{E}_2$.

Table 3.1 Axioms of BATC.

No.	Axiom
$A1$	$x+y=y+x$
$A2$	$(x+y)+z=x+(y+z)$
$A3$	$x+x=x$
$A4$	$(x+y)\cdot z=x\cdot z+y\cdot z$
$A5$	$(x\cdot y)\cdot z=x\cdot(y\cdot z)$

Table 3.2 Transition rules of BATC.

$$\frac{}{e\xrightarrow{e}\surd}$$

$$\frac{x\xrightarrow{e}\surd}{x+y\xrightarrow{e}\surd} \quad \frac{x\xrightarrow{e}x'}{x+y\xrightarrow{e}x'} \quad \frac{y\xrightarrow{e}\surd}{x+y\xrightarrow{e}\surd} \quad \frac{y\xrightarrow{e}y'}{x+y\xrightarrow{e}y'}$$

$$\frac{x\xrightarrow{e}\surd}{x\cdot y\xrightarrow{e}y} \quad \frac{x\xrightarrow{e}x'}{x\cdot y\xrightarrow{e}x'\cdot y}$$

Definition 3.17 (Posetal product). Given two PESs $\mathcal{E}_1, \mathcal{E}_2$, the posetal product of their configurations, denoted $\mathcal{C}(\mathcal{E}_1)\overline{\times}\mathcal{C}(\mathcal{E}_2)$, is defined as

$$\{(C_1, f, C_2)|C_1 \in \mathcal{C}(\mathcal{E}_1), C_2 \in \mathcal{C}(\mathcal{E}_2), f : C_1 \to C_2 \text{ isomorphism}\}.$$

A subset $R \subseteq \mathcal{C}(\mathcal{E}_1)\overline{\times}\mathcal{C}(\mathcal{E}_2)$ is called a posetal relation. We say that R is downward closed when for any $(C_1, f, C_2), (C_1', f', C_2') \in \mathcal{C}(\mathcal{E}_1)\overline{\times}\mathcal{C}(\mathcal{E}_2)$, if $(C_1, f, C_2) \subseteq (C_1', f', C_2')$ pointwise and $(C_1', f', C_2') \in R$, then $(C_1, f, C_2) \in R$.

For $f : X_1 \to X_2$, we define $f[x_1 \mapsto x_2] : X_1 \cup \{x_1\} \to X_2 \cup \{x_2\}$, $z \in X_1 \cup \{x_1\}$, (1) $f[x_1 \mapsto x_2](z) = x_2$, if $z = x_1$; (2) $f[x_1 \mapsto x_2](z) = f(z)$, otherwise. Where $X_1 \subseteq \mathbb{E}_1$, $X_2 \subseteq \mathbb{E}_2$, $x_1 \in \mathbb{E}_1$, $x_2 \in \mathbb{E}_2$.

Definition 3.18 ((Hereditary) history-preserving bisimulation). A history-preserving (hp-)bisimulation is a posetal relation $R \subseteq \mathcal{C}(\mathcal{E}_1)\overline{\times}\mathcal{C}(\mathcal{E}_2)$ such that if $(C_1, f, C_2) \in R$, and $C_1 \xrightarrow{e_1} C_1'$, then $C_2 \xrightarrow{e_2} C_2'$, with $(C_1', f[e_1 \mapsto e_2], C_2') \in R$, and vice-versa. $\mathcal{E}_1, \mathcal{E}_2$ are history-preserving (hp-)bisimilar and are written $\mathcal{E}_1 \sim_{hp} \mathcal{E}_2$ if there exists a hp-bisimulation R such that $(\emptyset, \emptyset, \emptyset) \in R$.

A hereditary history-preserving (hhp-)bisimulation is a downward closed hp-bisimulation. $\mathcal{E}_1, \mathcal{E}_2$ are hereditary history-preserving (hhp-)bisimilar and are written $\mathcal{E}_1 \sim_{hhp} \mathcal{E}_2$.

In the following, let $e_1, e_2, e_1', e_2' \in \mathbb{E}$, and let variables x, y, z range over the set of terms for true concurrency, p, q, s range over the set of closed terms. The set of axioms of BATC consists of the laws given in Table 3.1.

We give the operational transition rules of operators $\cdot$ and $+$ as Table 3.2 shows. And the predicate $\xrightarrow{e}\surd$ represents successful termination after execution of the event e.

Theorem 3.19 (Soundness of BATC modulo truly concurrent bisimulation equivalences). *The axiomatization of BATC is sound modulo truly concurrent bisimulation equivalences* $\sim_p$, $\sim_s$, $\sim_{hp}$, *and* $\sim_{hhp}$. *That is,*

1. *let* x *and* y *be BATC terms. If* BATC $\vdash x = y$, *then* $x \sim_p y$;
2. *let* x *and* y *be BATC terms. If* BATC $\vdash x = y$, *then* $x \sim_s y$;
3. *let* x *and* y *be BATC terms. If* BATC $\vdash x = y$, *then* $x \sim_{hp} y$;
4. *let* x *and* y *be BATC terms. If* BATC $\vdash x = y$, *then* $x \sim_{hhp} y$.

Theorem 3.20 (Completeness of BATC modulo truly concurrent bisimulation equivalences). *The axiomatization of BATC is complete modulo truly concurrent bisimulation equivalences* $\sim_p$, $\sim_s$, $\sim_{hp}$, *and* $\sim_{hhp}$. *That is,*

1. *let* p *and* q *be closed BATC terms, if* $p \sim_p q$ *then* $p = q$;
2. *let* p *and* q *be closed BATC terms, if* $p \sim_s q$ *then* $p = q$;
3. *let* p *and* q *be closed BATC terms, if* $p \sim_{hp} q$ *then* $p = q$;
4. *let* p *and* q *be closed BATC terms, if* $p \sim_{hhp} q$ *then* $p = q$.

3.4 Algebra for parallelism in true concurrency

APTC uses the whole parallel operator $\between$, the auxiliary binary parallel $\parallel$ to model parallelism, and the communication merge $\mid$ to model communications among different parallel branches, and also the unary conflict elimination operator Θ and the binary unless operator $\triangleleft$ to eliminate conflictions among different parallel branches. Since a communication may be blocked, a new constant called deadlock δ is extended to A, and also a new unary encapsulation operator ∂_H is introduced to eliminate δ, which may exist in the processes. The algebraic laws on these operators are also sound and complete modulo truly concurrent bisimulation equivalences (including pomset bisimulation, step bisimulation, hp-bisimulation, but not hhp-bisimulation). Note that, the parallel operator $\parallel$ in a process cannot be eliminated by deductions on the process using axioms of APTC, but other operators can eventually be steadied by $\cdot$, $+$, and $\parallel$, this is also why truly concurrent bisimulations are called an *truly concurrent* semantics.

We design the axioms of APTC in Table 3.3, including algebraic laws of parallel operator $\parallel$, communication operator $\mid$, conflict elimination operator Θ and unless operator $\triangleleft$, encapsulation operator ∂_H, the deadlock constant δ, and also the whole parallel operator $\between$.

We give the transition rules of APTC in Table 3.4, it is suitable for all truly concurrent behavioral equivalence, including pomset bisimulation, step bisimulation, hp-bisimulation, and hhp-bisimulation.

Theorem 3.21 (Soundness of APTC modulo truly concurrent bisimulation equivalences). *The axiomatization of APTC is sound modulo truly concurrent bisimulation equiva-*

Table 3.3 Axioms of APTC.

No.	**Axiom**
$A6$	$x + \delta = x$
$A7$	$\delta \cdot x = \delta$
$P1$	$x \between y = x \parallel y + x \mid y$
$P2$	$x \parallel y = y \parallel x$
$P3$	$(x \parallel y) \parallel z = x \parallel (y \parallel z)$
$P4$	$e_1 \parallel (e_2 \cdot y) = (e_1 \parallel e_2) \cdot y$
$P5$	$(e_1 \cdot x) \parallel e_2 = (e_1 \parallel e_2) \cdot x$
$P6$	$(e_1 \cdot x) \parallel (e_2 \cdot y) = (e_1 \parallel e_2) \cdot (x \between y)$
$P7$	$(x + y) \parallel z = (x \parallel z) + (y \parallel z)$
$P8$	$x \parallel (y + z) = (x \parallel y) + (x \parallel z)$
$P9$	$\delta \parallel x = \delta$
$P10$	$x \parallel \delta = \delta$
$C11$	$e_1 \mid e_2 = \gamma(e_1, e_2)$
$C12$	$e_1 \mid (e_2 \cdot y) = \gamma(e_1, e_2) \cdot y$
$C13$	$(e_1 \cdot x) \mid e_2 = \gamma(e_1, e_2) \cdot x$
$C14$	$(e_1 \cdot x) \mid (e_2 \cdot y) = \gamma(e_1, e_2) \cdot (x \between y)$
$C15$	$(x + y) \mid z = (x \mid z) + (y \mid z)$
$C16$	$x \mid (y + z) = (x \mid y) + (x \mid z)$
$C17$	$\delta \mid x = \delta$
$C18$	$x \mid \delta = \delta$
$CE19$	$\Theta(e) = e$
$CE20$	$\Theta(\delta) = \delta$
$CE21$	$\Theta(x + y) = \Theta(x) + \Theta(y)$
$CE22$	$\Theta(x \cdot y) = \Theta(x) \cdot \Theta(y)$
$CE23$	$\Theta(x \parallel y) = ((\Theta(x) \triangleleft y) \parallel y) + ((\Theta(y) \triangleleft x) \parallel x)$
$CE24$	$\Theta(x \mid y) = ((\Theta(x) \triangleleft y) \mid y) + ((\Theta(y) \triangleleft x) \mid x)$
$U25$	$(\sharp(e_1, e_2)) \quad e_1 \triangleleft e_2 = \tau$
$U26$	$(\sharp(e_1, e_2), e_2 \leq e_3) \quad e_1 \triangleleft e_3 = \tau$
$U27$	$(\sharp(e_1, e_2), e_2 \leq e_3) \quad e3 \triangleleft e_1 = \tau$
$U28$	$e \triangleleft \delta = e$
$U29$	$\delta \triangleleft e = \delta$
$U30$	$(x + y) \triangleleft z = (x \triangleleft z) + (y \triangleleft z)$
$U31$	$(x \cdot y) \triangleleft z = (x \triangleleft z) \cdot (y \triangleleft z)$
$U32$	$(x \parallel y) \triangleleft z = (x \triangleleft z) \parallel (y \triangleleft z)$
$U33$	$(x \mid y) \triangleleft z = (x \triangleleft z) \mid (y \triangleleft z)$
$U34$	$x \triangleleft (y + z) = (x \triangleleft y) \triangleleft z$
$U35$	$x \triangleleft (y \cdot z) = (x \triangleleft y) \triangleleft z$
$U36$	$x \triangleleft (y \parallel z) = (x \triangleleft y) \triangleleft z$
$U37$	$x \triangleleft (y \mid z) = (x \triangleleft y) \triangleleft z$
$D1$	$e \notin H \quad \partial_H(e) = e$
$D2$	$e \in H \quad \partial_H(e) = \delta$
$D3$	$\partial_H(\delta) = \delta$
$D4$	$\partial_H(x + y) = \partial_H(x) + \partial_H(y)$
$D5$	$\partial_H(x \cdot y) = \partial_H(x) \cdot \partial_H(y)$
$D6$	$\partial_H(x \parallel y) = \partial_H(x) \parallel \partial_H(y)$

Table 3.4 Transition rules of APTC.

$$\frac{x \xrightarrow{e_1} \surd \quad y \xrightarrow{e_2} \surd}{x \parallel y \xrightarrow{\{e_1,e_2\}} \surd} \qquad \frac{x \xrightarrow{e_1} x' \quad y \xrightarrow{e_2} \surd}{x \parallel y \xrightarrow{\{e_1,e_2\}} x'}$$

$$\frac{x \xrightarrow{e_1} \surd \quad y \xrightarrow{e_2} y'}{x \parallel y \xrightarrow{\{e_1,e_2\}} y'} \qquad \frac{x \xrightarrow{e_1} x' \quad y \xrightarrow{e_2} y'}{x \parallel y \xrightarrow{\{e_1,e_2\}} x' \between y'}$$

$$\frac{x \xrightarrow{e_1} \surd \quad y \xrightarrow{e_2} \surd}{x \mid y \xrightarrow{\gamma(e_1,e_2)} \surd} \qquad \frac{x \xrightarrow{e_1} x' \quad y \xrightarrow{e_2} \surd}{x \mid y \xrightarrow{\gamma(e_1,e_2)} x'}$$

$$\frac{x \xrightarrow{e_1} \surd \quad y \xrightarrow{e_2} y'}{x \mid y \xrightarrow{\gamma(e_1,e_2)} y'} \qquad \frac{x \xrightarrow{e_1} x' \quad y \xrightarrow{e_2} y'}{x \mid y \xrightarrow{\gamma(e_1,e_2)} x' \between y'}$$

$$\frac{x \xrightarrow{e_1} \surd \quad (\sharp(e_1,e_2))}{\Theta(x) \xrightarrow{e_1} \surd} \qquad \frac{x \xrightarrow{e_2} \surd \quad (\sharp(e_1,e_2))}{\Theta(x) \xrightarrow{e_2} \surd}$$

$$\frac{x \xrightarrow{e_1} x' \quad (\sharp(e_1,e_2))}{\Theta(x) \xrightarrow{e_1} \Theta(x')} \qquad \frac{x \xrightarrow{e_2} x' \quad (\sharp(e_1,e_2))}{\Theta(x) \xrightarrow{e_2} \Theta(x')}$$

$$\frac{x \xrightarrow{e_1} \surd \quad y \nrightarrow^{e_2} \quad (\sharp(e_1,e_2))}{x \triangleleft y \xrightarrow{\tau} \surd} \qquad \frac{x \xrightarrow{e_1} x' \quad y \nrightarrow^{e_2} \quad (\sharp(e_1,e_2))}{x \triangleleft y \xrightarrow{\tau} x'}$$

$$\frac{x \xrightarrow{e_1} \surd \quad y \nrightarrow^{e_3} \quad (\sharp(e_1,e_2), e_2 \le e_3)}{x \triangleleft y \xrightarrow{\tau} \surd} \qquad \frac{x \xrightarrow{e_1} x' \quad y \nrightarrow^{e_3} \quad (\sharp(e_1,e_2), e_2 \le e_3)}{x \triangleleft y \xrightarrow{\tau} x'}$$

$$\frac{x \xrightarrow{e_3} \surd \quad y \nrightarrow^{e_2} \quad (\sharp(e_1,e_2), e_1 \le e_3)}{x \triangleleft y \xrightarrow{\tau} \surd} \qquad \frac{x \xrightarrow{e_3} x' \quad y \nrightarrow^{e_2} \quad (\sharp(e_1,e_2), e_1 \le e_3)}{x \triangleleft y \xrightarrow{\tau} x'}$$

$$\frac{x \xrightarrow{e} \surd}{\partial_H(x) \xrightarrow{e} \surd} \quad (e \notin H) \qquad \frac{x \xrightarrow{e} x'}{\partial_H(x) \xrightarrow{e} \partial_H(x')} \quad (e \notin H)$$

lences $\sim_p$, $\sim_s$, and $\sim_{hp}$. That is,

1. *let x and y be APTC terms. If APTC $\vdash x = y$, then $x \sim_p y$;*
2. *let x and y be APTC terms. If APTC $\vdash x = y$, then $x \sim_s y$;*
3. *let x and y be APTC terms. If APTC $\vdash x = y$, then $x \sim_{hp} y$.*

Theorem 3.22 (Completeness of APTC modulo truly concurrent bisimulation equivalences). *The axiomatization of APTC is complete modulo truly concurrent bisimulation equivalences $\sim_p$, $\sim_s$, and $\sim_{hp}$. That is,*

1. *let p and q be closed APTC terms, if $p \sim_p q$ then $p = q$;*
2. *let p and q be closed APTC terms, if $p \sim_s q$ then $p = q$;*
3. *let p and q be closed APTC terms, if $p \sim_{hp} q$ then $p = q$.*

3.5 Recursion

To model infinite computation, recursion is introduced into APTC. In order to obtain a sound and complete theory, guarded recursion and linear recursion are needed. The cor-

Table 3.5 Transition rules of guarded recursion.

$$\frac{t_i(\langle X_1\|E\rangle,\cdots,\langle X_n\|E\rangle)\xrightarrow{\{e_1,\cdots,e_k\}}\surd}{\langle X_i\|E\rangle\xrightarrow{\{e_1,\cdots,e_k\}}\surd}$$
$$\frac{t_i(\langle X_1\|E\rangle,\cdots,\langle X_n\|E\rangle)\xrightarrow{\{e_1,\cdots,e_k\}}y}{\langle X_i\|E\rangle\xrightarrow{\{e_1,\cdots,e_k\}}y}$$

Table 3.6 Recursive definition and specification principle.

No.	Axiom
RDP	$\langle X_i\|E\rangle = t_i(\langle X_1\|E,\cdots,X_n\|E\rangle)\quad (i\in\{1,\cdots,n\})$
RSP	if $y_i = t_i(y_1,\cdots,y_n)$ for $i\in\{1,\cdots,n\}$, then $y_i=\langle X_i\|E\rangle\quad (i\in\{1,\cdots,n\})$

responding axioms are RSP (Recursive Specification Principle) and RDP (Recursive Definition Principle), RDP says the solutions of a recursive specification can represent the behaviors of the specification, while RSP says that a guarded recursive specification has only one solution, they are sound with respect to APTC with guarded recursion modulo several truly concurrent bisimulation equivalences (including pomset bisimulation, step bisimulation, and hp-bisimulation), and they are complete with respect to APTC with linear recursion modulo several truly concurrent bisimulation equivalences (including pomset bisimulation, step bisimulation, and hp-bisimulation). In the following, E, F, G are recursion specifications, X, Y, Z are recursive variables.

For a guarded recursive specifications E with the form

$$X_1 = t_1(X_1,\cdots,X_n)$$

$$\cdots$$

$$X_n = t_n(X_1,\cdots,X_n)$$

the behavior of the solution $\langle X_i|E\rangle$ for the recursion variable X_i in E, where $i\in\{1,\cdots,n\}$, is exactly the behavior of their right-hand sides $t_i(X_1,\cdots,X_n)$, which is captured by the two transition rules in Table 3.5.

The RDP (Recursive Definition Principle) and the RSP (Recursive Specification Principle) are shown in Table 3.6.

Theorem 3.23 (Soundness of $APTC$ with guarded recursion). *Let x and y be $APTC$ with guarded recursion terms. If $APTC$ with guarded recursion $\vdash x = y$, then*

1. $x \sim_s y$;
2. $x \sim_p y$;
3. $x \sim_{hp} y$.

Theorem 3.24 (Completeness of $APTC$ with linear recursion). *Let p and q be closed $APTC$ with linear recursion terms, then,*

1. *if* $p \sim_s q$ *then* $p = q$;
2. *if* $p \sim_p q$ *then* $p = q$;
3. *if* $p \sim_{hp} q$ *then* $p = q$.

3.6 Abstraction

To abstract away internal implementations from the external behaviors, a new constant τ called silent step is added to A, and also a new unary abstraction operator τ_I is used to rename actions in I into τ (the resulted APTC with silent step and abstraction operator is called APTC_τ). The recursive specification is adapted to guarded linear recursion to prevent infinite τ-loops specifically. The axioms of τ and τ_I are sound modulo rooted branching truly concurrent bisimulation equivalences (several kinds of weakly truly concurrent bisimulation equivalences, including rooted branching pomset bisimulation, rooted branching step bisimulation, and rooted branching hp-bisimulation). To eliminate infinite τ-loops caused by τ_I and obtain the completeness, CFAR (Cluster Fair Abstraction Rule) is used to prevent infinite τ-loops in a constructible way.

Definition 3.25 (Weak pomset transitions and weak step). Let $\mathcal{E}$ be a PES and let $C \in \mathcal{C}(\mathcal{E})$, and $\emptyset \neq X \subseteq \hat{\mathbb{E}}$, if $C \cap X = \emptyset$ and $\hat{C}' = \hat{C} \cup X \in \mathcal{C}(\mathcal{E})$, then $C \stackrel{X}{\Rightarrow} C'$ is called a weak pomset transition from C to C', where we define $\stackrel{e}{\Rightarrow} \triangleq \stackrel{\tau^*}{\longrightarrow}\stackrel{e}{\longrightarrow}\stackrel{\tau^*}{\longrightarrow}$. And $\stackrel{X}{\Rightarrow} \triangleq \stackrel{\tau^*}{\longrightarrow}\stackrel{e}{\longrightarrow}\stackrel{\tau^*}{\longrightarrow}$, for every $e \in X$. When the events in X are pairwise concurrent, we say that $C \stackrel{X}{\Rightarrow} C'$ is a weak step.

Definition 3.26 (Branching pomset, step bisimulation). Assume a special termination predicate $\downarrow$, and let $\surd$ represent a state with $\surd\downarrow$. Let $\mathcal{E}_1$, $\mathcal{E}_2$ be PESs. A branching pomset bisimulation is a relation $R \subseteq \mathcal{C}(\mathcal{E}_1) \times \mathcal{C}(\mathcal{E}_2)$, such that:

1. if $(C_1, C_2) \in R$, and $C_1 \xrightarrow{X} C_1'$ then
   - either $X \equiv \tau^*$, and $(C_1', C_2) \in R$;
   - or there is a sequence of (zero or more) τ-transitions $C_2 \xrightarrow{\tau^*} C_2^0$, such that $(C_1, C_2^0) \in R$ and $C_2^0 \stackrel{X}{\Rightarrow} C_2'$ with $(C_1', C_2') \in R$;
2. if $(C_1, C_2) \in R$, and $C_2 \xrightarrow{X} C_2'$ then
   - either $X \equiv \tau^*$, and $(C_1, C_2') \in R$;
   - or there is a sequence of (zero or more) τ-transitions $C_1 \xrightarrow{\tau^*} C_1^0$, such that $(C_1^0, C_2) \in R$ and $C_1^0 \stackrel{X}{\Rightarrow} C_1'$ with $(C_1', C_2') \in R$;
3. if $(C_1, C_2) \in R$ and $C_1 \downarrow$, then there is a sequence of (zero or more) τ-transitions $C_2 \xrightarrow{\tau^*} C_2^0$ such that $(C_1, C_2^0) \in R$ and $C_2^0 \downarrow$;
4. if $(C_1, C_2) \in R$ and $C_2 \downarrow$, then there is a sequence of (zero or more) τ-transitions $C_1 \xrightarrow{\tau^*} C_1^0$ such that $(C_1^0, C_2) \in R$ and $C_1^0 \downarrow$.

We say that $\mathcal{E}_1$, $\mathcal{E}_2$ are branching pomset bisimilar, written $\mathcal{E}_1 \approx_{bp} \mathcal{E}_2$, if there exists a branching pomset bisimulation R, such that $(\emptyset, \emptyset) \in R$.

By replacing pomset transitions with steps, we can get the definition of branching step bisimulation. When PESs $\mathcal{E}_1$ and $\mathcal{E}_2$ are branching step bisimilar, we write $\mathcal{E}_1 \approx_{bs} \mathcal{E}_2$.

Definition 3.27 (Rooted branching pomset, step bisimulation). Assume a special termination predicate $\downarrow$, and let $\surd$ represent a state with $\surd \downarrow$. Let $\mathcal{E}_1$, $\mathcal{E}_2$ be PESs. A branching pomset bisimulation is a relation $R \subseteq \mathcal{C}(\mathcal{E}_1) \times \mathcal{C}(\mathcal{E}_2)$, such that:

1. if $(C_1, C_2) \in R$, and $C_1 \xrightarrow{X} C_1'$ then $C_2 \xrightarrow{X} C_2'$ with $C_1' \approx_{bp} C_2'$;
2. if $(C_1, C_2) \in R$, and $C_2 \xrightarrow{X} C_2'$ then $C_1 \xrightarrow{X} C_1'$ with $C_1' \approx_{bp} C_2'$;
3. if $(C_1, C_2) \in R$ and $C_1 \downarrow$, then $C_2 \downarrow$;
4. if $(C_1, C_2) \in R$ and $C_2 \downarrow$, then $C_1 \downarrow$.

We say that $\mathcal{E}_1$, $\mathcal{E}_2$ are rooted branching pomset bisimilar, written $\mathcal{E}_1 \approx_{rbp} \mathcal{E}_2$, if there exists a rooted branching pomset bisimulation R, such that $(\emptyset, \emptyset) \in R$.

By replacing pomset transitions with steps, we can get the definition of rooted branching step bisimulation. When PESs $\mathcal{E}_1$ and $\mathcal{E}_2$ are rooted branching step bisimilar, we write $\mathcal{E}_1 \approx_{rbs} \mathcal{E}_2$.

Definition 3.28 (Branching (hereditary) history-preserving bisimulation). Assume a special termination predicate $\downarrow$, and let $\surd$ represent a state with $\surd \downarrow$. A branching history-preserving (hp-)bisimulation is a weakly posetal relation $R \subseteq \mathcal{C}(\mathcal{E}_1)\overline{\times}\mathcal{C}(\mathcal{E}_2)$ such that:

1. if $(C_1, f, C_2) \in R$, and $C_1 \xrightarrow{e_1} C_1'$ then
   - either $e_1 \equiv \tau$, and $(C_1', f[e_1 \mapsto \tau], C_2) \in R$;
   - or there is a sequence of (zero or more) τ-transitions $C_2 \xrightarrow{\tau^*} C_2^0$, such that $(C_1, f, C_2^0) \in R$ and $C_2^0 \xrightarrow{e_2} C_2'$ with $(C_1', f[e_1 \mapsto e_2], C_2') \in R$;
2. if $(C_1, f, C_2) \in R$, and $C_2 \xrightarrow{e_2} C_2'$ then
   - either $X \equiv \tau$, and $(C_1, f[e_2 \mapsto \tau], C_2') \in R$;
   - or there is a sequence of (zero or more) τ-transitions $C_1 \xrightarrow{\tau^*} C_1^0$, such that $(C_1^0, f, C_2) \in R$ and $C_1^0 \xrightarrow{e_1} C_1'$ with $(C_1', f[e_2 \mapsto e_1], C_2') \in R$;
3. if $(C_1, f, C_2) \in R$ and $C_1 \downarrow$, then there is a sequence of (zero or more) τ-transitions $C_2 \xrightarrow{\tau^*} C_2^0$ such that $(C_1, f, C_2^0) \in R$ and $C_2^0 \downarrow$;
4. if $(C_1, f, C_2) \in R$ and $C_2 \downarrow$, then there is a sequence of (zero or more) τ-transitions $C_1 \xrightarrow{\tau^*} C_1^0$ such that $(C_1^0, f, C_2) \in R$ and $C_1^0 \downarrow$.

$\mathcal{E}_1$, $\mathcal{E}_2$ are branching history-preserving (hp-)bisimilar and are written $\mathcal{E}_1 \approx_{bhp} \mathcal{E}_2$ if there exists a branching hp-bisimulation R such that $(\emptyset, \emptyset, \emptyset) \in R$.

Table 3.7 Axioms of APTC$_\tau$.

No.	Axiom
$B1$	$e \cdot \tau = e$
$B2$	$e \cdot (\tau \cdot (x + y) + x) = e \cdot (x + y)$
$B3$	$x \parallel \tau = x$
$TI1$	$e \notin I \quad \tau_I(e) = e$
$TI2$	$e \in I \quad \tau_I(e) = \tau$
$TI3$	$\tau_I(\delta) = \delta$
$TI4$	$\tau_I(x + y) = \tau_I(x) + \tau_I(y)$
$TI5$	$\tau_I(x \cdot y) = \tau_I(x) \cdot \tau_I(y)$
$TI6$	$\tau_I(x \parallel y) = \tau_I(x) \parallel \tau_I(y)$
$CFAR$	If X is in a cluster for I with exits $\{(a_{11} \parallel \cdots \parallel a_{1i})Y_1, \cdots, (a_{m1} \parallel \cdots \parallel a_{mi})Y_m, b_{11} \parallel \cdots \parallel b_{1j}, \cdots, b_{n1} \parallel \cdots \parallel b_{nj}\}$, then $\tau \cdot \tau_I(\langle X\|E\rangle) =$ $\tau \cdot \tau_I((a_{11} \parallel \cdots \parallel a_{1i})\langle Y_1\|E\rangle + \cdots + (a_{m1} \parallel \cdots \parallel a_{mi})\langle Y_m\|E\rangle + b_{11} \parallel \cdots \parallel b_{1j} + \cdots + b_{n1} \parallel \cdots \parallel b_{nj})$

A branching hereditary history-preserving (hhp-)bisimulation is a downward closed branching hhp-bisimulation. $\mathcal{E}_1, \mathcal{E}_2$ are branching hereditary history-preserving (hhp-)bisimilar and are written $\mathcal{E}_1 \approx_{bhhp} \mathcal{E}_2$.

Definition 3.29 (Rooted branching (hereditary) history-preserving bisimulation). Assume a special termination predicate $\downarrow$, and let $\surd$ represent a state with $\surd \downarrow$. A rooted branching history-preserving (hp-)bisimulation is a weakly posetal relation $R \subseteq \mathcal{C}(\mathcal{E}_1)\overline{\times}\mathcal{C}(\mathcal{E}_2)$ such that:

1. if $(C_1, f, C_2) \in R$, and $C_1 \xrightarrow{e_1} C_1'$, then $C_2 \xrightarrow{e_2} C_2'$ with $C_1' \approx_{bhp} C_2'$;
2. if $(C_1, f, C_2) \in R$, and $C_2 \xrightarrow{e_2} C_1'$, then $C_1 \xrightarrow{e_1} C_2'$ with $C_1' \approx_{bhp} C_2'$;
3. if $(C_1, f, C_2) \in R$ and $C_1 \downarrow$, then $C_2 \downarrow$;
4. if $(C_1, f, C_2) \in R$ and $C_2 \downarrow$, then $C_1 \downarrow$.

$\mathcal{E}_1, \mathcal{E}_2$ are rooted branching history-preserving (hp-)bisimilar and are written $\mathcal{E}_1 \approx_{rbhp} \mathcal{E}_2$ if there exists rooted a branching hp-bisimulation R such that $(\emptyset, \emptyset, \emptyset) \in R$.

A rooted branching hereditary history-preserving (hhp-)bisimulation is a downward closed rooted branching hhp-bisimulation. $\mathcal{E}_1, \mathcal{E}_2$ are rooted branching hereditary history-preserving (hhp-)bisimilar and are written $\mathcal{E}_1 \approx_{rbhhp} \mathcal{E}_2$.

The axioms and transition rules of APTC$_\tau$ are shown in Table 3.7 and Table 3.8.

Theorem 3.30 (Soundness of $APTC_\tau$ with guarded linear recursion). *Let x and y be $APTC_\tau$ with guarded linear recursion terms. If $APTC_\tau$ with guarded linear recursion $\vdash x = y$, then*

1. $x \approx_{rbs} y$;
2. $x \approx_{rbp} y$;
3. $x \approx_{rbhp} y$.

Table 3.8 Transition rule of $APTC_\tau$.

$$\frac{}{\tau\xrightarrow{\tau}\surd}$$

$$\frac{x\xrightarrow{e}\surd}{\tau_I(x)\xrightarrow{e}\surd}\quad e\notin I \qquad \frac{x\xrightarrow{e}x'}{\tau_I(x)\xrightarrow{e}\tau_I(x')}\quad e\notin I$$

$$\frac{x\xrightarrow{e}\surd}{\tau_I(x)\xrightarrow{\tau}\surd}\quad e\in I \qquad \frac{x\xrightarrow{e}x'}{\tau_I(x)\xrightarrow{\tau}\tau_I(x')}\quad e\in I$$

Table 3.9 Transition rule of the shadow constant.

$$\frac{}{\circledS\rightarrow\surd}$$

Theorem 3.31 (Soundness of $CFAR$). *$CFAR$ is sound modulo rooted branching truly concurrent bisimulation equivalences $\approx_{rbs}$, $\approx_{rbp}$, and $\approx_{rbhp}$.*

Theorem 3.32 (Completeness of $APTC_\tau$ with guarded linear recursion and $CFAR$). *Let p and q be closed $APTC_\tau$ with guarded linear recursion and $CFAR$ terms, then,*

1. *if $p\approx_{rbs} q$ then $p=q$;*
2. *if $p\approx_{rbp} q$ then $p=q$;*
3. *if $p\approx_{rbhp} q$ then $p=q$.*

3.7 Placeholder

We introduce a constant called shadow constant $\circledS$ to act for the placeholder that we ever used to deal entanglement in quantum process algebra. The transition rule of the shadow constant $\circledS$ is shown in Table 3.9. The rule says that $\circledS$ can terminate successfully without executing any action.

We need to adjust the definition of guarded linear recursive specification to the following one.

Definition 3.33 (Guarded linear recursive specification). A linear recursive specification E is guarded if there does not exist an infinite sequence of τ-transitions $\langle X|E\rangle\xrightarrow{\tau}\langle X'|E\rangle\xrightarrow{\tau}\langle X''|E\rangle\xrightarrow{\tau}\cdots$, and there does not exist an infinite sequence of $\circledS$-transitions $\langle X|E\rangle\rightarrow\langle X'|E\rangle\rightarrow\langle X''|E\rangle\rightarrow\cdots$.

Theorem 3.34 (Conservativity of $APTC$ with respect to the shadow constant). *$APTC_\tau$ with guarded linear recursion and shadow constant is a conservative extension of $APTC_\tau$ with guarded linear recursion.*

We design the axioms for the shadow constant $\circledS$ in Table 3.10. And for $\circledS_i^e$, we add superscript e to denote $\circledS$ is belonging to e and subscript i to denote that it is the i-th shadow of e. And we extend the set $\mathbb{E}$ to the set $\mathbb{E}\cup\{\tau\}\cup\{\delta\}\cup\{\circledS_i^e\}$.

Table 3.10 Axioms of shadow constant.

No.	Axiom
$SC1$	$Ⓢ \cdot x = x$
$SC2$	$x \cdot Ⓢ = x$
$SC3$	$Ⓢ^e \parallel e = e$
$SC4$	$e \parallel (Ⓢ^e \cdot y) = e \cdot y$
$SC5$	$Ⓢ^e \parallel (e \cdot y) = e \cdot y$
$SC6$	$(e \cdot x) \parallel Ⓢ^e = e \cdot x$
$SC7$	$(Ⓢ^e \cdot x) \parallel e = e \cdot x$
$SC8$	$(e \cdot x) \parallel (Ⓢ^e \cdot y) = e \cdot (x \between y)$
$SC9$	$(Ⓢ^e \cdot x) \parallel (e \cdot y) = e \cdot (x \between y)$

The mismatch of action and its shadows in parallelism will cause deadlock, that is, $e \parallel Ⓢ^{e'} = \delta$ with $e \neq e'$. We must make all shadows $Ⓢ^e_i$ are distinct, to ensure f in hp-bisimulation is an isomorphism.

Theorem 3.35 (Soundness of the shadow constant). *Let x and y be $APTC_\tau$ with guarded linear recursion and the shadow constant terms. If $APTC_\tau$ with guarded linear recursion and the shadow constant $\vdash x = y$, then*

1. $x \approx_{rbs} y$;
2. $x \approx_{rbp} y$;
3. $x \approx_{rbhp} y$.

Theorem 3.36 (Completeness of the shadow constant). *Let p and q be closed $APTC_\tau$ with guarded linear recursion and $CFAR$ and the shadow constant terms, then,*

1. *if* $p \approx_{rbs} q$ *then* $p = q$;
2. *if* $p \approx_{rbp} q$ *then* $p = q$;
3. *if* $p \approx_{rbhp} q$ *then* $p = q$.

With the shadow constant, we have

$$\begin{aligned}\partial_H((a \cdot r_b) \between w_b) &= \partial_H((a \cdot r_b) \between (Ⓢ^a_1 \cdot w_b)) \\ &= a \cdot c_b\end{aligned}$$

with $H = \{r_b, w_b\}$ and $\gamma(r_b, w_b) \triangleq c_b$.

And we see the following example:

$$\begin{aligned}a \between b &= a \parallel b + a \mid b \\ &= a \parallel b + a \parallel b + a \parallel b + a \mid b \\ &= a \parallel (Ⓢ^a_1 \cdot b) + (Ⓢ^b_1 \cdot a) \parallel b + a \parallel b + a \mid b \\ &= (a \parallel Ⓢ^a_1) \cdot b + (Ⓢ^b_1 \parallel b) \cdot a + a \parallel b + a \mid b \\ &= a \cdot b + b \cdot a + a \parallel b + a \mid b\end{aligned}$$

Table 3.11 Transition rules of left parallel operator $\mathbin{\|\!\!\lfloor}$.

$$\frac{x \xrightarrow{e_1} \surd \quad y \xrightarrow{e_2} \surd \quad (e_1 \leq e_2)}{x \mathbin{\|\!\!\lfloor} y \xrightarrow{\{e_1, e_2\}} \surd} \qquad \frac{x \xrightarrow{e_1} x' \quad y \xrightarrow{e_2} \surd \quad (e_1 \leq e_2)}{x \mathbin{\|\!\!\lfloor} y \xrightarrow{\{e_1, e_2\}} x'}$$

$$\frac{x \xrightarrow{e_1} \surd \quad y \xrightarrow{e_2} y' \quad (e_1 \leq e_2)}{x \mathbin{\|\!\!\lfloor} y \xrightarrow{\{e_1, e_2\}} y'} \qquad \frac{x \xrightarrow{e_1} x' \quad y \xrightarrow{e_2} y' \quad (e_1 \leq e_2)}{x \mathbin{\|\!\!\lfloor} y \xrightarrow{\{e_1, e_2\}} x' \between y'}$$

What do we see? Yes. The parallelism contains both interleaving and true concurrency. This may be why true concurrency is called ***true** concurrency*.

3.8 Axiomatization for hhp-bisimilarity

Since hhp-bisimilarity is a downward closed hp-bisimilarity and can be downward closed to single atomic event, which implies bisimilarity. As Moller [23] proven, there is not a finite sound and complete axiomatization for parallelism $\parallel$ modulo bisimulation equivalence, so there is not a finite sound and complete axiomatization for parallelism $\parallel$ modulo hhp-bisimulation equivalence either. Inspired by the way of left merge to modeling the full merge for bisimilarity, we introduce a left parallel composition $\mathbin{\|\!\!\lfloor}$ to model the full parallelism $\parallel$ for hhp-bisimilarity.

In the following subsection, we add left parallel composition $\mathbin{\|\!\!\lfloor}$ to the whole theory. Because the resulting theory is similar to the former, we only list the significant differences, and all proofs of the conclusions are left to the reader.

3.8.1 $APTC$ with left parallel composition

The transition rules of left parallel composition $\mathbin{\|\!\!\lfloor}$ are shown in Table 3.11. With a little abuse, we extend the causal order relation $\leq$ on $\mathbb{E}$ to include the original partial order (denoted by $<$) and concurrency (denoted by $=$).

The new axioms for parallelism are listed in Table 3.12.

Definition 3.37 (Basic terms of $APTC$ with left parallel composition). The set of basic terms of $APTC$, $\mathcal{B}(APTC)$, is inductively defined as follows:

1. $\mathbb{E} \subset \mathcal{B}(APTC)$;
2. if $e \in \mathbb{E}, t \in \mathcal{B}(APTC)$ then $e \cdot t \in \mathcal{B}(APTC)$;
3. if $t, s \in \mathcal{B}(APTC)$ then $t + s \in \mathcal{B}(APTC)$;
4. if $t, s \in \mathcal{B}(APTC)$ then $t \mathbin{\|\!\!\lfloor} s \in \mathcal{B}(APTC)$.

Theorem 3.38 (Generalization of the algebra for left parallelism with respect to $BATC$). *The algebra for left parallelism is a generalization of $BATC$.*

Table 3.12 Axioms of parallelism with left parallel composition.

No.	Axiom
$A6$	$x + \delta = x$
$A7$	$\delta \cdot x = \delta$
$P1$	$x \between y = x \parallel y + x \mid y$
$P2$	$x \parallel y = y \parallel x$
$P3$	$(x \parallel y) \parallel z = x \parallel (y \parallel z)$
$P4$	$x \parallel y = x \talloblong y + y \talloblong x$
$P5$	$(e_1 \leq e_2) \quad e_1 \talloblong (e_2 \cdot y) = (e_1 \talloblong e_2) \cdot y$
$P6$	$(e_1 \leq e_2) \quad (e_1 \cdot x) \talloblong e_2 = (e_1 \talloblong e_2) \cdot x$
$P7$	$(e_1 \leq e_2) \quad (e_1 \cdot x) \talloblong (e_2 \cdot y) = (e_1 \talloblong e_2) \cdot (x \between y)$
$P8$	$(x + y) \talloblong z = (x \talloblong z) + (y \talloblong z)$
$P9$	$\delta \talloblong x = \delta$
$C10$	$e_1 \mid e_2 = \gamma(e_1, e_2)$
$C11$	$e_1 \mid (e_2 \cdot y) = \gamma(e_1, e_2) \cdot y$
$C12$	$(e_1 \cdot x) \mid e_2 = \gamma(e_1, e_2) \cdot x$
$C13$	$(e_1 \cdot x) \mid (e_2 \cdot y) = \gamma(e_1, e_2) \cdot (x \between y)$
$C14$	$(x + y) \mid z = (x \mid z) + (y \mid z)$
$C15$	$x \mid (y + z) = (x \mid y) + (x \mid z)$
$C16$	$\delta \mid x = \delta$
$C17$	$x \mid \delta = \delta$
$CE18$	$\Theta(e) = e$
$CE19$	$\Theta(\delta) = \delta$
$CE20$	$\Theta(x + y) = \Theta(x) + \Theta(y)$
$CE21$	$\Theta(x \cdot y) = \Theta(x) \cdot \Theta(y)$
$CE22$	$\Theta(x \talloblong y) = ((\Theta(x) \triangleleft y) \talloblong y) + ((\Theta(y) \triangleleft x) \talloblong x)$
$CE23$	$\Theta(x \mid y) = ((\Theta(x) \triangleleft y) \mid y) + ((\Theta(y) \triangleleft x) \mid x)$
$U24$	$(\sharp(e_1, e_2)) \quad e_1 \triangleleft e_2 = \tau$
$U25$	$(\sharp(e_1, e_2), e_2 \leq e_3) \quad e_1 \triangleleft e_3 = \tau$
$U26$	$(\sharp(e_1, e_2), e_2 \leq e_3) \quad e3 \triangleleft e_1 = \tau$
$U27$	$e \triangleleft \delta = e$
$U28$	$\delta \triangleleft e = \delta$
$U29$	$(x + y) \triangleleft z = (x \triangleleft z) + (y \triangleleft z)$
$U30$	$(x \cdot y) \triangleleft z = (x \triangleleft z) \cdot (y \triangleleft z)$
$U31$	$(x \talloblong y) \triangleleft z = (x \triangleleft z) \talloblong (y \triangleleft z)$
$U32$	$(x \mid y) \triangleleft z = (x \triangleleft z) \mid (y \triangleleft z)$
$U33$	$x \triangleleft (y + z) = (x \triangleleft y) \triangleleft z$
$U34$	$x \triangleleft (y \cdot z) = (x \triangleleft y) \triangleleft z$
$U35$	$x \triangleleft (y \talloblong z) = (x \triangleleft y) \triangleleft z$
$U36$	$x \triangleleft (y \mid z) = (x \triangleleft y) \triangleleft z$

Table 3.13 Axioms of encapsulation operator with left parallel composition.

No.	Axiom
$D1$	$e \notin H \quad \partial_H(e) = e$
$D2$	$e \in H \quad \partial_H(e) = \delta$
$D3$	$\partial_H(\delta) = \delta$
$D4$	$\partial_H(x + y) = \partial_H(x) + \partial_H(y)$
$D5$	$\partial_H(x \cdot y) = \partial_H(x) \cdot \partial_H(y)$
$D6$	$\partial_H(x \mathbin{\|\!\!\lfloor} y) = \partial_H(x) \mathbin{\|\!\!\lfloor} \partial_H(y)$

Theorem 3.39 (Congruence theorem of $APTC$ with left parallel composition). *Truly concurrent bisimulation equivalences $\sim_p$, $\sim_s$, $\sim_{hp}$, and $\sim_{hhp}$ are all congruences with respect to $APTC$ with left parallel composition.*

Theorem 3.40 (Elimination theorem of parallelism with left parallel composition). *Let p be a closed $APTC$ with left parallel composition term. Then there is a basic $APTC$ term q such that $APTC \vdash p = q$.*

Theorem 3.41 (Soundness of parallelism with left parallel composition modulo truly concurrent bisimulation equivalences). *Let x and y be $APTC$ with left parallel composition terms. If $APTC \vdash x = y$, then*

1. $x \sim_s y$;
2. $x \sim_p y$;
3. $x \sim_{hp} y$;
4. $x \sim_{hhp} y$.

Theorem 3.42 (Completeness of parallelism with left parallel composition modulo truly concurrent bisimulation equivalences). *Let x and y be $APTC$ terms.*

1. *If $x \sim_s y$, then $APTC \vdash x = y$;*
2. *if $x \sim_p y$, then $APTC \vdash x = y$;*
3. *if $x \sim_{hp} y$, then $APTC \vdash x = y$;*
4. *if $x \sim_{hhp} y$, then $APTC \vdash x = y$.*

The transition rules of encapsulation operator are the same, and the axioms are shown in Table 3.13.

Theorem 3.43 (Conservativity of $APTC$ with respect to the algebra for parallelism with left parallel composition). *$APTC$ is a conservative extension of the algebra for parallelism with left parallel composition.*

Theorem 3.44 (Congruence theorem of encapsulation operator ∂_H). *Truly concurrent bisimulation equivalences $\sim_p$, $\sim_s$, $\sim_{hp}$, and $\sim_{hhp}$ are all congruences with respect to encapsulation operator ∂_H.*

Theorem 3.45 (Elimination theorem of $APTC$). *Let p be a closed $APTC$ term including the encapsulation operator ∂_H. Then there is a basic $APTC$ term q such that $APTC \vdash p = q$.*

Theorem 3.46 (Soundness of $APTC$ modulo truly concurrent bisimulation equivalences). *Let x and y be $APTC$ terms including encapsulation operator ∂_H. If $APTC \vdash x = y$, then*

1. $x \sim_s y$;
2. $x \sim_p y$;
3. $x \sim_{hp} y$;
4. $x \sim_{hhp} y$.

Theorem 3.47 (Completeness of $APTC$ modulo truly concurrent bisimulation equivalences). *Let p and q be closed $APTC$ terms including encapsulation operator ∂_H,*

1. *if $p \sim_s q$ then $p = q$;*
2. *if $p \sim_p q$ then $p = q$;*
3. *if $p \sim_{hp} q$ then $p = q$;*
4. *if $p \sim_{hhp} q$ then $p = q$.*

3.8.2 Recursion

Definition 3.48 (Recursive specification). A recursive specification is a finite set of recursive equations

$$X_1 = t_1(X_1, \cdots, X_n)$$

$$\cdots$$

$$X_n = t_n(X_1, \cdots, X_n)$$

where the left-hand sides of X_i are called recursion variables, and the right-hand sides $t_i(X_1, \cdots, X_n)$ are process terms in $APTC$ with possible occurrences of the recursion variables $X_1, \cdots, X_n$.

Definition 3.49 (Solution). Processes $p_1, \cdots, p_n$ are a solution for a recursive specification $\{X_i = t_i(X_1, \cdots, X_n) | i \in \{1, \cdots, n\}\}$ (with respect to truly concurrent bisimulation equivalences $\sim_s (\sim_p, \sim_{hp}, \sim_{hhp})$) if $p_i \sim_s (\sim_p, \sim_{hp}, \sim hhp) t_i(p_1, \cdots, p_n)$ for $i \in \{1, \cdots, n\}$.

Definition 3.50 (Guarded recursive specification). A recursive specification

$$X_1 = t_1(X_1, \cdots, X_n)$$

$$\cdots$$

$$X_n = t_n(X_1, \cdots, X_n)$$

is guarded if the right-hand sides of its recursive equations can be adapted to the form by applications of the axioms in $APTC$ and replacing recursion variables by the right-hand sides of their recursive equations,

$$(a_{11} \between \cdots \between a_{1i_1}) \cdot s_1(X_1, \cdots, X_n) + \cdots + (a_{k1} \between \cdots \between a_{ki_k}) \cdot s_k(X_1, \cdots, X_n)$$
$$+ (b_{11} \between \cdots \between b_{1j_1}) + \cdots + (b_{1j_1} \between \cdots \between b_{lj_l})$$

where $a_{11}, \cdots, a_{1i_1}, a_{k1}, \cdots, a_{ki_k}, b_{11}, \cdots, b_{1j_1}, b_{1j_1}, \cdots, b_{lj_l} \in \mathbb{E}$, and the sum above is allowed to be empty, in which case it represents the deadlock δ.

Definition 3.51 (Linear recursive specification). A recursive specification is linear if its recursive equations are of the form

$$(a_{11} \between \cdots \between a_{1i_1})X_1 + \cdots + (a_{k1} \between \cdots \between a_{ki_k})X_k + (b_{11} \between \cdots \between b_{1j_1}) + \cdots + (b_{1j_1} \between \cdots \between b_{lj_l})$$

where $a_{11}, \cdots, a_{1i_1}, a_{k1}, \cdots, a_{ki_k}, b_{11}, \cdots, b_{1j_1}, b_{1j_1}, \cdots, b_{lj_l} \in \mathbb{E}$, and the sum above is allowed to be empty, in which case it represents the deadlock δ.

Theorem 3.52 (Conservativity of $APTC$ with guarded recursion). *$APTC$ with guarded recursion is a conservative extension of $APTC$.*

Theorem 3.53 (Congruence theorem of $APTC$ with guarded recursion). *Truly concurrent bisimulation equivalences $\sim_p$, $\sim_s$, $\sim_{hp}$, $\sim_{hhp}$ are all congruences with respect to $APTC$ with guarded recursion.*

Theorem 3.54 (Elimination theorem of $APTC$ with linear recursion). *Each process term in $APTC$ with linear recursion is equal to a process term $\langle X_1|E\rangle$ with E a linear recursive specification.*

Theorem 3.55 (Soundness of $APTC$ with guarded recursion). *Let x and y be $APTC$ with guarded recursion terms. If $APTC$ with guarded recursion $\vdash x = y$, then*

1. $x \sim_s y$;
2. $x \sim_p y$;
3. $x \sim_{hp} y$;
4. $x \sim_{hhp} y$.

Theorem 3.56 (Completeness of $APTC$ with linear recursion). *Let p and q be closed $APTC$ with linear recursion terms, then,*

1. *if* $p \sim_s q$ *then* $p = q$;
2. *if* $p \sim_p q$ *then* $p = q$;
3. *if* $p \sim_{hp} q$ *then* $p = q$;
4. *if* $p \sim_{hhp} q$ *then* $p = q$.

Table 3.14 Axioms of silent step.

No.	Axiom
$B1$	$e \cdot \tau = e$
$B2$	$e \cdot (\tau \cdot (x + y) + x) = e \cdot (x + y)$
$B3$	$x \parallel \tau = x$

3.8.3 Abstraction

Definition 3.57 (Guarded linear recursive specification). A recursive specification is linear if its recursive equations are of the form

$$(a_{11} \parallel \cdots \parallel a_{1i_1})X_1 + \cdots + (a_{k1} \parallel \cdots \parallel a_{ki_k})X_k + (b_{11} \parallel \cdots \parallel b_{1j_1}) + \cdots + (b_{1j_1} \parallel \cdots \parallel b_{lj_l})$$

where $a_{11}, \cdots, a_{1i_1}, a_{k1}, \cdots, a_{ki_k}, b_{11}, \cdots, b_{1j_1}, b_{1j_1}, \cdots, b_{lj_l} \in \mathbb{E} \cup \{\tau\}$, and the sum above is allowed to be empty, in which case it represents the deadlock δ.

A linear recursive specification E is guarded if there does not exist an infinite sequence of τ-transitions $\langle X|E\rangle \xrightarrow{\tau} \langle X'|E\rangle \xrightarrow{\tau} \langle X''|E\rangle \xrightarrow{\tau} \cdots$.

The transition rules of τ are the same, and axioms of τ are as Table 3.14 shows.

Theorem 3.58 (Conservativity of $APTC$ with silent step and guarded linear recursion). *$APTC$ with silent step and guarded linear recursion is a conservative extension of $APTC$ with linear recursion.*

Theorem 3.59 (Congruence theorem of $APTC$ with silent step and guarded linear recursion). *Rooted branching truly concurrent bisimulation equivalences $\approx_{rbp}$, $\approx_{rbs}$, $\approx_{rbhp}$, and $\approx_{rbhhp}$ are all congruences with respect to $APTC$ with silent step and guarded linear recursion.*

Theorem 3.60 (Elimination theorem of $APTC$ with silent step and guarded linear recursion). *Each process term in $APTC$ with silent step and guarded linear recursion is equal to a process term $\langle X_1|E\rangle$ with E a guarded linear recursive specification.*

Theorem 3.61 (Soundness of $APTC$ with silent step and guarded linear recursion). *Let x and y be $APTC$ with silent step and guarded linear recursion terms. If $APTC$ with silent step and guarded linear recursion $\vdash x = y$, then*

1. $x \approx_{rbs} y$;
2. $x \approx_{rbp} y$;
3. $x \approx_{rbhp} y$;
4. $x \approx_{rbhhp} y$.

Theorem 3.62 (Completeness of $APTC$ with silent step and guarded linear recursion). *Let p and q be closed $APTC$ with silent step and guarded linear recursion terms, then,*

Table 3.15 Axioms of abstraction operator.

No.	Axiom
$TI1$	$e \notin I \quad \tau_I(e) = e$
$TI2$	$e \in I \quad \tau_I(e) = \tau$
$TI3$	$\tau_I(\delta) = \delta$
$TI4$	$\tau_I(x + y) = \tau_I(x) + \tau_I(y)$
$TI5$	$\tau_I(x \cdot y) = \tau_I(x) \cdot \tau_I(y)$
$TI6$	$\tau_I(x \between y) = \tau_I(x) \between \tau_I(y)$

1. *if $p \approx_{rbs} q$ then $p = q$;*
2. *if $p \approx_{rbp} q$ then $p = q$;*
3. *if $p \approx_{rbhp} q$ then $p = q$;*
4. *if $p \approx_{rbhhp} q$ then $p = q$.*

The transition rules of τ_I are the same, and the axioms are shown in Table 3.15.

Theorem 3.63 (Conservativity of $APTC_\tau$ with guarded linear recursion). *$APTC_\tau$ with guarded linear recursion is a conservative extension of $APTC$ with silent step and guarded linear recursion.*

Theorem 3.64 (Congruence theorem of $APTC_\tau$ with guarded linear recursion). *Rooted branching truly concurrent bisimulation equivalences $\approx_{rbp}$, $\approx_{rbs}$, $\approx_{rbhp}$, and $\approx_{rbhhp}$ are all congruences with respect to $APTC_\tau$ with guarded linear recursion.*

Theorem 3.65 (Soundness of $APTC_\tau$ with guarded linear recursion). *Let x and y be $APTC_\tau$ with guarded linear recursion terms. If $APTC_\tau$ with guarded linear recursion $\vdash x = y$, then*

1. $x \approx_{rbs} y$;
2. $x \approx_{rbp} y$;
3. $x \approx_{rbhp} y$;
4. $x \approx_{rbhhp} y$.

Definition 3.66 (Cluster). Let E be a guarded linear recursive specification, and $I \subseteq \mathbb{E}$. Two recursion variable X and Y in E are in the same cluster for I iff there exist sequences of transitions $\langle X|E\rangle \xrightarrow{\{b_{11},\cdots,b_{1i}\}} \cdots \xrightarrow{\{b_{m1},\cdots,b_{mi}\}} \langle Y|E\rangle$ and $\langle Y|E\rangle \xrightarrow{\{c_{11},\cdots,c_{1j}\}} \cdots \xrightarrow{\{c_{n1},\cdots,c_{nj}\}} \langle X|E\rangle$, where $b_{11},\cdots,b_{mi},c_{11},\cdots,c_{nj} \in I \cup \{\tau\}$.

$a_1 \between \cdots \between a_k$ or $(a_1 \between \cdots \between a_k)X$ is an exit for the cluster C iff: (1) $a_1 \between \cdots \between a_k$ or $(a_1 \between \cdots \between a_k)X$ is a summand at the right-hand side of the recursive equation for a recursion variable in C, and (2) in the case of $(a_1 \between \cdots \between a_k)X$, either $a_l \notin I \cup \{\tau\} (l \in \{1,2,\cdots,k\})$ or $X \notin C$.

The CFAR are shown in Table 3.16.

Theorem 3.67 (Soundness of $CFAR$). *$CFAR$ is sound modulo rooted branching truly concurrent bisimulation equivalences $\approx_{rbs}$, $\approx_{rbp}$, $\approx_{rbhp}$, and $\approx_{rbhhp}$.*

Table 3.16 Cluster fair abstraction rule.

No.	Axiom
$CFAR$	If X is in a cluster for I with exits $\{(a_{11} \between \cdots \between a_{1i})Y_1, \cdots, (a_{m1} \between \cdots \between a_{mi})Y_m, b_{11} \between \cdots \between b_{1j}, \cdots, b_{n1} \between \cdots \between b_{nj}\}$, then $\tau \cdot \tau_I(\langle X\|E\rangle) =$ $\tau \cdot \tau_I((a_{11} \between \cdots \between a_{1i})\langle Y_1\|E\rangle + \cdots + (a_{m1} \between \cdots \between a_{mi})\langle Y_m\|E\rangle + b_{11} \between \cdots \between b_{1j} + \cdots + b_{n1} \between \cdots \between b_{nj})$

Theorem 3.68 (Completeness of $APTC_\tau$ with guarded linear recursion and $CFAR$). *Let p and q be closed $APTC_\tau$ with guarded linear recursion and $CFAR$ terms, then,*

1. *if $p \approx_{rbs} q$ then $p = q$;*
2. *if $p \approx_{rbp} q$ then $p = q$;*
3. *if $p \approx_{rbhp} q$ then $p = q$;*
4. *if $p \approx_{rbhhp} q$ then $p = q$.*

3.9 APTC with asynchronous communication

Let c be a channel, Δ be a finite set of data. For $d \in \Delta$, $c \uparrow d$ is a potential action to send data d via channel c, $c \Uparrow d$ is an actual action to send data d via channel c; and $c \downarrow d$ is a potential action to receive data d via channel c, $c \Downarrow d$ is an actual action to receive data d via channel c. Let the action $b \in \mathbb{B}$ be not related to channel c, and $\mathbb{E} = \mathbb{B} \cup \{\delta\} \cup \{c \uparrow d\} \cup \{c \Uparrow d\} \cup \{c \downarrow d\} \cup \{c \Downarrow d\}$. Let σ be the sequence of data and $\sigma_1 * \sigma_2$ be the concatenation of data sequences σ_1 and σ_2. For $\sigma =< d_1, \cdots, d_n >$, $last(\sigma) = d_n$ if $1 \leq n$. For a queue-like channel, the unary operator $\mu_c^\sigma(x)$ denotes that in x, the channel c initially contains the data sequence σ and outside x, no communications via c are performed. For a bag-like channel, the unary operator $\mu_c^M(x)$ denoted the similar thing, but M is a multiset of data. We remain the synchronous communication merge $|$, and for causality-based asynchronous communication, we just add the causal constraints on the send and receive actions, any violation of the constraints will cause deadlock, that is, $\{\delta | c \downarrow d \leq c \uparrow d, c \Downarrow d \leq c \Uparrow d\}$.

We give the transition rules of APTC with asynchronous communication as Table 3.17 shows.

We define the basic terms for APTC with asynchronous communication.

Definition 3.69 (Basic terms of APTC with asynchronous communication). The set of basic terms of APTC with asynchronous communication, $\mathcal{B}(APTCAC)$, is inductively defined as follows:

1. $\mathbb{E} \subset \mathcal{B}(APTCAC)$;
2. if $e \in \mathbb{E}, t \in \mathcal{B}(APTCAC)$ then $e \cdot t \in \mathcal{B}(APTCAC)$;
3. if $t, s \in \mathcal{B}(APTCAC)$ then $t + s \in \mathcal{B}(APTCAC)$;
4. if $t, s \in \mathcal{B}(APTCAC)$ then $t \between s \in \mathcal{B}(APTCAC)$.

Table 3.17 Transition rules of APTC with asynchronous communication.

$$\frac{x \xrightarrow{e_1} \surd \quad y \xrightarrow{e_2} \surd}{x \parallel y \xrightarrow{\{e_1,e_2\}} \surd} \qquad \frac{x \xrightarrow{e_1} x' \quad y \xrightarrow{e_2} \surd}{x \parallel y \xrightarrow{\{e_1,e_2\}} x'}$$

$$\frac{x \xrightarrow{e_1} \surd \quad y \xrightarrow{e_2} y'}{x \parallel y \xrightarrow{\{e_1,e_2\}} y'} \qquad \frac{x \xrightarrow{e_1} x' \quad y \xrightarrow{e_2} y'}{x \parallel y \xrightarrow{\{e_1,e_2\}} x' \between y'}$$

$$\frac{x \xrightarrow{e_1} \surd \quad y \xrightarrow{e_2} \surd \quad (e_1 \leq e_2)}{x \mathbin{\underline{\parallel}} y \xrightarrow{\{e_1,e_2\}} \surd} \qquad \frac{x \xrightarrow{e_1} x' \quad y \xrightarrow{e_2} \surd \quad (e_1 \leq e_2)}{x \mathbin{\underline{\parallel}} y \xrightarrow{\{e_1,e_2\}} x'}$$

$$\frac{x \xrightarrow{e_1} \surd \quad y \xrightarrow{e_2} y' \quad (e_1 \leq e_2)}{x \mathbin{\underline{\parallel}} y \xrightarrow{\{e_1,e_2\}} y'} \qquad \frac{x \xrightarrow{e_1} x' \quad y \xrightarrow{e_2} y' \quad (e_1 \leq e_2)}{x \mathbin{\underline{\parallel}} y \xrightarrow{\{e_1,e_2\}} x' \between y'}$$

$$\frac{x \xrightarrow{e_1} \surd \quad y \xrightarrow{e_2} \surd}{x \mid y \xrightarrow{\gamma(e_1,e_2)} \surd} \qquad \frac{x \xrightarrow{e_1} x' \quad y \xrightarrow{e_2} \surd}{x \mid y \xrightarrow{\gamma(e_1,e_2)} x'}$$

$$\frac{x \xrightarrow{e_1} \surd \quad y \xrightarrow{e_2} y'}{x \mid y \xrightarrow{\gamma(e_1,e_2)} y'} \qquad \frac{x \xrightarrow{e_1} x' \quad y \xrightarrow{e_2} y'}{x \mid y \xrightarrow{\gamma(e_1,e_2)} x' \between y'}$$

$$\frac{x \xrightarrow{e_1} \surd \quad (\sharp(e_1,e_2))}{\Theta(x) \xrightarrow{e_1} \surd} \qquad \frac{x \xrightarrow{e_2} \surd \quad (\sharp(e_1,e_2))}{\Theta(x) \xrightarrow{e_2} \surd}$$

$$\frac{x \xrightarrow{e_1} x' \quad (\sharp(e_1,e_2))}{\Theta(x) \xrightarrow{e_1} \Theta(x')} \qquad \frac{x \xrightarrow{e_2} x' \quad (\sharp(e_1,e_2))}{\Theta(x) \xrightarrow{e_2} \Theta(x')}$$

$$\frac{x \xrightarrow{e_1} \surd \quad y \nrightarrow^{e_2} \quad (\sharp(e_1,e_2))}{x \triangleleft y \xrightarrow{\tau} \surd} \qquad \frac{x \xrightarrow{e_1} x' \quad y \nrightarrow^{e_2} \quad (\sharp(e_1,e_2))}{x \triangleleft y \xrightarrow{\tau} x'}$$

$$\frac{x \xrightarrow{e_1} \surd \quad y \nrightarrow^{e_3} \quad (\sharp(e_1,e_2), e_2 \leq e_3)}{x \triangleleft y \xrightarrow{\tau} \surd} \qquad \frac{x \xrightarrow{e_1} x' \quad y \nrightarrow^{e_3} \quad (\sharp(e_1,e_2), e_2 \leq e_3)}{x \triangleleft y \xrightarrow{\tau} x'}$$

$$\frac{x \xrightarrow{e_3} \surd \quad y \nrightarrow^{e_2} \quad (\sharp(e_1,e_2), e_1 \leq e_3)}{x \triangleleft y \xrightarrow{\tau} \surd} \qquad \frac{x \xrightarrow{e_3} x' \quad y \nrightarrow^{e_2} \quad (\sharp(e_1,e_2), e_1 \leq e_3)}{x \triangleleft y \xrightarrow{\tau} x'}$$

$$\frac{x \xrightarrow{e} \surd \quad e \neq c \uparrow d \neq c \downarrow d}{\mu_c^{\sigma}(x) \xrightarrow{e} \surd} \qquad \frac{x \xrightarrow{e} x' \quad e \neq c \uparrow d \neq c \downarrow d}{\mu_c^{\sigma}(x) \xrightarrow{e} \mu_c^{\sigma}(x')}$$

$$\frac{x \xrightarrow{c\uparrow d} \surd}{\mu_c^{\sigma}(x) \xrightarrow{c\Uparrow d} \surd} \qquad \frac{x \xrightarrow{c\uparrow d} x'}{\mu_c^{\sigma}(x) \xrightarrow{c\Uparrow d} \mu_c^{d*\sigma}(x')}$$

$$\frac{x \xrightarrow{c\downarrow d} \surd}{\mu_c^{\sigma}(x) \xrightarrow{c\Downarrow d} \surd} \qquad \frac{x \xrightarrow{c\Downarrow d} x'}{\mu_c^{\sigma*d}(x) \xrightarrow{c\Downarrow d} \mu_c^{\sigma}(x')}$$

$$\frac{x \xrightarrow{e} \surd \quad e \neq c \uparrow d \neq c \downarrow d}{\mu_c^{M}(x) \xrightarrow{e} \surd} \qquad \frac{x \xrightarrow{e} x' \quad e \neq c \uparrow d \neq c \downarrow d}{\mu_c^{M}(x) \xrightarrow{e} \mu_c^{M}(x')}$$

$$\frac{x \xrightarrow{c\uparrow d} \surd}{\mu_c^{M}(x) \xrightarrow{c\Uparrow d} \surd} \qquad \frac{x \xrightarrow{c\uparrow d} x'}{\mu_c^{M}(x) \xrightarrow{c\Uparrow d} \mu_c^{M\cup\{d\}}(x')}$$

$$\frac{x \xrightarrow{c\downarrow d} \surd}{\mu_c^{M}(x) \xrightarrow{c\Downarrow d} \surd} \qquad \frac{x \xrightarrow{c\Downarrow d} x'}{\mu_c^{M\cup\{d\}}(x) \xrightarrow{c\Downarrow d} \mu_c^{M}(x')}$$

Theorem 3.70 (Congruence theorem of APTC with asynchronous communication). *Truly concurrent bisimulation equivalences* $\sim_p$, $\sim_s$, $\sim_{hp}$, *and* $\sim_{hhp}$ *are all congruences with respect to APTC with asynchronous communication.*

So, we design the axioms of parallelism in Table 3.18, including algebraic laws for parallel operator $\parallel$, communication operator $\mid$, conflict elimination operator Θ and unless operator $\triangleleft$, and also the whole parallel operator $\between$. Since the communication between two communicating events in different parallel branches may cause deadlock (a state of inactivity), which is caused by mismatch of two communicating events or the imperfectness of the communication channel. We use the constant δ to denote the deadlock, and let the atomic event $e \in \mathbb{E}$.

Based on the definition of basic terms for APTC with asynchronous communication (see Definition 3.69) and axioms of parallelism (see Table 3.18), we can prove the elimination theorem of parallelism.

Theorem 3.71 (Elimination theorem of parallelism). *Let* p *be a closed APTC with asynchronous communication term. Then there is a basic APTC with asynchronous communication term* q *such that APTC with asynchronous communication* $\vdash p = q$.

Theorem 3.72 (Generalization of APTC with asynchronous communication with respect to BATC). *APTC with asynchronous communication is a generalization of BATC.*

Theorem 3.73 (Soundness of APTC with asynchronous communication modulo pomset bisimulation equivalence). *Let* x *and* y *be APTC with asynchronous communication terms. If APTC with asynchronous communication* $\vdash x = y$, *then* $x \sim_p y$.

Theorem 3.74 (Completeness of APTC with asynchronous communication modulo pomset bisimulation equivalence). *Let* p *and* q *be closed APTC with asynchronous communication terms, if* $p \sim_p q$ *then* $p = q$.

Theorem 3.75 (Soundness of APTC with asynchronous communication modulo step bisimulation equivalence). *Let* x *and* y *be APTC with asynchronous communication terms. If APTC with asynchronous communication* $\vdash x = y$, *then* $x \sim_s y$.

Theorem 3.76 (Completeness of APTC with asynchronous communication modulo step bisimulation equivalence). *Let* p *and* q *be closed APTC with asynchronous communication terms, if* $p \sim_s q$ *then* $p = q$.

Theorem 3.77 (Soundness of APTC with asynchronous communication modulo hp-bisimulation equivalence). *Let* x *and* y *be APTC with asynchronous communication terms. If APTC with asynchronous communication* $\vdash x = y$, *then* $x \sim_{hp} y$.

Table 3.18 Axioms of parallelism.

No.	Axiom
$A6$	$x+\delta=x$
$A7$	$\delta\cdot x=\delta$
$P1$	$x \between y = x \parallel y + x \mid y$
$P2$	$x \parallel y = y \parallel x$
$P3$	$(x \parallel y) \parallel z = x \parallel (y \parallel z)$
$P4$	$x \parallel y = x \mathbin{\lfloor\!\lfloor} y + y \mathbin{\lfloor\!\lfloor} x$
$P5$	$(e_1 \leq e_2) \quad e_1 \mathbin{\lfloor\!\lfloor} (e_2\cdot y) = (e_1 \mathbin{\lfloor\!\lfloor} e_2)\cdot y$
$P6$	$(e_1 \leq e_2) \quad (e_1\cdot x) \mathbin{\lfloor\!\lfloor} e_2 = (e_1 \mathbin{\lfloor\!\lfloor} e_2)\cdot x$
$P7$	$(e_1 \leq e_2) \quad (e_1\cdot x) \mathbin{\lfloor\!\lfloor} (e_2\cdot y) = (e_1 \mathbin{\lfloor\!\lfloor} e_2)\cdot (x \between y)$
$P8$	$(x+y) \mathbin{\lfloor\!\lfloor} z = (x \mathbin{\lfloor\!\lfloor} z) + (y \mathbin{\lfloor\!\lfloor} z)$
$P9$	$\delta \mathbin{\lfloor\!\lfloor} x = \delta$
$C1$	$e_1 \mid e_2 = \gamma(e_1, e_2)$
$C2$	$e_1 \mid (e_2\cdot y) = \gamma(e_1, e_2)\cdot y$
$C3$	$(e_1\cdot x) \mid e_2 = \gamma(e_1, e_2)\cdot x$
$C4$	$(e_1\cdot x) \mid (e_2\cdot y) = \gamma(e_1, e_2)\cdot (x \between y)$
$C5$	$(x+y) \mid z = (x \mid z) + (y \mid z)$
$C6$	$x \mid (y+z) = (x \mid y) + (x \mid z)$
$C7$	$\delta \mid x = \delta$
$C8$	$x \mid \delta = \delta$
$CE1$	$\Theta(e)=e$
$CE2$	$\Theta(\delta)=\delta$
$CE3$	$\Theta(x+y)=\Theta(x)+\Theta(y)$
$CE4$	$\Theta(x\cdot y)=\Theta(x)\cdot\Theta(y)$
$CE5$	$\Theta(x \parallel y) = ((\Theta(x) \triangleleft y) \parallel y) + ((\Theta(y) \triangleleft x) \parallel x)$
$CE6$	$\Theta(x \mid y) = ((\Theta(x) \triangleleft y) \mid y) + ((\Theta(y) \triangleleft x) \mid x)$
$U1$	$(\sharp(e_1, e_2)) \quad e_1 \triangleleft e_2 = \tau$
$U2$	$(\sharp(e_1, e_2), e_2 \leq e_3) \quad e_1 \triangleleft e_3 = \tau$
$U3$	$(\sharp(e_1, e_2), e_2 \leq e_3) \quad e3 \triangleleft e_1 = \tau$
$U4$	$e \triangleleft \delta = e$
$U5$	$\delta \triangleleft e = \delta$
$U6$	$(x+y) \triangleleft z = (x \triangleleft z) + (y \triangleleft z)$
$U7$	$(x\cdot y) \triangleleft z = (x \triangleleft z)\cdot(y \triangleleft z)$
$U8$	$(x \mathbin{\lfloor\!\lfloor} y) \triangleleft z = (x \triangleleft z) \mathbin{\lfloor\!\lfloor} (y \triangleleft z)$
$U9$	$(x \mid y) \triangleleft z = (x \triangleleft z) \mid (y \triangleleft z)$
$U10$	$x \triangleleft (y+z) = (x \triangleleft y) \triangleleft z$
$U11$	$x \triangleleft (y\cdot z) = (x \triangleleft y) \triangleleft z$
$U12$	$x \triangleleft (y \mathbin{\lfloor\!\lfloor} z) = (x \triangleleft y) \triangleleft z$
$U13$	$x \triangleleft (y \mid z) = (x \triangleleft y) \triangleleft z$
$AM1$	$(e \neq c \uparrow d \neq c \downarrow d) \quad \mu_c^{\sigma}(e)=e$
$AM2$	$(e \neq c \uparrow d \neq c \downarrow d) \quad \mu_c^{\sigma}(e\cdot x)=e\cdot\mu_c^{\sigma}(x)$
$AM3$	$(e \neq c \uparrow d \neq c \downarrow d) \quad \mu_c^{\sigma}(e \mathbin{\lfloor\!\lfloor} x)=e \mathbin{\lfloor\!\lfloor} \mu_c^{\sigma}(x)$
$AM4$	$\mu_c^{\sigma}(c \uparrow d) = c \Uparrow d$

continued on next page

Table 3.18 (continued)

No.	Axiom
$AM5$	$\mu_c^{\sigma}(c \uparrow d \cdot x) = c \Uparrow d \cdot \mu_c^{d*\sigma}(x)$
$AM6$	$\mu_c^{\sigma}(c \uparrow d \between x) = c \Uparrow d \between \mu_c^{d*\sigma}(x)$
$AM7$	$\mu_c^{\sigma*d}(c \downarrow d) = c \Downarrow d$
$AM8$	$\mu_c^{\sigma*d}(c \downarrow d \cdot x) = c \Downarrow d \cdot \mu_c^{\sigma}(x)$
$AM9$	$\mu_c^{\sigma*d}(c \downarrow d \between x) = c \Downarrow d \between \mu_c^{\sigma}(x)$
$AM10$	$(d \neq last(\sigma) \text{ or } \sigma = \emptyset) \quad \mu_c^{\sigma}(c \downarrow d) = \delta$
$AM11$	$(d \neq last(\sigma) \text{ or } \sigma = \emptyset) \quad \mu_c^{\sigma}(c \downarrow d \cdot x) = \delta$
$AM12$	$(d \neq last(\sigma) \text{ or } \sigma = \emptyset) \quad \mu_c^{\sigma}(c \downarrow d \between x) = \delta$
$AM13$	$\mu_c^{\sigma}(x + y) = \mu_c^{\sigma}(x) + \mu_c^{\sigma}(y)$
$AM14$	$(e \neq c \uparrow d \neq c \downarrow d) \quad \mu_c^{M}(e) = e$
$AM15$	$(e \neq c \uparrow d \neq c \downarrow d) \quad \mu_c^{M}(e \cdot x) = e \cdot \mu_c^{M}(x)$
$AM16$	$(e \neq c \uparrow d \neq c \downarrow d) \quad \mu_c^{M}(e \between x) = e \between \mu_c^{M}(x)$
$AM17$	$\mu_c^{M}(c \uparrow d) = c \Uparrow d$
$AM18$	$\mu_c^{M}(c \uparrow d \cdot x) = c \Uparrow d \cdot \mu_c^{M \cup \{d\}}(x)$
$AM19$	$\mu_c^{M}(c \uparrow d \between x) = c \Uparrow d \between \mu_c^{M \cup \{d\}}(x)$
$AM20$	$\mu_c^{M \cup \{d\}}(c \downarrow d) = c \Downarrow d$
$AM21$	$\mu_c^{M \cup \{d\}}(c \downarrow d \cdot x) = c \Downarrow d \cdot \mu_c^{M}(x)$
$AM22$	$\mu_c^{M \cup \{d\}}(c \downarrow d \between x) = c \Downarrow d \between \mu_c^{M}(x)$
$AM23$	$(d \notin M) \quad \mu_c^{M}(c \downarrow d) = \delta$
$AM24$	$(d \notin M) \quad \mu_c^{M}(c \downarrow d \cdot x) = \delta$
$AM25$	$(d \notin M) \quad \mu_c^{M}(c \downarrow d \between x) = \delta$
$AM26$	$\mu_c^{M}(x + y) = \mu_c^{M}(x) + \mu_c^{M}(y)$
$AM27$	$\mu_c^{\sigma}(\delta) = \delta$
$AM27$	$\mu_c^{M}(\delta) = \delta$

Theorem 3.78 (Completeness of APTC with asynchronous communication modulo hp-bisimulation equivalence). *Let p and q be closed APTC with asynchronous communication terms, if $p \sim_{hp} q$ then $p = q$.*

Theorem 3.79 (Soundness of APTC with asynchronous communication modulo hhp-bisimulation equivalence). *Let x and y be APTC with asynchronous communication terms. If APTC with asynchronous communication $\vdash x = y$, then $x \sim_{hhp} y$.*

Theorem 3.80 (Completeness of APTC with asynchronous communication modulo hhp-bisimulation equivalence). *Let p and q be closed APTC with asynchronous communication terms, if $p \sim_{hhp} q$ then $p = q$.*

3.10 Applications

APTC provides a formal framework based on truly concurrent behavioral semantics, which can be used to verify the correctness of system behaviors. In this subsection, we tend to choose alternating bit protocol (ABP) [24].

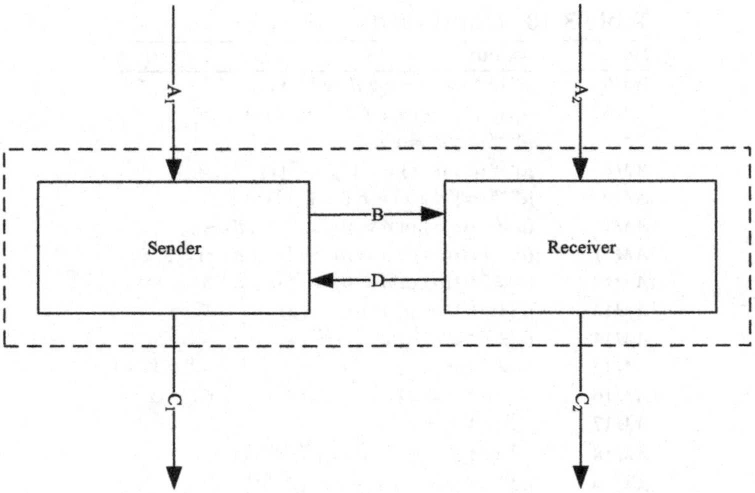

FIGURE 3.1 Alternating bit protocol.

The ABP protocol is used to ensure successful transmission of data through a corrupted channel. This success is based on the assumption that data can be resent an unlimited number of times, which is illustrated in Fig. 3.1, we alter it into the true concurrency situation.

1. Data elements $d_1, d_2, d_3, \cdots$ from a finite set Δ are communicated between a Sender and a Receiver.
2. If the Sender reads a datum from channel A_1, then this datum is sent to the Receiver in parallel through channel A_2.
3. The Sender processes the data in Δ, forms new data, and sends them to the Receiver through channel B.
4. And the Receiver sends the datum into channel C_2.
5. If channel B is corrupted, the message communicated through B can be turn into an error message $\perp$.
6. Every time the Receiver receives a message via channel B, it sends an acknowledgment to the Sender via channel D, which is also corrupted.
7. Finally, then Sender and the Receiver send out their outputs in parallel through channels C_1 and C_2.

In the truly concurrent ABP, the Sender sends its data to the Receiver; and the Receiver can also send its data to the Sender, for simplicity and without loss of generality, we assume that only the Sender sends its data and the Receiver only receives the data from the Sender. The Sender attaches a bit 0 to data elements d_{2k-1} and a bit 1 to data elements d_{2k}, when they are sent into channel B. When the Receiver reads a datum, it sends back the attached bit via channel D. If the Receiver receives a corrupted message, then it sends back the previous acknowledgment to the Sender.

Then the state transition of the Sender can be described by $APTC$ as follows.

$$S_b = \sum_{d\in\Delta} r_{A_1}(d) \cdot T_{db}$$

$$T_{db} = (\sum_{d'\in\Delta} (s_B(d', b) \cdot s_{C_1}(d')) + s_B(\bot)) \cdot U_{db}$$

$$U_{db} = r_D(b) \cdot S_{1-b} + (r_D(1-b) + r_D(\bot)) \cdot T_{db}$$

where s_B denotes sending data through channel B, r_D denotes receiving data through channel D, similarly, r_{A_1} means receiving data via channel A_1, s_{C_1} denotes sending data via channel C_1, and $b \in \{0, 1\}$.

And the state transition of the Receiver can be described by $APTC$ as follows.

$$R_b = \sum_{d\in\Delta} r_{A_2}(d) \cdot R'_b$$

$$R'_b = \sum_{d'\in\Delta} \{r_B(d', b) \cdot s_{C_2}(d') \cdot Q_b + r_B(d', 1-b) \cdot Q_{1-b}\} + r_B(\bot) \cdot Q_{1-b}$$

$$Q_b = (s_D(b) + s_D(\bot)) \cdot R_{1-b}$$

where r_{A_2} denotes receiving data via channel A_2, r_B denotes receiving data via channel B, s_{C_2} denotes sending data via channel C_2, s_D denotes sending data via channel D, and $b \in \{0, 1\}$.

The send action and receive action of the same data through the same channel can communicate each other, otherwise, a deadlock δ will be caused. We define the following communication functions.

$$\gamma(s_B(d', b), r_B(d', b)) \triangleq c_B(d', b)$$

$$\gamma(s_B(\bot), r_B(\bot)) \triangleq c_B(\bot)$$

$$\gamma(s_D(b), r_D(b)) \triangleq c_D(b)$$

$$\gamma(s_D(\bot), r_D(\bot)) \triangleq c_D(\bot)$$

Let R_0 and S_0 be in parallel, then the system $R_0 S_0$ can be represented by the following process term.

$$\tau_I(\partial_H(\Theta(R_0 \between S_0))) = \tau_I(\partial_H(R_0 \between S_0))$$

where $H = \{s_B(d', b), r_B(d', b), s_D(b), r_D(b) | d' \in \Delta, b \in \{0, 1\}\}$
$\{s_B(\bot), r_B(\bot), s_D(\bot), r_D(\bot)\}$
$I = \{c_B(d', b), c_D(b) | d' \in \Delta, b \in \{0, 1\}\} \cup \{c_B(\bot), c_D(\bot)\}$.

Then we get the following conclusion.

Theorem 3.81 (Correctness of the ABP protocol). *The ABP protocol $\tau_I(\partial_H(R_0 \between S_0))$ can exhibit desired external behaviors.*

Proof. By use of the algebraic laws of $APTC$, we have the following expansions.

$$\begin{aligned}
R_0 \between S_0 &\overset{\text{P1}}{=} R_0 \parallel S_0 + R_0 \mid S_0\\
&\overset{\text{RDP}}{=} (\sum_{d\in\Delta} r_{A_2}(d)\cdot R_0') \parallel (\sum_{d\in\Delta} r_{A_1}(d) T_{d0})\\
&+ (\sum_{d\in\Delta} r_{A_2}(d)\cdot R_0') \mid (\sum_{d\in\Delta} r_{A_1}(d) T_{d0})\\
&\overset{\text{P6,C14}}{=} \sum_{d\in\Delta}(r_{A_2}(d) \parallel r_{A_1}(d)) R_0' \between T_{d0} + \delta\cdot R_0' \between T_{d0}\\
&\overset{\text{A6,A7}}{=} \sum_{d\in\Delta}(r_{A_2}(d) \parallel r_{A_1}(d)) R_0' \between T_{d0}
\end{aligned}$$

$$\begin{aligned}
\partial_H(R_0 \between S_0) &= \partial_H(\sum_{d\in\Delta}(r_{A_2}(d) \parallel r_{A_1}(d)) R_0' \between T_{d0})\\
&= \sum_{d\in\Delta}(r_{A_2}(d) \parallel r_{A_1}(d)) \partial_H(R_0' \between T_{d0})
\end{aligned}$$

Similarly, we can get the following equations.

$$\begin{aligned}
\partial_H(R_0 \between S_0) &= \sum_{d\in\Delta}(r_{A_2}(d) \parallel r_{A_1}(d))\cdot \partial_H(T_{d0} \between R_0')\\
\partial_H(T_{d0} \between R_0') &= c_B(d',0)\cdot(s_{C_1}(d') \parallel s_{C_2}(d'))\cdot \partial_H(U_{d0} \between Q_0) + c_B(\bot)\cdot \partial_H(U_{d0} \between Q_1)\\
\partial_H(U_{d0} \between Q_1) &= (c_D(1) + c_D(\bot))\cdot \partial_H(T_{d0} \between R_0')\\
\partial_H(Q_0 \between U_{d0}) &= c_D(0)\cdot \partial_H(R_1 \between S_1) + c_D(\bot)\cdot \partial_H(R_1' \between T_{d0})\\
\partial_H(R_1' \between T_{d0}) &= (c_B(d',0) + c_B(\bot))\cdot \partial_H(Q_0 \between U_{d0})\\
\partial_H(R_1 \between S_1) &= \sum_{d\in\Delta}(r_{A_2}(d) \parallel r_{A_1}(d))\cdot \partial_H(T_{d1} \between R_1')\\
\partial_H(T_{d1} \between R_1') &= c_B(d',1)\cdot(s_{C_1}(d') \parallel s_{C_2}(d'))\cdot \partial_H(U_{d1} \between Q_1) + c_B(\bot)\cdot \partial_H(U_{d1} \between Q_0')\\
\partial_H(U_{d1} \between Q_0') &= (c_D(0) + c_D(\bot))\cdot \partial_H(T_{d1} \between R_1')\\
\partial_H(Q_1 \between U_{d1}) &= c_D(1)\cdot \partial_H(R_0 \between S_0) + c_D(\bot)\cdot \partial_H(R_0' \between T_{d1})\\
\partial_H(R_0' \between T_{d1}) &= (c_B(d',1) + c_B(\bot))\cdot \partial_H(Q_1 \between U_{d1})
\end{aligned}$$

Let $\partial_H(R_0 \between S_0) = \langle X_1 | E\rangle$, where E is the following guarded linear recursion specification:

$$\begin{aligned}
\{X_1 &= \sum_{d\in\Delta}(r_{A_2}(d) \parallel r_{A_1}(d))\cdot X_{2d}, Y_1 = \sum_{d\in\Delta}(r_{A_2}(d) \parallel r_{A_1}(d))\cdot Y_{2d},\\
X_{2d} &= c_B(d',0)\cdot X_{4d} + c_B(\bot)\cdot X_{3d}, Y_{2d} = c_B(d',1)\cdot Y_{4d} + c_B(\bot)\cdot Y_{3d},
\end{aligned}$$

$$X_{3d} = (c_D(1) + c_D(\bot)) \cdot X_{2d}, Y_{3d} = (c_D(0) + c_D(\bot)) \cdot Y_{2d},$$
$$X_{4d} = (s_{C_1}(d') \parallel s_{C_2}(d')) \cdot X_{5d}, Y_{4d} = (s_{C_1}(d') \parallel s_{C_2}(d')) \cdot Y_{5d},$$
$$X_{5d} = c_D(0) \cdot Y_1 + c_D(\bot) \cdot X_{6d}, Y_{5d} = c_D(1) \cdot X_1 + c_D(\bot) \cdot Y_{6d},$$
$$X_{6d} = (c_B(d,0) + c_B(\bot)) \cdot X_{5d}, Y_{6d} = (c_B(d,1) + c_B(\bot)) \cdot Y_{5d}$$
$$|d, d' \in \Delta\}$$

Then we apply abstraction operator τ_I into $\langle X_1|E\rangle$.

$$\begin{aligned}\tau_I(\langle X_1|E\rangle) &= \sum_{d\in\Delta}(r_{A_1}(d) \parallel r_{A_2}(d)) \cdot \tau_I(\langle X_{2d}|E\rangle)\\ &= \sum_{d\in\Delta}(r_{A_1}(d) \parallel r_{A_2}(d)) \cdot \tau_I(\langle X_{4d}|E\rangle)\\ &= \sum_{d,d'\in\Delta}(r_{A_1}(d) \parallel r_{A_2}(d)) \cdot (s_{C_1}(d') \parallel s_{C_2}(d')) \cdot \tau_I(\langle X_{5d}|E\rangle)\\ &= \sum_{d,d'\in\Delta}(r_{A_1}(d) \parallel r_{A_2}(d)) \cdot (s_{C_1}(d') \parallel s_{C_2}(d')) \cdot \tau_I(\langle Y_1|E\rangle)\end{aligned}$$

Similarly, we can get $\tau_I(\langle Y_1|E\rangle) = \sum_{d,d'\in\Delta}(r_{A_1}(d) \parallel r_{A_2}(d)) \cdot (s_{C_1}(d') \parallel s_{C_2}(d')) \cdot \tau_I(\langle X_1|E\rangle)$.

We get $\tau_I(\partial_H(R_0 \between S_0)) = \sum_{d,d'\in\Delta}(r_{A_1}(d) \parallel r_{A_2}(d)) \cdot (s_{C_1}(d') \parallel s_{C_2}(d')) \cdot \tau_I(\partial_H(R_0 \between S_0))$. So, the ABP protocol $\tau_I(\partial_H(R_0 \between S_0))$ can exhibit desired external behaviors. □

With the help of shadow constant, now we can verify the traditional alternating bit protocol (ABP) [24].

The ABP protocol is used to ensure successful transmission of data through a corrupted channel. This success is based on the assumption that data can be resent an unlimited number of times, which is illustrated in Fig. 3.2, we alter it into the true concurrency situation.

1. Data elements $d_1, d_2, d_3, \cdots$ from a finite set Δ are communicated between a Sender and a Receiver.
2. If the Sender reads a datum from channel A.
3. The Sender processes the data in Δ, forms new data, and sends them to the Receiver through channel B.
4. And the Receiver sends the datum into channel C.
5. If channel B is corrupted, the message communicated through B can be turn into an error message $\bot$.
6. Every time the Receiver receives a message via channel B, it sends an acknowledgment to the Sender via channel D, which is also corrupted.

The Sender attaches a bit 0 to data elements d_{2k-1} and a bit 1 to data elements d_{2k}, when they are sent into channel B. When the Receiver reads a datum, it sends back the attached bit via channel D. If the Receiver receives a corrupted message, then it sends back the previous acknowledgment to the Sender.

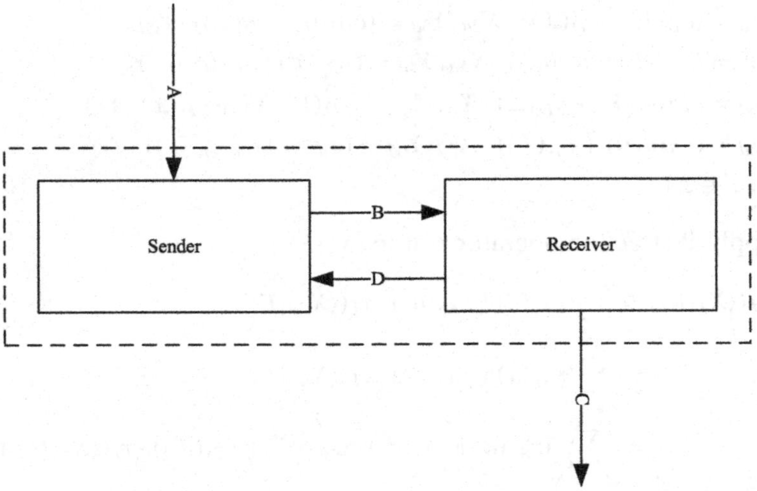

FIGURE 3.2 Alternating bit protocol.

Then the state transition of the Sender can be described by $APTC$ as follows.

$$S_b = \sum_{d \in \Delta} r_A(d) \cdot T_{db}$$

$$T_{db} = (\sum_{d' \in \Delta} (s_B(d', b) \cdot ⓢ^{s_C(d')}) + s_B(\bot)) \cdot U_{db}$$

$$U_{db} = r_D(b) \cdot S_{1-b} + (r_D(1-b) + r_D(\bot)) \cdot T_{db}$$

where s_B denotes sending data through channel B, r_D denotes receiving data through channel D, similarly, r_A means receiving data via channel A, $ⓢ^{s_C(d')}$ denotes the shadow of $s_C(d')$.

And the state transition of the Receiver can be described by $APTC$ as follows.

$$R_b = \sum_{d \in \Delta} ⓢ^{r_A(d)} \cdot R'_b$$

$$R'_b = \sum_{d' \in \Delta} \{r_B(d', b) \cdot s_C(d') \cdot Q_b + r_B(d', 1-b) \cdot Q_{1-b}\} + r_B(\bot) \cdot Q_{1-b}$$

$$Q_b = (s_D(b) + s_D(\bot)) \cdot R_{1-b}$$

where $ⓢ^{r_A(d)}$ denotes the shadow of $r_A(d)$, r_B denotes receiving data via channel B, s_C denotes sending data via channel C, s_D denotes sending data via channel D, and $b \in \{0, 1\}$.

The send action and receive action of the same data through the same channel can communicate each other, otherwise, a deadlock δ will be caused. We define the following communication functions.

$$\gamma(s_B(d',b), r_B(d',b)) \triangleq c_B(d',b)$$
$$\gamma(s_B(\perp), r_B(\perp)) \triangleq c_B(\perp)$$
$$\gamma(s_D(b), r_D(b)) \triangleq c_D(b)$$
$$\gamma(s_D(\perp), r_D(\perp)) \triangleq c_D(\perp)$$

Let R_0 and S_0 be in parallel, then the system $R_0 S_0$ can be represented by the following process term.

$$\tau_I(\partial_H(\Theta(R_0 \between S_0))) = \tau_I(\partial_H(R_0 \between S_0))$$

where $H = \{s_B(d',b), r_B(d',b), s_D(b), r_D(b) | d' \in \Delta, b \in \{0,1\}\}$
$\{s_B(\perp), r_B(\perp), s_D(\perp), r_D(\perp)\}$
$I = \{c_B(d',b), c_D(b) | d' \in \Delta, b \in \{0,1\}\} \cup \{c_B(\perp), c_D(\perp)\}$.

Then we get the following conclusion.

Theorem 3.82 (Correctness of the ABP protocol). *The ABP protocol $\tau_I(\partial_H(R_0 \between S_0))$ can exhibit desired external behaviors.*

Proof. Similarly, we can get $\tau_I(\langle X_1|E\rangle) = \sum_{d,d'\in\Delta} r_A(d) \cdot s_C(d') \cdot \tau_I(\langle Y_1|E\rangle)$ and $\tau_I(\langle Y_1|E\rangle) = \sum_{d,d'\in\Delta} r_A(d) \cdot s_C(d') \cdot \tau_I(\langle X_1|E\rangle)$.

So, the ABP protocol $\tau_I(\partial_H(R_0 \between S_0))$ can exhibit desired external behaviors. □

4 Guarded APTC

This chapter is organized as follows. We introduce the operational semantics of guards in Section 4.1, $BATC$ with Guards in Section 4.2, $APTC$ with Guards 4.3, recursion in Section 4.4, abstraction in Section 4.5.

4.1 Operational semantics

In this section, we extend truly concurrent bisimilarities to the ones containing data states.

Definition 4.1 (Prime event structure with silent event and empty event). Let Λ be a fixed set of labels, ranged over $a, b, c, \cdots$ and τ, ϵ. A (Λ-labeled) prime event structure with silent event τ and empty event ϵ is a tuple $\mathcal{E} = \langle \mathbb{E}, \leq, \sharp, \lambda \rangle$, where $\mathbb{E}$ is a denumerable set of events, including the silent event τ and empty event ϵ. Let $\hat{\mathbb{E}} = \mathbb{E} \backslash \{\tau, \epsilon\}$, exactly excluding τ and ϵ, it is obvious that $\hat{\tau^*} = \epsilon$. Let $\lambda : \mathbb{E} \to \Lambda$ be a labeling function and let $\lambda(\tau) = \tau$ and $\lambda(\epsilon) = \epsilon$. And $\leq$, $\sharp$ are binary relations on $\mathbb{E}$, called causality and conflict respectively, such that:

1. $\leq$ is a partial order and $\lceil e \rceil = \{e' \in \mathbb{E} | e' \leq e\}$ is finite for all $e \in \mathbb{E}$. It is easy to see that $e \leq \tau^* \leq e' = e \leq \tau \leq \cdots \leq \tau \leq e'$, then $e \leq e'$.
2. $\sharp$ is irreflexive, symmetric, and hereditary with respect to $\leq$, that is, for all $e, e', e'' \in \mathbb{E}$, if $e \sharp e' \leq e''$, then $e \sharp e''$.

Then, the concepts of consistency and concurrency can be drawn from the above definition:

1. $e, e' \in \mathbb{E}$ are consistent, denoted as $e \frown e'$, if $\neg(e \sharp e')$. A subset $X \subseteq \mathbb{E}$ is called consistent, if $e \frown e'$ for all $e, e' \in X$.
2. $e, e' \in \mathbb{E}$ are concurrent, denoted as $e \parallel e'$, if $\neg(e \leq e')$, $\neg(e' \leq e)$, and $\neg(e \sharp e')$.

Definition 4.2 (Configuration). Let $\mathcal{E}$ be a PES. A (finite) configuration in $\mathcal{E}$ is a (finite) consistent subset of events $C \subseteq \mathcal{E}$, closed with respect to causality (i.e. $\lceil C \rceil = C$), and a data state $s \in S$ with S the set of all data states, denoted $\langle C, s \rangle$. The set of finite configurations of $\mathcal{E}$ is denoted by $\langle \mathcal{C}(\mathcal{E}), S \rangle$. We let $\hat{C} = C \backslash \{\tau\} \cup \{\epsilon\}$.

A consistent subset of $X \subseteq \mathbb{E}$ of events can be seen as a pomset. Given $X, Y \subseteq \mathbb{E}$, $\hat{X} \sim \hat{Y}$ if $\hat{X}$ and $\hat{Y}$ are isomorphic as pomsets. In the following of the paper, we say $C_1 \sim C_2$, we mean $\hat{C_1} \sim \hat{C_2}$.

Definition 4.3 (Pomset transitions and step). Let $\mathcal{E}$ be a PES and let $C \in \mathcal{C}(\mathcal{E})$, and $\emptyset \neq X \subseteq \mathbb{E}$, if $C \cap X = \emptyset$ and $C' = C \cup X \in \mathcal{C}(\mathcal{E})$, then $\langle C, s \rangle \xrightarrow{X} \langle C', s' \rangle$ is called a pomset transition from $\langle C, s \rangle$ to $\langle C', s' \rangle$. When the events in X are pairwise concurrent, we say that $\langle C, s \rangle \xrightarrow{X} \langle C', s' \rangle$ is a step. It is obvious that $\to^* \xrightarrow{X} \to^* = \xrightarrow{X}$ and $\to^* \xrightarrow{e} \to^* = \xrightarrow{e}$ for any $e \in \mathbb{E}$ and $X \subseteq \mathbb{E}$.

Theory of Structured Parallel Programming. https://doi.org/10.1016/B978-0-44-324814-6.00008-3

Definition 4.4 (Weak pomset transitions and weak step). Let $\mathcal{E}$ be a PES and let $C \in \mathcal{C}(\mathcal{E})$, and $\emptyset \neq X \subseteq \hat{\mathbb{E}}$, if $C \cap X = \emptyset$ and $\hat{C}' = \hat{C} \cup X \in \mathcal{C}(\mathcal{E})$, then $\langle C, s\rangle \overset{X}{\Rightarrow} \langle C', s'\rangle$ is called a weak pomset transition from $\langle C, s\rangle$ to $\langle C', s'\rangle$, where we define $\overset{e}{\Rightarrow} \triangleq \overset{\tau^*}{\rightarrow}\overset{e}{\rightarrow}\overset{\tau^*}{\rightarrow}$. And $\overset{X}{\Rightarrow} \triangleq \overset{\tau^*}{\rightarrow}\overset{e}{\rightarrow}\overset{\tau^*}{\rightarrow}$, for every $e \in X$. When the events in X are pairwise concurrent, we say that $\langle C, s\rangle \overset{X}{\Rightarrow} \langle C', s'\rangle$ is a weak step.

We will also suppose that all the PESs in this paper are image finite, that is, for any PES $\mathcal{E}$ and $C \in \mathcal{C}(\mathcal{E})$ and $a \in \Lambda$, $\{e \in \mathbb{E} | \langle C, s\rangle \overset{e}{\rightarrow} \langle C', s'\rangle \wedge \lambda(e) = a\}$, and $\{e \in \hat{\mathbb{E}} | \langle C, s\rangle \overset{e}{\Rightarrow} \langle C', s'\rangle \wedge \lambda(e) = a\}$ is finite.

Definition 4.5 (Pomset, step bisimulation). Let $\mathcal{E}_1$, $\mathcal{E}_2$ be PESs. A pomset bisimulation is a relation $R \subseteq \langle \mathcal{C}(\mathcal{E}_1), S\rangle \times \langle \mathcal{C}(\mathcal{E}_2), S\rangle$, such that if $(\langle C_1, s\rangle, \langle C_2, s\rangle) \in R$, and $\langle C_1, s\rangle \xrightarrow{X_1} \langle C_1', s'\rangle$ then $\langle C_2, s\rangle \xrightarrow{X_2} \langle C_2', s'\rangle$, with $X_1 \subseteq \mathbb{E}_1$, $X_2 \subseteq \mathbb{E}_2$, $X_1 \sim X_2$, and $(\langle C_1', s'\rangle, \langle C_2', s'\rangle) \in R$ for all $s, s' \in S$, and vice-versa. We say that $\mathcal{E}_1$, $\mathcal{E}_2$ are pomset bisimilar, written $\mathcal{E}_1 \sim_p \mathcal{E}_2$, if there exists a pomset bisimulation R, such that $(\langle \emptyset, \emptyset\rangle, \langle \emptyset, \emptyset\rangle) \in R$. By replacing pomset transitions with steps, we can get the definition of step bisimulation. When PESs $\mathcal{E}_1$ and $\mathcal{E}_2$ are step bisimilar, we write $\mathcal{E}_1 \sim_s \mathcal{E}_2$.

Definition 4.6 (Weak pomset, step bisimulation). Let $\mathcal{E}_1$, $\mathcal{E}_2$ be PESs. A weak pomset bisimulation is a relation $R \subseteq \langle \mathcal{C}(\mathcal{E}_1), S\rangle \times \langle \mathcal{C}(\mathcal{E}_2), S\rangle$, such that if $(\langle C_1, s\rangle, \langle C_2, s\rangle) \in R$, and $\langle C_1, s\rangle \overset{X_1}{\Rightarrow} \langle C_1', s'\rangle$ then $\langle C_2, s\rangle \overset{X_2}{\Rightarrow} \langle C_2', s'\rangle$, with $X_1 \subseteq \hat{\mathbb{E}_1}$, $X_2 \subseteq \hat{\mathbb{E}_2}$, $X_1 \sim X_2$, and $(\langle C_1', s'\rangle, \langle C_2', s'\rangle) \in R$ for all $s, s' \in S$, and vice-versa. We say that $\mathcal{E}_1$, $\mathcal{E}_2$ are weak pomset bisimilar, written $\mathcal{E}_1 \approx_p \mathcal{E}_2$, if there exists a weak pomset bisimulation R, such that $(\langle \emptyset, \emptyset\rangle, \langle \emptyset, \emptyset\rangle) \in R$. By replacing weak pomset transitions with weak steps, we can get the definition of weak step bisimulation. When PESs $\mathcal{E}_1$ and $\mathcal{E}_2$ are weak step bisimilar, we write $\mathcal{E}_1 \approx_s \mathcal{E}_2$.

Definition 4.7 (Posetal product). Given two PESs $\mathcal{E}_1$, $\mathcal{E}_2$, the posetal product of their configurations, denoted $\langle \mathcal{C}(\mathcal{E}_1), S\rangle \overline{\times} \langle \mathcal{C}(\mathcal{E}_2), S\rangle$, is defined as

$$\{(\langle C_1, s\rangle, f, \langle C_2, s\rangle) | C_1 \in \mathcal{C}(\mathcal{E}_1), C_2 \in \mathcal{C}(\mathcal{E}_2), f : C_1 \to C_2 \text{ isomorphism}\}.$$

A subset $R \subseteq \langle \mathcal{C}(\mathcal{E}_1), S\rangle \overline{\times} \langle \mathcal{C}(\mathcal{E}_2), S\rangle$ is called a posetal relation. We say that R is downward closed when for any $(\langle C_1, s\rangle, f, \langle C_2, s\rangle), (\langle C_1', s'\rangle, f', \langle C_2', s'\rangle) \in \langle \mathcal{C}(\mathcal{E}_1), S\rangle \overline{\times} \langle \mathcal{C}(\mathcal{E}_2), S\rangle$, if $(\langle C_1, s\rangle, f, \langle C_2, s\rangle) \subseteq (\langle C_1', s'\rangle, f', \langle C_2', s'\rangle)$ pointwise and $(\langle C_1', s'\rangle, f', \langle C_2', s'\rangle) \in R$, then $(\langle C_1, s\rangle, f, \langle C_2, s\rangle) \in R$.

For $f : X_1 \to X_2$, we define $f[x_1 \mapsto x_2] : X_1 \cup \{x_1\} \to X_2 \cup \{x_2\}$, $z \in X_1 \cup \{x_1\}$, (1) $f[x_1 \mapsto x_2](z) = x_2$, if $z = x_1$; (2) $f[x_1 \mapsto x_2](z) = f(z)$, otherwise. Where $X_1 \subseteq \mathbb{E}_1$, $X_2 \subseteq \mathbb{E}_2$, $x_1 \in \mathbb{E}_1$, $x_2 \in \mathbb{E}_2$.

Definition 4.8 (Weakly posetal product). Given two PESs $\mathcal{E}_1$, $\mathcal{E}_2$, the weakly posetal product of their configurations, denoted $\langle \mathcal{C}(\mathcal{E}_1), S\rangle \overline{\times} \langle \mathcal{C}(\mathcal{E}_2), S\rangle$, is defined as

$$\{(\langle C_1, s\rangle, f, \langle C_2, s\rangle) | C_1 \in \mathcal{C}(\mathcal{E}_1), C_2 \in \mathcal{C}(\mathcal{E}_2), f : \hat{C_1} \to \hat{C_2} \text{ isomorphism}\}.$$

A subset $R \subseteq \langle \mathcal{C}(\mathcal{E}_1), S\rangle \overline{\times} \langle \mathcal{C}(\mathcal{E}_2), S\rangle$ is called a weakly posetal relation. We say that R is downward closed when for any $(\langle C_1, s\rangle, f, \langle C_2, s\rangle), (\langle C_1', s'\rangle, f, \langle C_2', s'\rangle) \in \langle \mathcal{C}(\mathcal{E}_1), S\rangle \overline{\times} \langle \mathcal{C}(\mathcal{E}_2), S\rangle$, if $(\langle C_1, s\rangle, f, \langle C_2, s\rangle) \subseteq (\langle C_1', s'\rangle, f', \langle C_2', s'\rangle)$ pointwise and $(\langle C_1', s'\rangle, f', \langle C_2', s'\rangle) \in R$, then $(\langle C_1, s\rangle, f, \langle C_2, s\rangle) \in R$.

For $f : X_1 \to X_2$, we define $f[x_1 \mapsto x_2] : X_1 \cup \{x_1\} \to X_2 \cup \{x_2\}$, $z \in X_1 \cup \{x_1\}$, (1) $f[x_1 \mapsto x_2](z) = x_2$, if $z = x_1$; (2) $f[x_1 \mapsto x_2](z) = f(z)$, otherwise. Where $X_1 \subseteq \hat{\mathbb{E}}_1$, $X_2 \subseteq \hat{\mathbb{E}}_2$, $x_1 \in \hat{\mathbb{E}}_1$, $x_2 \in \hat{\mathbb{E}}_2$. Also, we define $f(\tau^*) = f(\tau^*)$.

Definition 4.9 ((Hereditary) history-preserving bisimulation). A history-preserving (hp-)bisimulation is a posetal relation $R \subseteq \langle \mathcal{C}(\mathcal{E}_1), S\rangle \overline{\times} \langle \mathcal{C}(\mathcal{E}_2), S\rangle$ such that if $(\langle C_1, s\rangle, f, \langle C_2, s\rangle) \in R$, and $\langle C_1, s\rangle \xrightarrow{e_1} \langle C_1', s'\rangle$, then $\langle C_2, s\rangle \xrightarrow{e_2} \langle C_2', s'\rangle$, with $(\langle C_1', s'\rangle, f[e_1 \mapsto e_2], \langle C_2', s'\rangle) \in R$ for all $s, s' \in S$, and vice-versa. $\mathcal{E}_1, \mathcal{E}_2$ are history-preserving (hp-)bisimilar and are written $\mathcal{E}_1 \sim_{hp} \mathcal{E}_2$ if there exists a hp-bisimulation R such that $(\langle \emptyset, \emptyset\rangle, \emptyset, \langle \emptyset, \emptyset\rangle) \in R$.

A hereditary history-preserving (hhp-)bisimulation is a downward closed hp-bisimulation. $\mathcal{E}_1, \mathcal{E}_2$ are hereditary history-preserving (hhp-)bisimilar and are written $\mathcal{E}_1 \sim_{hhp} \mathcal{E}_2$.

Definition 4.10 (Weak (hereditary) history-preserving bisimulation). A weak history-preserving (hp-)bisimulation is a weakly posetal relation $R \subseteq \langle \mathcal{C}(\mathcal{E}_1), S\rangle \overline{\times} \langle \mathcal{C}(\mathcal{E}_2), S\rangle$ such that if $(\langle C_1, s\rangle, f, \langle C_2, s\rangle) \in R$, and $\langle C_1, s\rangle \xRightarrow{e_1} \langle C_1', s'\rangle$, then $\langle C_2, s\rangle \xRightarrow{e_2} \langle C_2', s'\rangle$, with $(\langle C_1', s'\rangle, f[e_1 \mapsto e_2], \langle C_2', s'\rangle) \in R$ for all $s, s' \in S$, and vice-versa. $\mathcal{E}_1, \mathcal{E}_2$ are weak history-preserving (hp-)bisimilar and are written $\mathcal{E}_1 \approx_{hp} \mathcal{E}_2$ if there exists a weak hp-bisimulation R such that $(\langle \emptyset, \emptyset\rangle, \emptyset, \langle \emptyset, \emptyset\rangle) \in R$.

A weakly hereditary history-preserving (hhp-)bisimulation is a downward closed weak hp-bisimulation. $\mathcal{E}_1, \mathcal{E}_2$ are weakly hereditary history-preserving (hhp-)bisimilar and are written $\mathcal{E}_1 \approx_{hhp} \mathcal{E}_2$.

4.2 $BATC$ with guards

In this section, we will discuss the guards for $BATC$, which is denoted as $BATC_G$. Let $\mathbb{E}$ be the set of atomic events (actions), and we assume that there is a data set Δ and data $D_1, \cdots, D_n \in \Delta$, the data variable $d_1, \cdots, d_n$ range over Δ, and d_i has the same data type as D_i and can have a substitution D_i/d_i, for process x, $x[D_i/d_i]$ denotes that all occurrences of d_i in x are replaced by D_i. And also the atomic action e may manipulate on data and has the form $e(d_1, \cdots, d_n)$ or $e(D_1, \cdots, D_n)$. G_{at} be the set of atomic guards, δ be the deadlock constant, and ϵ be the empty event. We extend G_{at} to the set of basic guards G with element $\phi, \psi, \cdots$, which is generated by the following formation rules:

$$\phi ::= \delta | \epsilon | \neg\phi | \psi \in G_{at} | \phi + \psi | \phi \cdot \psi$$

In the following, let $e_1, e_2, e_1', e_2' \in \mathbb{E}$, $\phi, \psi \in G$ and let variables x, y, z range over the set of terms for true concurrency, p, q, s range over the set of closed terms. The predicate $test(\phi, s)$ represents that ϕ holds in the state s, and $test(\epsilon, s)$ holds and $test(\delta, s)$ does not

Table 4.1 Axioms of $BATC_G$.

No.	Axiom
$A1$	$x + y = y + x$
$A2$	$(x + y) + z = x + (y + z)$
$A3$	$x + x = x$
$A4$	$(x + y) \cdot z = x \cdot z + y \cdot z$
$A5$	$(x \cdot y) \cdot z = x \cdot (y \cdot z)$
$A6$	$x + \delta = x$
$A7$	$\delta \cdot x = \delta$
$A8$	$\epsilon \cdot x = x$
$A9$	$x \cdot \epsilon = x$
$G1$	$\phi \cdot \neg\phi = \delta$
$G2$	$\phi + \neg\phi = \epsilon$
$G3$	$\phi\delta = \delta$
$G4$	$\phi(x + y) = \phi x + \phi y$
$G5$	$\phi(x \cdot y) = \phi x \cdot y$
$G6$	$(\phi + \psi)x = \phi x + \psi x$
$G7$	$(\phi \cdot \psi) \cdot x = \phi \cdot (\psi \cdot x)$
$G8$	$\phi = \epsilon$ if $\forall s \in S.test(\phi, s)$
$G9$	$\phi_0 \cdot \cdots \cdot \phi_n = \delta$ if $\forall s \in S, \exists i \leq n.test(\neg\phi_i, s)$
$G10$	$wp(e, \phi)e\phi = wp(e, \phi)e$
$G11$	$\neg wp(e, \phi)e\neg\phi = \neg wp(e, \phi)e$

hold. $effect(e, s) \in S$ denotes s' in $s \xrightarrow{e} s'$. The predicate weakest precondition $wp(e, \phi)$ denotes that $\forall s \in S, test(\phi, effect(e, s))$ holds.

The set of axioms of $BATC_G$ consists of the laws given in Table 4.1.

Note that, by eliminating atomic event from the process terms, the axioms in Table 4.1 will lead to a Boolean Algebra. And $G9$ is a precondition of e and ϕ, $G10$ is the weakest precondition of e and ϕ. A data environment with $effect$ function is sufficiently deterministic, and it is obvious that if the weakest precondition is expressible and $G9$, $G10$ are sound, then the related data environment is sufficiently deterministic.

Definition 4.11 (Basic terms of $BATC_G$). The set of basic terms of $BATC_G$, $\mathcal{B}(BATC_G)$, is inductively defined as follows:

1. $\mathbb{E} \subset \mathcal{B}(BATC_G)$;
2. $G \subset \mathcal{B}(BATC_G)$;
3. if $e \in \mathbb{E}, t \in \mathcal{B}(BATC_G)$ then $e \cdot t \in \mathcal{B}(BATC_G)$;
4. if $\phi \in G, t \in \mathcal{B}(BATC_G)$ then $\phi \cdot t \in \mathcal{B}(BATC_G)$;
5. if $t, s \in \mathcal{B}(BATC_G)$ then $t + s \in \mathcal{B}(BATC_G)$.

Theorem 4.12 (Elimination theorem of $BATC_G$). *Let p be a closed $BATC_G$ term. Then there is a basic $BATC_G$ term q such that $BATC_G \vdash p = q$.*

Table 4.2 Single event transition rules of $BATC_G$.

$$\frac{}{\langle \epsilon, s\rangle \rightarrow \langle \surd, s\rangle}$$

$$\frac{}{\langle e, s\rangle \xrightarrow{e} \langle \surd, s'\rangle} \text{ if } s' \in effect(e,s)$$

$$\frac{}{\langle \phi, s\rangle \rightarrow \langle \surd, s\rangle} \text{ if } test(\phi,s)$$

$$\frac{\langle x, s\rangle \xrightarrow{e} \langle \surd, s'\rangle}{\langle x+y, s\rangle \xrightarrow{e} \langle \surd, s'\rangle} \quad \frac{\langle x, s\rangle \xrightarrow{e} \langle x', s'\rangle}{\langle x+y, s\rangle \xrightarrow{e} \langle x', s'\rangle}$$

$$\frac{\langle y, s\rangle \xrightarrow{e} \langle \surd, s'\rangle}{\langle x+y, s\rangle \xrightarrow{e} \langle \surd, s'\rangle} \quad \frac{\langle y, s\rangle \xrightarrow{e} \langle y', s'\rangle}{\langle x+y, s\rangle \xrightarrow{e} \langle y', s'\rangle}$$

$$\frac{\langle x, s\rangle \xrightarrow{e} \langle \surd, s'\rangle}{\langle x\cdot y, s\rangle \xrightarrow{e} \langle y, s'\rangle} \quad \frac{\langle x, s\rangle \xrightarrow{e} \langle x', s'\rangle}{\langle x\cdot y, s\rangle \xrightarrow{e} \langle x'\cdot y, s'\rangle}$$

We will define a term-deduction system which gives the operational semantics of $BATC_G$. We give the operational transition rules for ϵ, atomic guard $\phi \in G_{at}$, atomic event $e \in \mathbb{E}$, operators $\cdot$ and $+$ as Table 4.2 shows. And the predicate $\xrightarrow{e} \surd$ represents successful termination after execution of the event e.

Note that, we replace the single atomic event $e \in \mathbb{E}$ by $X \subseteq \mathbb{E}$, we can obtain the pomset transition rules of $BATC_G$, and omit them.

Theorem 4.13 (Congruence of $BATC_G$ with respect to truly concurrent bisimulation equivalences). *(1) Pomset bisimulation equivalence* $\sim_p$ *is a congruence with respect to* $BATC_G$.

(2) Step bisimulation equivalence $\sim_s$ *is a congruence with respect to* $BATC_G$.

(3) hp-bisimulation equivalence $\sim_{hp}$ *is a congruence with respect to* $BATC_G$.

(4) hhp-bisimulation equivalence $\sim_{hhp}$ *is a congruence with respect to* $BATC_G$.

Theorem 4.14 (Soundness of $BATC_G$ modulo truly concurrent bisimulation equivalences). *(1) Let x and y be* $BATC_G$ *terms. If* $BATC \vdash x = y$, *then* $x \sim_p y$.

(2) Let x and y be $BATC_G$ *terms. If* $BATC \vdash x = y$, *then* $x \sim_s y$.

(3) Let x and y be $BATC_G$ *terms. If* $BATC \vdash x = y$, *then* $x \sim_{hp} y$.

(4) Let x and y be $BATC_G$ *terms. If* $BATC \vdash x = y$, *then* $x \sim_{hhp} y$.

Theorem 4.15 (Completeness of $BATC_G$ modulo truly concurrent bisimulation equivalences). *(1) Let p and q be closed* $BATC_G$ *terms, if* $p \sim_p q$ *then* $p = q$.

(2) Let p and q be closed $BATC_G$ *terms, if* $p \sim_s q$ *then* $p = q$.

(3) Let p and q be closed $BATC_G$ *terms, if* $p \sim_{hp} q$ *then* $p = q$.

(4) Let p and q be closed $BATC_G$ *terms, if* $p \sim_{hhp} q$ *then* $p = q$.

Theorem 4.16 (Sufficient determinacy). *All related data environments with respect to* $BATC_G$ *can be sufficiently deterministic.*

4.3 $APTC$ with guards

In this section, we will extend $APTC$ with guards, which is abbreviated $APTC_G$. The set of basic guards G with element $\phi, \psi, \cdots$, which is extended by the following formation rules:

$$\phi ::= \delta|\epsilon|\neg\phi|\psi \in G_{at}|\phi + \psi|\phi \cdot \psi|\phi \parallel \psi$$

The set of axioms of $APTC_G$ including axioms of $BATC_G$ in Table 4.1 and the axioms are shown in Table 4.3.

Definition 4.17 (Basic terms of $APTC_G$). The set of basic terms of $APTC_G$, $\mathcal{B}(APTC_G)$, is inductively defined as follows:

1. $\mathbb{E} \subset \mathcal{B}(APTC_G)$;
2. $G \subset \mathcal{B}(APTC_G)$;
3. if $e \in \mathbb{E}, t \in \mathcal{B}(APTC_G)$ then $e \cdot t \in \mathcal{B}(APTC_G)$;
4. if $\phi \in G, t \in \mathcal{B}(APTC_G)$ then $\phi \cdot t \in \mathcal{B}(APTC_G)$;
5. if $t, s \in \mathcal{B}(APTC_G)$ then $t + s \in \mathcal{B}(APTC_G)$.
6. if $t, s \in \mathcal{B}(APTC_G)$ then $t \parallel s \in \mathcal{B}(APTC_G)$.

Based on the definition of basic terms for $APTC_G$ (see Definition 4.17) and axioms of $APTC_G$, we can prove the elimination theorem of $APTC_G$.

Theorem 4.18 (Elimination theorem of $APTC_G$). *Let p be a closed $APTC_G$ term. Then there is a basic $APTC_G$ term q such that $APTC_G \vdash p = q$.*

We will define a term-deduction system which gives the operational semantics of $APTC_G$. Two atomic events e_1 and e_2 are in race condition, which are denoted $e_1\%e_2$. (See Table 4.4.)

Theorem 4.19 (Generalization of $APTC_G$ with respect to $BATC_G$). *$APTC_G$ is a generalization of $BATC_G$.*

Theorem 4.20 (Congruence of $APTC_G$ with respect to truly concurrent bisimulation equivalences). *(1) Pomset bisimulation equivalence $\sim_p$ is a congruence with respect to $APTC_G$.*

(2) Step bisimulation equivalence $\sim_s$ is a congruence with respect to $APTC_G$.

(3) hp-bisimulation equivalence $\sim_{hp}$ is a congruence with respect to $APTC_G$.

(4) hhp-bisimulation equivalence $\sim_{hhp}$ is a congruence with respect to $APTC_G$.

Theorem 4.21 (Soundness of $APTC_G$ modulo truly concurrent bisimulation equivalences). *(1) Let x and y be $APTC_G$ terms. If $APTC \vdash x = y$, then $x \sim_p y$.*

(2) Let x and y be $APTC_G$ terms. If $APTC \vdash x = y$, then $x \sim_s y$.

(3) Let x and y be $APTC_G$ terms. If $APTC \vdash x = y$, then $x \sim_{hp} y$.

Table 4.3 Axioms of $APTC_G$.

No.	Axiom
$P1$	$x \between y = x \parallel y + x \mid y$
$P2$	$e_1 \parallel (e_2 \cdot y) = (e_1 \parallel e_2) \cdot y$
$P3$	$(e_1 \cdot x) \parallel e_2 = (e_1 \parallel e_2) \cdot x$
$P4$	$(e_1 \cdot x) \parallel (e_2 \cdot y) = (e_1 \parallel e_2) \cdot (x \between y)$
$P5$	$(x + y) \parallel z = (x \parallel z) + (y \parallel z)$
$P6$	$x \parallel (y + z) = (x \parallel y) + (x \parallel z)$
$P7$	$\delta \parallel x = \delta$
$P8$	$x \parallel \delta = \delta$
$P9$	$\epsilon \parallel x = x$
$P10$	$x \parallel \epsilon = x$
$C1$	$e_1 \mid e_2 = \gamma(e_1, e_2)$
$C2$	$e_1 \mid (e_2 \cdot y) = \gamma(e_1, e_2) \cdot y$
$C3$	$(e_1 \cdot x) \mid e_2 = \gamma(e_1, e_2) \cdot x$
$C4$	$(e_1 \cdot x) \mid (e_2 \cdot y) = \gamma(e_1, e_2) \cdot (x \between y)$
$C5$	$(x + y) \mid z = (x \mid z) + (y \mid z)$
$C6$	$x \mid (y + z) = (x \mid y) + (x \mid z)$
$C7$	$\delta \mid x = \delta$
$C8$	$x \mid \delta = \delta$
$C9$	$\epsilon \mid x = \delta$
$C10$	$x \mid \epsilon = \delta$
$CE1$	$\Theta(e) = e$
$CE2$	$\Theta(\delta) = \delta$
$CE3$	$\Theta(\epsilon) = \epsilon$
$CE4$	$\Theta(x + y) = \Theta(x) + \Theta(y)$
$CE5$	$\Theta(x \cdot y) = \Theta(x) \cdot \Theta(y)$
$CE6$	$\Theta(x \parallel y) = ((\Theta(x) \triangleleft y) \parallel y) + ((\Theta(y) \triangleleft x) \parallel x)$
$CE7$	$\Theta(x \mid y) = ((\Theta(x) \triangleleft y) \mid y) + ((\Theta(y) \triangleleft x) \mid x)$
$U1$	$(\sharp(e_1, e_2)) \quad e_1 \triangleleft e_2 = \tau$
$U2$	$(\sharp(e_1, e_2), e_2 \leq e_3) \quad e_1 \triangleleft e_3 = \tau$
$U3$	$(\sharp(e_1, e_2), e_2 \leq e_3) \quad e3 \triangleleft e_1 = \tau$
$U4$	$e \triangleleft \delta = e$
$U5$	$\delta \triangleleft e = \delta$
$U6$	$e \triangleleft \epsilon = e$
$U7$	$\epsilon \triangleleft e = e$
$U8$	$(x + y) \triangleleft z = (x \triangleleft z) + (y \triangleleft z)$
$U9$	$(x \cdot y) \triangleleft z = (x \triangleleft z) \cdot (y \triangleleft z)$
$U10$	$(x \parallel y) \triangleleft z = (x \triangleleft z) \parallel (y \triangleleft z)$
$U11$	$(x \mid y) \triangleleft z = (x \triangleleft z) \mid (y \triangleleft z)$
$U12$	$x \triangleleft (y + z) = (x \triangleleft y) \triangleleft z$
$U13$	$x \triangleleft (y \cdot z) = (x \triangleleft y) \triangleleft z$
$U14$	$x \triangleleft (y \parallel z) = (x \triangleleft y) \triangleleft z$
$U15$	$x \triangleleft (y \mid z) = (x \triangleleft y) \triangleleft z$

continued on next page

Table 4.3 (continued)

No.	Axiom
$D1$	$e \notin H \quad \partial_H(e) = e$
$D2$	$e \in H \quad \partial_H(e) = \delta$
$D3$	$\partial_H(\delta) = \delta$
$D4$	$\partial_H(x + y) = \partial_H(x) + \partial_H(y)$
$D5$	$\partial_H(x \cdot y) = \partial_H(x) \cdot \partial_H(y)$
$D6$	$\partial_H(x \parallel y) = \partial_H(x) \parallel \partial_H(y)$
$G12$	$\phi(x \parallel y) = \phi x \parallel \phi y$
$G13$	$\phi(x \mid y) = \phi x \mid \phi y$
$G14$	$\phi \parallel \delta = \delta$
$G15$	$\delta \parallel \phi = \delta$
$G16$	$\phi \mid \delta = \delta$
$G17$	$\delta \mid \phi = \delta$
$G18$	$\phi \parallel \epsilon = \phi$
$G19$	$\epsilon \parallel \phi = \phi$
$G20$	$\phi \mid \epsilon = \delta$
$G21$	$\epsilon \mid \phi = \delta$
$G22$	$\phi \parallel \neg\phi = \delta$
$G23$	$\Theta(\phi) = \phi$
$G24$	$\partial_H(\phi) = \phi$
$G25$	$\phi_0 \parallel \cdots \parallel \phi_n = \delta$ if $\forall s_0, \cdots, s_n \in S$, $\exists i \leq n.test(\neg\phi_i, s_0 \cup \cdots \cup s_n)$

Theorem 4.22 (Completeness of $APTC_G$ modulo truly concurrent bisimulation equivalences). *(1) Let p and q be closed $APTC_G$ terms, if $p \sim_p q$ then $p = q$.*

(2) Let p and q be closed $APTC_G$ terms, if $p \sim_s q$ then $p = q$.

(3) Let p and q be closed $APTC_G$ terms, if $p \sim_{hp} q$ then $p = q$.

Theorem 4.23 (Sufficient determinacy). *All related data environments with respect to $APTC_G$ can be sufficiently deterministic.*

4.4 Recursion

In this section, we introduce recursion to capture infinite processes based on $APTC_G$. In the following, E, F, G are recursion specifications, X, Y, Z are recursive variables. (See Table 4.5.)

Definition 4.24 (Guarded recursive specification). A recursive specification

$$X_1 = t_1(X_1, \cdots, X_n)$$

$$\ldots$$

$$X_n = t_n(X_1, \cdots, X_n)$$

is guarded if the right-hand sides of its recursive equations can be adapted to the form by applications of the axioms in $APTC$ and replacing recursion variables by the right-hand

Table 4.4 Transition rules of $APTC_G$.

$$\frac{}{\langle e_1 \parallel \cdots \parallel e_n, s\rangle \xrightarrow{\{e_1,\cdots,e_n\}} \langle \surd, s'\rangle} \text{ if } s' \in effect(e_1, s) \cup \cdots \cup effect(e_n, s)$$

$$\frac{}{\langle \phi_1 \parallel \cdots \parallel \phi_n, s\rangle \rightarrow \langle \surd, s\rangle} \text{ if } test(\phi_1, s), \cdots, test(\phi_n, s)$$

$$\frac{\langle x, s\rangle \xrightarrow{e_1} \langle \surd, s'\rangle \quad \langle y, s\rangle \xrightarrow{e_2} \langle \surd, s''\rangle}{\langle x \parallel y, s\rangle \xrightarrow{\{e_1,e_2\}} \langle \surd, s' \cup s''\rangle} \qquad \frac{\langle x, s\rangle \xrightarrow{e_1} \langle x', s'\rangle \quad \langle y, s\rangle \xrightarrow{e_2} \langle \surd, s''\rangle}{\langle x \parallel y, s\rangle \xrightarrow{\{e_1,e_2\}} \langle x', s' \cup s''\rangle}$$

$$\frac{\langle x, s\rangle \xrightarrow{e_1} \langle \surd, s'\rangle \quad \langle y, s\rangle \xrightarrow{e_2} \langle y', s''\rangle}{\langle x \parallel y, s\rangle \xrightarrow{\{e_1,e_2\}} \langle y', s' \cup s''\rangle} \qquad \frac{\langle x, s\rangle \xrightarrow{e_1} \langle x', s'\rangle \quad \langle y, s\rangle \xrightarrow{e_2} \langle y', s''\rangle}{\langle x \parallel y, s\rangle \xrightarrow{\{e_1,e_2\}} \langle x' \between y', s' \cup s''\rangle}$$

$$\frac{\langle x, s\rangle \xrightarrow{e_1} \langle \surd, s'\rangle \quad \langle y, s\rangle \overset{e_2}{\nrightarrow} \quad (e_1 \% e_2)}{\langle x \parallel y, s\rangle \xrightarrow{e_1} \langle y, s'\rangle} \qquad \frac{\langle x, s\rangle \xrightarrow{e_1} \langle x', s'\rangle \quad \langle y, s\rangle \overset{e_2}{\nrightarrow} \quad (e_1 \% e_2)}{\langle x \parallel y, s\rangle \xrightarrow{e_1} \langle x' \between y, s'\rangle}$$

$$\frac{\langle x, s\rangle \overset{e_1}{\nrightarrow} \quad \langle y, s\rangle \xrightarrow{e_2} \langle \surd, s''\rangle \quad (e_1 \% e_2)}{\langle x \parallel y, s\rangle \xrightarrow{e_2} \langle x, s''\rangle} \qquad \frac{\langle x, s\rangle \overset{e_1}{\nrightarrow} \quad \langle y, s\rangle \xrightarrow{e_2} \langle y', s''\rangle \quad (e_1 \% e_2)}{\langle x \parallel y, s\rangle \xrightarrow{e_2} \langle x \between y', s''\rangle}$$

$$\frac{\langle x, s\rangle \xrightarrow{e_1} \langle \surd, s'\rangle \quad \langle y, s\rangle \xrightarrow{e_2} \langle \surd, s''\rangle}{\langle x \mid y, s\rangle \xrightarrow{\gamma(e_1,e_2)} \langle \surd, effect(\gamma(e_1, e_2), s)\rangle} \qquad \frac{\langle x, s\rangle \xrightarrow{e_1} \langle x', s'\rangle \quad \langle y, s\rangle \xrightarrow{e_2} \langle \surd, s''\rangle}{\langle x \mid y, s\rangle \xrightarrow{\gamma(e_1,e_2)} \langle x', effect(\gamma(e_1, e_2), s)\rangle}$$

$$\frac{\langle x, s\rangle \xrightarrow{e_1} \langle \surd, s'\rangle \quad \langle y, s\rangle \xrightarrow{e_2} \langle y', s''\rangle}{\langle x \mid y, s\rangle \xrightarrow{\gamma(e_1,e_2)} \langle y', effect(\gamma(e_1, e_2), s)\rangle} \qquad \frac{\langle x, s\rangle \xrightarrow{e_1} \langle x', s'\rangle \quad \langle y, s\rangle \xrightarrow{e_2} \langle y', s''\rangle}{\langle x \mid y, s\rangle \xrightarrow{\gamma(e_1,e_2)} \langle x' \between y', effect(\gamma(e_1, e_2), s)\rangle}$$

$$\frac{\langle x, s\rangle \xrightarrow{e_1} \langle \surd, s'\rangle \quad (\sharp(e_1, e_2))}{\langle \Theta(x), s\rangle \xrightarrow{e_1} \langle \surd, s'\rangle} \qquad \frac{\langle x, s\rangle \xrightarrow{e_2} \langle \surd, s''\rangle \quad (\sharp(e_1, e_2))}{\langle \Theta(x), s\rangle \xrightarrow{e_2} \langle \surd, s''\rangle}$$

$$\frac{\langle x, s\rangle \xrightarrow{e_1} \langle x', s'\rangle \quad (\sharp(e_1, e_2))}{\langle \Theta(x), s\rangle \xrightarrow{e_1} \langle \Theta(x'), s'\rangle} \qquad \frac{\langle x, s\rangle \xrightarrow{e_2} \langle x'', s''\rangle \quad (\sharp(e_1, e_2))}{\langle \Theta(x), s\rangle \xrightarrow{e_2} \langle \Theta(x''), s''\rangle}$$

$$\frac{\langle x, s\rangle \xrightarrow{e_1} \langle \surd, s'\rangle \quad \langle y, s\rangle \nrightarrow^{e_2} \quad (\sharp(e_1, e_2))}{\langle x \triangleleft y, s\rangle \xrightarrow{\tau} \langle \surd, s'\rangle} \qquad \frac{\langle x, s\rangle \xrightarrow{e_1} \langle x', s'\rangle \quad \langle y, s\rangle \nrightarrow^{e_2} \quad (\sharp(e_1, e_2))}{\langle x \triangleleft y, s\rangle \xrightarrow{\tau} \langle x', s'\rangle}$$

$$\frac{\langle x, s\rangle \xrightarrow{e_1} \langle \surd, s\rangle \quad \langle y, s\rangle \nrightarrow^{e_3} \quad (\sharp(e_1, e_2), e_2 \le e_3)}{\langle x \triangleleft y, s\rangle \xrightarrow{\tau} \langle \surd, s'\rangle} \qquad \frac{\langle x, s\rangle \xrightarrow{e_1} \langle x', s'\rangle \quad \langle y, s\rangle \nrightarrow^{e_3} \quad (\sharp(e_1, e_2), e_2 \le e_3)}{\langle x \triangleleft y, s\rangle \xrightarrow{\tau} \langle x', s'\rangle}$$

$$\frac{\langle x, s\rangle \xrightarrow{e_3} \langle \surd, s'\rangle \quad \langle y, s\rangle \nrightarrow^{e_2} \quad (\sharp(e_1, e_2), e_1 \le e_3)}{\langle x \triangleleft y, s\rangle \xrightarrow{\tau} \langle \surd, s'\rangle} \qquad \frac{\langle x, s\rangle \xrightarrow{e_3} \langle x', s'\rangle \quad \langle y, s\rangle \nrightarrow^{e_2} \quad (\sharp(e_1, e_2), e_1 \le e_3)}{\langle x \triangleleft y, s\rangle \xrightarrow{\tau} \langle x', s'\rangle}$$

$$\frac{\langle x, s\rangle \xrightarrow{e} \langle \surd, s'\rangle}{\langle \partial_H(x), s\rangle \xrightarrow{e} \langle \surd, s'\rangle} \quad (e \notin H) \qquad \frac{\langle x, s\rangle \xrightarrow{e} \langle x', s'\rangle}{\langle \partial_H(x), s\rangle \xrightarrow{e} \langle \partial_H(x'), s'\rangle} \quad (e \notin H)$$

sides of their recursive equations,

$$\begin{aligned}&(a_{11} \parallel \cdots \parallel a_{1i_1}) \cdot s_1(X_1, \cdots, X_n) + \cdots + (a_{k1} \parallel \cdots \parallel a_{ki_k}) \cdot s_k(X_1, \cdots, X_n)\\ &+ (b_{11} \parallel \cdots \parallel b_{1j_1}) + \cdots + (b_{1j_1} \parallel \cdots \parallel b_{lj_l})\end{aligned}$$

where $a_{11}, \cdots, a_{1i_1}, a_{k1}, \cdots, a_{ki_k}, b_{11}, \cdots, b_{1j_1}, b_{1j_1}, \cdots, b_{lj_l} \in \mathbb{E}$, and the sum above is allowed to be empty, in which case it represents the deadlock δ. And there does not exist an infinite sequence of ϵ-transitions $\langle X|E\rangle \rightarrow \langle X'|E\rangle \rightarrow \langle X''|E\rangle \rightarrow \cdots$.

Table 4.5 Transition rules of guarded recursion.

$$\frac{\langle t_i(\langle X_1|E\rangle,\cdots,\langle X_n|E\rangle),s\rangle \xrightarrow{\{e_1,\cdots,e_k\}} \langle\surd,s'\rangle}{\langle\langle X_i|E\rangle,s\rangle \xrightarrow{\{e_1,\cdots,e_k\}} \langle\surd,s'\rangle}$$

$$\frac{\langle t_i(\langle X_1|E\rangle,\cdots,\langle X_n|E\rangle),s\rangle \xrightarrow{\{e_1,\cdots,e_k\}} \langle y,s'\rangle}{\langle\langle X_i|E\rangle,s\rangle \xrightarrow{\{e_1,\cdots,e_k\}} \langle y,s'\rangle}$$

Theorem 4.25 (Conservativity of $APTC_G$ with guarded recursion). *$APTC_G$ with guarded recursion is a conservative extension of $APTC_G$.*

Theorem 4.26 (Congruence theorem of $APTC_G$ with guarded recursion). *Truly concurrent bisimulation equivalences $\sim_p$, $\sim_s$ and $\sim_{hp}$ are all congruences with respect to $APTC_G$ with guarded recursion.*

Theorem 4.27 (Elimination theorem of $APTC_G$ with linear recursion). *Each process term in $APTC_G$ with linear recursion is equal to a process term $\langle X_1|E\rangle$ with E a linear recursive specification.*

Theorem 4.28 (Soundness of $APTC_G$ with guarded recursion). *Let x and y be $APTC_G$ with guarded recursion terms. If $APTC_G$ with guarded recursion $\vdash x = y$, then*

(1) $x \sim_s y$;

(2) $x \sim_p y$;

(3) $x \sim_{hp} y$.

Theorem 4.29 (Completeness of $APTC_G$ with linear recursion). *Let p and q be closed $APTC_G$ with linear recursion terms, then,*

(1) if $p \sim_s q$ then $p = q$;

(2) if $p \sim_p q$ then $p = q$;

(3) if $p \sim_{hp} q$ then $p = q$.

4.5 Abstraction

To abstract away from the internal implementations of a program, and verify that the program exhibits the desired external behaviors, the silent step τ and abstraction operator τ_I are introduced, where $I \subseteq \mathbb{E} \cup G_{at}$ denotes the internal events or guards. The silent step τ represents the internal events, and τ_ϕ for internal guards, when we consider the external behaviors of a process, τ steps can be removed, that is, τ steps must keep silent. The transition rule of τ is shown in Table 4.6. In the following, let the atomic event e range over $\mathbb{E} \cup \{\epsilon\} \cup \{\delta\} \cup \{\tau\}$, and ϕ range over $G \cup \{\tau\}$, and let the communication function $\gamma : \mathbb{E} \cup \{\tau\} \times \mathbb{E} \cup \{\tau\} \to \mathbb{E} \cup \{\delta\}$, with each communication involved τ resulting in δ. We use $\tau(s)$ to denote $effect(\tau, s)$, for the fact that τ only change the state of internal data environment, that is, for the external data environments, $s = \tau(s)$.

Table 4.6 Transition rule of the silent step.

$$\frac{}{\langle\tau_\phi, s\rangle \rightarrow \langle\surd, s\rangle}\text{if } test(\tau_\phi, s)$$

$$\frac{}{\langle\tau, s\rangle \xrightarrow{\tau} \langle\surd, \tau(s)\rangle}$$

In Section 4.1, we introduce τ into event structure, and also give the concept of weakly true concurrency. In this section, we give the concepts of rooted branching truly concurrent bisimulation equivalences, based on these concepts, we can design the axiom system of the silent step τ and the abstraction operator τ_I.

Definition 4.30 (Branching pomset, step bisimulation). Assume a special termination predicate $\downarrow$, and let $\surd$ represent a state with $\surd\downarrow$. Let $\mathcal{E}_1$, $\mathcal{E}_2$ be PESs. A branching pomset bisimulation is a relation $R \subseteq \langle\mathcal{C}(\mathcal{E}_1), S\rangle \times \langle\mathcal{C}(\mathcal{E}_2), S\rangle$, such that:

1. if $(\langle C_1, s\rangle, \langle C_2, s\rangle) \in R$, and $\langle C_1, s\rangle \xrightarrow{X} \langle C_1', s'\rangle$ then
   - either $X \equiv \tau^*$, and $(\langle C_1', s'\rangle, \langle C_2, s\rangle) \in R$ with $s' \in \tau(s)$;
   - or there is a sequence of (zero or more) τ-transitions $\langle C_2, s\rangle \xrightarrow{\tau^*} \langle C_2^0, s^0\rangle$, such that $(\langle C_1, s\rangle, \langle C_2^0, s^0\rangle) \in R$ and $\langle C_2^0, s^0\rangle \xRightarrow{X} \langle C_2', s'\rangle$ with $(\langle C_1', s'\rangle, \langle C_2', s'\rangle) \in R$;
2. if $(\langle C_1, s\rangle, \langle C_2, s\rangle) \in R$, and $\langle C_2, s\rangle \xrightarrow{X} \langle C_2', s'\rangle$ then
   - either $X \equiv \tau^*$, and $(\langle C_1, s\rangle, \langle C_2', s'\rangle) \in R$;
   - or there is a sequence of (zero or more) τ-transitions $\langle C_1, s\rangle \xrightarrow{\tau^*} \langle C_1^0, s^0\rangle$, such that $(\langle C_1^0, s^0\rangle, \langle C_2, s\rangle) \in R$ and $\langle C_1^0, s^0\rangle \xRightarrow{X} \langle C_1', s'\rangle$ with $(\langle C_1', s'\rangle, \langle C_2', s'\rangle) \in R$;
3. if $(\langle C_1, s\rangle, \langle C_2, s\rangle) \in R$ and $\langle C_1, s\rangle\downarrow$, then there is a sequence of (zero or more) τ-transitions $\langle C_2, s\rangle \xrightarrow{\tau^*} \langle C_2^0, s^0\rangle$ such that $(\langle C_1, s\rangle, \langle C_2^0, s^0\rangle) \in R$ and $\langle C_2^0, s^0\rangle\downarrow$;
4. if $(\langle C_1, s\rangle, \langle C_2, s\rangle) \in R$ and $\langle C_2, s\rangle\downarrow$, then there is a sequence of (zero or more) τ-transitions $\langle C_1, s\rangle \xrightarrow{\tau^*} \langle C_1^0, s^0\rangle$ such that $(\langle C_1^0, s^0\rangle, \langle C_2, s\rangle) \in R$ and $\langle C_1^0, s^0\rangle\downarrow$.

We say that $\mathcal{E}_1$, $\mathcal{E}_2$ are branching pomset bisimilar, written $\mathcal{E}_1 \approx_{bp} \mathcal{E}_2$, if there exists a branching pomset bisimulation R, such that $(\langle\emptyset, \emptyset\rangle, \langle\emptyset, \emptyset\rangle) \in R$.

By replacing pomset transitions with steps, we can get the definition of branching step bisimulation. When PESs $\mathcal{E}_1$ and $\mathcal{E}_2$ are branching step bisimilar, we write $\mathcal{E}_1 \approx_{bs} \mathcal{E}_2$.

Definition 4.31 (Rooted branching pomset, step bisimulation). Assume a special termination predicate $\downarrow$, and let $\surd$ represent a state with $\surd\downarrow$. Let $\mathcal{E}_1$, $\mathcal{E}_2$ be PESs. A rooted branching pomset bisimulation is a relation $R \subseteq \langle\mathcal{C}(\mathcal{E}_1), S\rangle \times \langle\mathcal{C}(\mathcal{E}_2), S\rangle$, such that:

1. if $(\langle C_1, s\rangle, \langle C_2, s\rangle) \in R$, and $\langle C_1, s\rangle \xrightarrow{X} \langle C_1', s'\rangle$ then $\langle C_2, s\rangle \xrightarrow{X} \langle C_2', s'\rangle$ with $\langle C_1', s'\rangle \approx_{bp} \langle C_2', s'\rangle$;

2. if $(\langle C_1, s\rangle, \langle C_2, s\rangle) \in R$, and $\langle C_2, s\rangle \xrightarrow{X} \langle C_2', s'\rangle$ then $\langle C_1, s\rangle \xrightarrow{X} \langle C_1', s'\rangle$ with $\langle C_1', s'\rangle \approx_{bp} \langle C_2', s'\rangle$;
3. if $(\langle C_1, s\rangle, \langle C_2, s\rangle) \in R$ and $\langle C_1, s\rangle \downarrow$, then $\langle C_2, s\rangle \downarrow$;
4. if $(\langle C_1, s\rangle, \langle C_2, s\rangle) \in R$ and $\langle C_2, s\rangle \downarrow$, then $\langle C_1, s\rangle \downarrow$.

We say that $\mathcal{E}_1$, $\mathcal{E}_2$ are rooted branching pomset bisimilar, written $\mathcal{E}_1 \approx_{rbp} \mathcal{E}_2$, if there exists a rooted branching pomset bisimulation R, such that $(\langle\emptyset, \emptyset\rangle, \langle\emptyset, \emptyset\rangle) \in R$.

By replacing pomset transitions with steps, we can get the definition of rooted branching step bisimulation. When PESs $\mathcal{E}_1$ and $\mathcal{E}_2$ are rooted branching step bisimilar, we write $\mathcal{E}_1 \approx_{rbs} \mathcal{E}_2$.

Definition 4.32 (Branching (hereditary) history-preserving bisimulation). Assume a special termination predicate $\downarrow$, and let $\surd$ represent a state with $\surd \downarrow$. A branching history-preserving (hp-)bisimulation is a weakly posetal relation $R \subseteq \langle \mathcal{C}(\mathcal{E}_1), S\rangle \overline{\times} \langle \mathcal{C}(\mathcal{E}_2), S\rangle$ such that:

1. if $(\langle C_1, s\rangle, f, \langle C_2, s\rangle) \in R$, and $\langle C_1, s\rangle \xrightarrow{e_1} \langle C_1', s'\rangle$ then
   - either $e_1 \equiv \tau$, and $(\langle C_1', s'\rangle, f[e_1 \mapsto \tau], \langle C_2, s\rangle) \in R$;
   - or there is a sequence of (zero or more) τ-transitions $\langle C_2, s\rangle \xrightarrow{\tau^*} \langle C_2^0, s^0\rangle$, such that $(\langle C_1, s\rangle, f, \langle C_2^0, s^0\rangle) \in R$ and $\langle C_2^0, s^0\rangle \xrightarrow{e_2} \langle C_2', s'\rangle$ with $(\langle C_1', s'\rangle, f[e_1 \mapsto e_2], \langle C_2', s'\rangle) \in R$;
2. if $(\langle C_1, s\rangle, f, \langle C_2, s\rangle) \in R$, and $\langle C_2, s\rangle \xrightarrow{e_2} \langle C_2', s'\rangle$ then
   - either $e_2 \equiv \tau$, and $(\langle C_1, s\rangle, f[e_2 \mapsto \tau], \langle C_2', s'\rangle) \in R$;
   - or there is a sequence of (zero or more) τ-transitions $\langle C_1, s\rangle \xrightarrow{\tau^*} \langle C_1^0, s^0\rangle$, such that $(\langle C_1^0, s^0\rangle, f, \langle C_2, s\rangle) \in R$ and $\langle C_1^0, s^0\rangle \xrightarrow{e_1} \langle C_1', s'\rangle$ with $(\langle C_1', s'\rangle, f[e_2 \mapsto e_1], \langle C_2', s'\rangle) \in R$;
3. if $(\langle C_1, s\rangle, f, \langle C_2, s\rangle) \in R$ and $\langle C_1, s\rangle \downarrow$, then there is a sequence of (zero or more) τ-transitions $\langle C_2, s\rangle \xrightarrow{\tau^*} \langle C_2^0, s^0\rangle$ such that $(\langle C_1, s\rangle, f, \langle C_2^0, s^0\rangle) \in R$ and $\langle C_2^0, s^0\rangle \downarrow$;
4. if $(\langle C_1, s\rangle, f, \langle C_2, s\rangle) \in R$ and $\langle C_2, s\rangle \downarrow$, then there is a sequence of (zero or more) τ-transitions $\langle C_1, s\rangle \xrightarrow{\tau^*} \langle C_1^0, s^0\rangle$ such that $(\langle C_1^0, s^0\rangle, f, \langle C_2, s\rangle) \in R$ and $\langle C_1^0, s^0\rangle \downarrow$.

$\mathcal{E}_1, \mathcal{E}_2$ are branching history-preserving (hp-)bisimilar and are written $\mathcal{E}_1 \approx_{bhp} \mathcal{E}_2$ if there exists a branching hp-bisimulation R such that $(\langle\emptyset, \emptyset\rangle, \emptyset, \langle\emptyset, \emptyset\rangle) \in R$.

A branching hereditary history-preserving (hhp-)bisimulation is a downward closed branching hp-bisimulation. $\mathcal{E}_1, \mathcal{E}_2$ are branching hereditary history-preserving (hhp-)bisimilar and are written $\mathcal{E}_1 \approx_{bhhp} \mathcal{E}_2$.

Definition 4.33 (Rooted branching (hereditary) history-preserving bisimulation). Assume a special termination predicate $\downarrow$, and let $\surd$ represent a state with $\surd \downarrow$. A rooted branching history-preserving (hp-)bisimulation is a weakly posetal relation $R \subseteq \langle \mathcal{C}(\mathcal{E}_1), S\rangle \overline{\times} \langle \mathcal{C}(\mathcal{E}_2), S\rangle$ such that:

1. if $(\langle C_1, s\rangle, f, \langle C_2, s\rangle) \in R$, and $\langle C_1, s\rangle \xrightarrow{e_1} \langle C_1', s'\rangle$, then $\langle C_2, s\rangle \xrightarrow{e_2} \langle C_2', s'\rangle$ with $\langle C_1', s'\rangle \approx_{bhp} \langle C_2', s'\rangle$;

Table 4.7 Axioms of silent step.

No.	Axiom
$B1$	$e \cdot \tau = e$
$B2$	$e \cdot (\tau \cdot (x + y) + x) = e \cdot (x + y)$
$B3$	$x \parallel \tau = x$
$G26$	$\tau_\phi \cdot x = x$
$G27$	$x \cdot \tau_\phi = x$
$G28$	$x \parallel \tau_\phi = x$

2. if $(\langle C_1, s\rangle, f, \langle C_2, s\rangle) \in R$, and $\langle C_2, s\rangle \xrightarrow{e_2} \langle C_2', s'\rangle$, then $\langle C_1, s\rangle \xrightarrow{e_1} \langle C_1', s'\rangle$ with $\langle C_1', s'\rangle \approx_{bhp} \langle C_2', s'\rangle$;
3. if $(\langle C_1, s\rangle, f, \langle C_2, s\rangle) \in R$ and $\langle C_1, s\rangle \downarrow$, then $\langle C_2, s\rangle \downarrow$;
4. if $(\langle C_1, s\rangle, f, \langle C_2, s\rangle) \in R$ and $\langle C_2, s\rangle \downarrow$, then $\langle C_1, s\rangle \downarrow$.

$\mathcal{E}_1, \mathcal{E}_2$ are rooted branching history-preserving (hp-)bisimilar and are written $\mathcal{E}_1 \approx_{rbhp} \mathcal{E}_2$ if there exists a rooted branching hp-bisimulation R such that $(\langle\emptyset, \emptyset\rangle, \emptyset, \langle\emptyset, \emptyset\rangle) \in R$.

A rooted branching hereditary history-preserving (hhp-)bisimulation is a downward closed rooted branching hp-bisimulation. $\mathcal{E}_1, \mathcal{E}_2$ are rooted branching hereditary history-preserving (hhp-)bisimilar and are written $\mathcal{E}_1 \approx_{rbhhp} \mathcal{E}_2$.

Definition 4.34 (Guarded linear recursive specification). A linear recursive specification E is guarded if there does not exist an infinite sequence of τ-transitions $\langle X|E\rangle \xrightarrow{\tau} \langle X'|E\rangle \xrightarrow{\tau} \langle X''|E\rangle \xrightarrow{\tau} \cdots$, and there does not exist an infinite sequence of ϵ-transitions $\langle X|E\rangle \rightarrow \langle X'|E\rangle \rightarrow \langle X''|E\rangle \rightarrow \cdots$.

Theorem 4.35 (Conservativity of $APTC_G$ with silent step and guarded linear recursion). *$APTC_G$ with silent step and guarded linear recursion is a conservative extension of $APTC_G$ with linear recursion.*

Theorem 4.36 (Congruence theorem of $APTC_G$ with silent step and guarded linear recursion). *Rooted branching truly concurrent bisimulation equivalences $\approx_{rbp}$, $\approx_{rbs}$ and $\approx_{rbhp}$ are all congruences with respect to $APTC_G$ with silent step and guarded linear recursion.*

We design the axioms for the silent step τ in Table 4.7.

Theorem 4.37 (Elimination theorem of $APTC_G$ with silent step and guarded linear recursion). *Each process term in $APTC_G$ with silent step and guarded linear recursion is equal to a process term $\langle X_1|E\rangle$ with E a guarded linear recursive specification.*

Theorem 4.38 (Soundness of $APTC_G$ with silent step and guarded linear recursion). *Let x and y be $APTC_G$ with silent step and guarded linear recursion terms. If $APTC_G$ with silent step and guarded linear recursion $\vdash x = y$, then*

(1) $x \approx_{rbs} y$;
(2) $x \approx_{rbp} y$;
(3) $x \approx_{rbhp} y$.

Table 4.8 Transition rule of the abstraction operator.

$$\frac{\langle x,s\rangle \xrightarrow{e} \langle\surd,s'\rangle}{\langle\tau_I(x),s\rangle \xrightarrow{e} \langle\surd,s'\rangle}\quad e\notin I \qquad \frac{\langle x,s\rangle \xrightarrow{e} \langle x',s'\rangle}{\langle\tau_I(x),s\rangle \xrightarrow{e} \langle\tau_I(x'),s'\rangle}\quad e\notin I$$

$$\frac{\langle x,s\rangle \xrightarrow{e} \langle\surd,s'\rangle}{\langle\tau_I(x),s\rangle \xrightarrow{\tau} \langle\surd,\tau(s)\rangle}\quad e\in I \qquad \frac{\langle x,s\rangle \xrightarrow{e} \langle x',s'\rangle}{\langle\tau_I(x),s\rangle \xrightarrow{\tau} \langle\tau_I(x'),\tau(s)\rangle}\quad e\in I$$

Table 4.9 Axioms of abstraction operator.

No.	Axiom
$TI1$	$e\notin I \quad \tau_I(e)=e$
$TI2$	$e\in I \quad \tau_I(e)=\tau$
$TI3$	$\tau_I(\delta)=\delta$
$TI4$	$\tau_I(x+y)=\tau_I(x)+\tau_I(y)$
$TI5$	$\tau_I(x\cdot y)=\tau_I(x)\cdot\tau_I(y)$
$TI6$	$\tau_I(x\parallel y)=\tau_I(x)\parallel\tau_I(y)$
$G29$	$\phi\notin I \quad \tau_I(\phi)=\phi$
$G30$	$\phi\in I \quad \tau_I(\phi)=\tau_\phi$

Theorem 4.39 (Completeness of $APTC_G$ with silent step and guarded linear recursion). *Let p and q be closed $APTC_G$ with silent step and guarded linear recursion terms, then,*

(1) if $p\approx_{rbs} q$ then $p=q$;

(2) if $p\approx_{rbp} q$ then $p=q$;

(3) if $p\approx_{rbhp} q$ then $p=q$.

The unary abstraction operator τ_I ($I\subseteq\mathbb{E}\cup G_{at}$) renames all atomic events or atomic guards in I into τ. $APTC_G$ with silent step and abstraction operator is called $APTC_{G_\tau}$. The transition rules of operator τ_I are shown in Table 4.8.

Theorem 4.40 (Conservativity of $APTC_{G_\tau}$ with guarded linear recursion). *$APTC_{G_\tau}$ with guarded linear recursion is a conservative extension of $APTC_G$ with silent step and guarded linear recursion.*

Theorem 4.41 (Congruence theorem of $APTC_{G_\tau}$ with guarded linear recursion). *Rooted branching truly concurrent bisimulation equivalences $\approx_{rbp}$, $\approx_{rbs}$, and $\approx_{rbhp}$ are all congruences with respect to $APTC_{G_\tau}$ with guarded linear recursion.*

We design the axioms for the abstraction operator τ_I in Table 4.9.

Theorem 4.42 (Soundness of $APTC_{G_\tau}$ with guarded linear recursion). *Let x and y be $APTC_{G_\tau}$ with guarded linear recursion terms. If $APTC_{G_\tau}$ with guarded linear recursion $\vdash x=y$, then*

(1) $x \approx_{rbs} y$;
(2) $x \approx_{rbp} y$;
(3) $x \approx_{rbhp} y$.

Though τ-loops are prohibited in guarded linear recursive specifications (see Definition 4.34) in a specifiable way, they can be constructed using the abstraction operator, for example, there exist τ-loops in the process term $\tau_{\{a\}}(\langle X|X = aX\rangle)$. To avoid τ-loops caused by τ_I and ensure fairness, the concepts of cluster and $CFAR$ (Cluster Fair Abstraction Rule) [25] are still needed.

Theorem 4.43 (Completeness of $APTC_{G_\tau}$ with guarded linear recursion and $CFAR$). *Let p and q be closed $APTC_{G_\tau}$ with guarded linear recursion and $CFAR$ terms, then,*
(1) if $p \approx_{rbs} q$ *then* $p = q$;
(2) if $p \approx_{rbp} q$ *then* $p = q$;
(3) if $p \approx_{rbhp} q$ *then* $p = q$.

5

Distributed APTC

Distributed APTC makes APTC to have the ability to express the locations or roles. Distributed APTC can be used to model the roles of participants in WS composition.

This chapter is organized as follows. We introduce the operational semantics of static location in Section 5.1, distributed $BATC$ in Section 5.2, distributed $APTC$ in Section 5.3, recursion in Section 5.4, abstraction in Section 5.5.

5.1 Static location bisimulations

Let Loc be the set of locations, and $u, v \in Loc^*$. Let $\ll$ be the sequential ordering on Loc^*, we call v is an extension or a sublocation of u in $u \ll v$; and if $u \not\ll v$ $v \not\ll u$, then u and v are independent and denoted $u \diamond v$.

Definition 5.1 (Consistent location association). A relation $\varphi \subseteq (Loc^* \times Loc^*)$ is a consistent location association (cla), if $(u, v) \in \varphi \& (u', v') \in \varphi$, then $u \diamond u' \Leftrightarrow v \diamond v'$.

Definition 5.2 (Static location pomset, step bisimulation). Let $\mathcal{E}_1, \mathcal{E}_2$ be PESs. A static location pomset bisimulation is a relation $R_\varphi \subseteq \mathcal{C}(\mathcal{E}_1) \times \mathcal{C}(\mathcal{E}_2)$, such that if $(C_1, C_2) \in R_\varphi$, and $C_1 \xrightarrow[u]{X_1} C_1'$ then $C_2 \xrightarrow[v]{X_2} C_2'$, with $X_1 \subseteq \mathbb{E}_1$, $X_2 \subseteq \mathbb{E}_2$, $X_1 \sim X_2$, and $(C_1', C_2') \in R_{\varphi \cup \{(u,v)\}}$, and vice-versa. We say that $\mathcal{E}_1, \mathcal{E}_2$ are static location pomset bisimilar, written $\mathcal{E}_1 \sim_p^{sl} \mathcal{E}_2$, if there exists a static location pomset bisimulation R_φ, such that $(\emptyset, \emptyset) \in R_\varphi$. By replacing pomset transitions with steps, we can get the definition of static location step bisimulation. When PESs $\mathcal{E}_1$ and $\mathcal{E}_2$ are static location step bisimilar, we write $\mathcal{E}_1 \sim_s^{sl} \mathcal{E}_2$.

Definition 5.3 (Static location (hereditary) history-preserving bisimulation). A static location history-preserving (hp-)bisimulation is a posetal relation $R_\varphi \subseteq \mathcal{C}(\mathcal{E}_1)\overline{\times}\mathcal{C}(\mathcal{E}_2)$ such that if $(C_1, f, C_2) \in R_\varphi$, and $C_1 \xrightarrow[u]{e_1} C_1'$, then $C_2 \xrightarrow[v]{e_2} C_2'$, with $(C_1', f[e_1 \mapsto e_2], C_2') \in R_{\varphi \cup \{(u,v)\}}$, and vice-versa. $\mathcal{E}_1, \mathcal{E}_2$ are static location history-preserving (hp-)bisimilar and are written $\mathcal{E}_1 \sim_{hp}^{sl} \mathcal{E}_2$ if there exists a static location hp-bisimulation R_φ such that $(\emptyset, \emptyset, \emptyset) \in R_\varphi$.

A static location hereditary history-preserving (hhp-)bisimulation is a downward closed static location hp-bisimulation. $\mathcal{E}_1, \mathcal{E}_2$ are static location hereditary history-preserving (hhp-)bisimilar and are written $\mathcal{E}_1 \sim_{hhp}^{sl} \mathcal{E}_2$.

Definition 5.4 (Weak static location pomset, step bisimulation). Let $\mathcal{E}_1, \mathcal{E}_2$ be PESs. A weak static location pomset bisimulation is a relation $R_\varphi \subseteq \mathcal{C}(\mathcal{E}_1) \times \mathcal{C}(\mathcal{E}_2)$, such that if $(C_1, C_2) \in R_\varphi$, and $C_1 \overset{X_1}{\underset{u}{\Longrightarrow}} C_1'$ then $C_2 \overset{X_2}{\underset{v}{\Longrightarrow}} C_2'$, with $X_1 \subseteq \hat{\mathbb{E}}_1$, $X_2 \subseteq \hat{\mathbb{E}}_2$, $X_1 \sim X_2$, and $(C_1', C_2') \in R_{\varphi \cup \{(u,v)\}}$, and vice-versa. We say that $\mathcal{E}_1, \mathcal{E}_2$ are weak static location pomset bisimilar, written $\mathcal{E}_1 \approx_p^{sl} \mathcal{E}_2$, if there exists a weak static location pomset bisimulation R_φ, such that $(\emptyset, \emptyset) \in R_\varphi$. By

Theory of Structured Parallel Programming. https://doi.org/10.1016/B978-0-44-324814-6.00009-5

replacing weak pomset transitions with weak steps, we can get the definition of weak static location step bisimulation. When PESs $\mathcal{E}_1$ and $\mathcal{E}_2$ are weak static location step bisimilar, we write $\mathcal{E}_1 \approx_s^{sl} \mathcal{E}_2$.

Definition 5.5 (Weak static location (hereditary) history-preserving bisimulation). A weak static location history-preserving (hp-)bisimulation is a weakly posetal relation $R_\varphi \subseteq \mathcal{C}(\mathcal{E}_1)\overline{\times}\mathcal{C}(\mathcal{E}_2)$ such that if $(C_1, f, C_2) \in R_\varphi$, and $C_1 \overset{e_1}{\underset{u}{\Rightarrow}} C_1'$, then $C_2 \overset{e_2}{\underset{v}{\Rightarrow}} C_2'$, with $(C_1', f[e_1 \mapsto e_2], C_2') \in R_{\varphi\cup\{(u,v)\}}$, and vice-versa. $\mathcal{E}_1, \mathcal{E}_2$ are weak static location history-preserving (hp-)bisimilar and are written $\mathcal{E}_1 \approx_{hp}^{sl} \mathcal{E}_2$ if there exists a weak static location hp-bisimulation R_φ such that $(\emptyset, \emptyset, \emptyset) \in R_\varphi$.

A weak static location hereditary history-preserving (hhp-)bisimulation is a downward closed weak static location hp-bisimulation. $\mathcal{E}_1, \mathcal{E}_2$ are weak static location hereditary history-preserving (hhp-)bisimilar and are written $\mathcal{E}_1 \approx_{hhp}^{sl} \mathcal{E}_2$.

Definition 5.6 (Branching static location pomset, step bisimulation). Assume a special termination predicate $\downarrow$, and let $\surd$ represent a state with $\surd\downarrow$. Let $\mathcal{E}_1, \mathcal{E}_2$ be PESs. A branching static location pomset bisimulation is a relation $R_\varphi \subseteq \mathcal{C}(\mathcal{E}_1) \times \mathcal{C}(\mathcal{E}_2)$, such that:

1. if $(C_1, C_2) \in R_\varphi$, and $C_1 \overset{X}{\underset{u}{\rightarrow}} C_1'$ then
   - either $X \equiv \tau^*$, and $(C_1', C_2) \in R_\varphi$;
   - or there is a sequence of (zero or more) τ-transitions $C_2 \overset{\tau^*}{\rightarrow} C_2^0$, such that $(C_1, C_2^0) \in R_\varphi$ and $C_2^0 \overset{X}{\underset{v}{\Rightarrow}} C_2'$ with $(C_1', C_2') \in R_{\varphi\cup\{(u,v)\}}$;
2. if $(C_1, C_2) \in R_\varphi$, and $C_2 \overset{X}{\underset{v}{\rightarrow}} C_2'$ then
   - either $X \equiv \tau^*$, and $(C_1, C_2') \in R_\varphi$;
   - or there is a sequence of (zero or more) τ-transitions $C_1 \overset{\tau^*}{\rightarrow} C_1^0$, such that $(C_1^0, C_2) \in R_\varphi$ and $C_1^0 \overset{X}{\underset{u}{\Rightarrow}} C_1'$ with $(C_1', C_2') \in R_{\varphi\cup\{(u,v)\}}$;
3. if $(C_1, C_2) \in R_\varphi$ and $C_1\downarrow$, then there is a sequence of (zero or more) τ-transitions $C_2 \overset{\tau^*}{\rightarrow} C_2^0$ such that $(C_1, C_2^0) \in R_\varphi$ and $C_2^0\downarrow$;
4. if $(C_1, C_2) \in R_\varphi$ and $C_2\downarrow$, then there is a sequence of (zero or more) τ-transitions $C_1 \overset{\tau^*}{\rightarrow} C_1^0$ such that $(C_1^0, C_2) \in R_\varphi$ and $C_1^0\downarrow$.

We say that $\mathcal{E}_1$, $\mathcal{E}_2$ are branching static location pomset bisimilar, written $\mathcal{E}_1 \approx_{bp}^{sl} \mathcal{E}_2$, if there exists a branching static location pomset bisimulation R_φ, such that $(\emptyset, \emptyset) \in R_\varphi$.

By replacing pomset transitions with steps, we can get the definition of branching static location step bisimulation. When PESs $\mathcal{E}_1$ and $\mathcal{E}_2$ are branching static location step bisimilar, we write $\mathcal{E}_1 \approx_{bs}^{sl} \mathcal{E}_2$.

Definition 5.7 (Rooted branching static location pomset, step bisimulation). Assume a special termination predicate $\downarrow$, and let $\surd$ represent a state with $\surd\downarrow$. Let $\mathcal{E}_1, \mathcal{E}_2$ be PESs.

A rooted branching static location pomset bisimulation is a relation $R_\varphi \subseteq \mathcal{C}(\mathcal{E}_1) \times \mathcal{C}(\mathcal{E}_2)$, such that:

1. if $(C_1, C_2) \in R_\varphi$, and $C_1 \xrightarrow[u]{X} C_1'$ then $C_2 \xrightarrow[v]{X} C_2'$ with $C_1' \approx_{bp}^{sl} C_2'$;
2. if $(C_1, C_2) \in R_\varphi$, and $C_2 \xrightarrow[v]{X} C_2'$ then $C_1 \xrightarrow[u]{X} C_1'$ with $C_1' \approx_{bp}^{sl} C_2'$;
3. if $(C_1, C_2) \in R_\varphi$ and $C_1 \downarrow$, then $C_2 \downarrow$;
4. if $(C_1, C_2) \in R_\varphi$ and $C_2 \downarrow$, then $C_1 \downarrow$.

We say that $\mathcal{E}_1, \mathcal{E}_2$ are rooted branching static location pomset bisimilar, written $\mathcal{E}_1 \approx_{rbp}^{sl} \mathcal{E}_2$, if there exists a rooted branching static location pomset bisimulation R_φ, such that $(\emptyset, \emptyset) \in R_\varphi$.

By replacing pomset transitions with steps, we can get the definition of rooted branching static location step bisimulation. When PESs $\mathcal{E}_1$ and $\mathcal{E}_2$ are rooted branching static location step bisimilar, we write $\mathcal{E}_1 \approx_{rbs}^{sl} \mathcal{E}_2$.

Definition 5.8 (Branching static location (hereditary) history-preserving bisimulation). Assume a special termination predicate $\downarrow$, and let $\surd$ represent a state with $\surd \downarrow$. A branching static location history-preserving (hp-)bisimulation is a posetal relation $R_\varphi \subseteq \mathcal{C}(\mathcal{E}_1)\overline{\times}\mathcal{C}(\mathcal{E}_2)$ such that:

1. if $(C_1, f, C_2) \in R$, and $C_1 \xrightarrow[u]{e_1} C_1'$ then
   - either $e_1 \equiv \tau$, and $(C_1', f[e_1 \mapsto \tau], C_2) \in R_\varphi$;
   - or there is a sequence of (zero or more) τ-transitions $C_2 \xrightarrow{\tau^*} C_2^0$, such that $(C_1, f, C_2^0) \in R_\varphi$ and $C_2^0 \xrightarrow[v]{e_2} C_2'$ with $(C_1', f[e_1 \mapsto e_2], C_2') \in R_{\varphi\cup\{(u,v)\}}$;
2. if $(C_1, f, C_2) \in R_\varphi$, and $C_2 \xrightarrow[v]{e_2} C_2'$ then
   - either $X \equiv \tau$, and $(C_1, f[e_2 \mapsto \tau], C_2') \in R_\varphi$;
   - or there is a sequence of (zero or more) τ-transitions $C_1 \xrightarrow{\tau^*} C_1^0$, such that $(C_1^0, f, C_2) \in R_\varphi$ and $C_1^0 \xrightarrow[u]{e_1} C_1'$ with $(C_1', f[e_2 \mapsto e_1], C_2') \in R_{\varphi\cup\{(u,v)\}}$;
3. if $(C_1, f, C_2) \in R_\varphi$ and $C_1 \downarrow$, then there is a sequence of (zero or more) τ-transitions $C_2 \xrightarrow{\tau^*} C_2^0$ such that $(C_1, f, C_2^0) \in R_\varphi$ and $C_2^0 \downarrow$;
4. if $(C_1, f, C_2) \in R_\varphi$ and $C_2 \downarrow$, then there is a sequence of (zero or more) τ-transitions $C_1 \xrightarrow{\tau^*} C_1^0$ such that $(C_1^0, f, C_2) \in R_\varphi$ and $C_1^0 \downarrow$.

$\mathcal{E}_1, \mathcal{E}_2$ are branching static location history-preserving (hp-)bisimilar and are written $\mathcal{E}_1 \approx_{bhp}^{sl} \mathcal{E}_2$ if there exists a branching static location hp-bisimulation R_φ such that $(\emptyset, \emptyset, \emptyset) \in R_\varphi$.

A branching static location hereditary history-preserving (hhp-)bisimulation is a downward closed branching static location hhp-bisimulation. $\mathcal{E}_1, \mathcal{E}_2$ are branching static location hereditary history-preserving (hhp-)bisimilar and are written $\mathcal{E}_1 \approx_{bhhp}^{sl} \mathcal{E}_2$.

Table 5.1 Axioms of BATC with static localities.

No.	Axiom
$A1$	$x+y=y+x$
$A2$	$(x+y)+z=x+(y+z)$
$A3$	$x+x=x$
$A4$	$(x+y)\cdot z=x\cdot z+y\cdot z$
$A5$	$(x\cdot y)\cdot z=x\cdot(y\cdot z)$
$L1$	$\epsilon :: x=x$
$L2$	$u :: (x\cdot y)=u :: x\cdot u :: y$
$L3$	$u :: (x+y)=u :: x+u :: y$
$L4$	$u :: (v :: x)=uv :: x$

Definition 5.9 (Rooted branching static location (hereditary) history-preserving bisimulation). Assume a special termination predicate $\downarrow$, and let $\surd$ represent a state with $\surd\downarrow$. A rooted branching static location history-preserving (hp-)bisimulation is a posetal relation $R_\varphi \subseteq \mathcal{C}(\mathcal{E}_1)\overline{\times}\mathcal{C}(\mathcal{E}_2)$ such that:

1. if $(C_1, f, C_2)\in R_\varphi$, and $C_1 \xrightarrow[u]{e_1} C_1'$, then $C_2 \xrightarrow[v]{e_2} C_2'$ with $C_1' \approx^{sl}_{bhp} C_2'$;
2. if $(C_1, f, C_2)\in R_\varphi$, and $C_2 \xrightarrow[v]{e_2} C_2'$, then $C_1 \xrightarrow[u]{e_1} C_1'$ with $C_1' \approx^{sl}_{bhp} C_2'$;
3. if $(C_1, f, C_2)\in R_\varphi$ and $C_1\downarrow$, then $C_2\downarrow$;
4. if $(C_1, f, C_2)\in R_\varphi$ and $C_2\downarrow$, then $C_1\downarrow$.

$\mathcal{E}_1, \mathcal{E}_2$ are rooted branching static location history-preserving (hp-)bisimilar and are written $\mathcal{E}_1 \approx^{sl}_{rbhp} \mathcal{E}_2$ if there exists a rooted branching static location hp-bisimulation R_φ such that $(\emptyset,\emptyset,\emptyset)\in R_\varphi$.

A rooted branching static location hereditary history-preserving (hhp-)bisimulation is a downward closed rooted branching static location hp-bisimulation. $\mathcal{E}_1, \mathcal{E}_2$ are rooted branching static location hereditary history-preserving (hhp-)bisimilar and are written $\mathcal{E}_1 \approx^{sl}_{rbhhp} \mathcal{E}_2$.

5.2 BATC with static localities

Let Loc be the set of locations, and $loc \in Loc$, $u, v \in Loc^*$, ϵ is the empty location. A distribution allocates a location $u \in Loc*$ to an action e denoted $u :: e$ or a process x denoted $u :: x$.

In the following, let $e_1, e_2, e_1', e_2' \in \mathbb{E}$, and let variables x, y, z range over the set of terms for true concurrency, p, q, s range over the set of closed terms. The set of axioms of BATC with static localities ($BATC^{sl}$) consists of the laws given in Table 5.1.

Definition 5.10 (Basic terms of BATC with static localities). The set of basic terms of BATC with static localities, $\mathcal{B}(BATC^{sl})$, is inductively defined as follows:

Table 5.2 Single event transition rules of BATC with static localities.

$$\frac{}{e \xrightarrow[\epsilon]{e} \surd} \quad \frac{}{loc :: e \xrightarrow[loc]{e} \surd}$$

$$\frac{x \xrightarrow[u]{e} x'}{loc :: x \xrightarrow[loc \ll u]{e} loc :: x'}$$

$$\frac{x \xrightarrow[u]{e} \surd}{x + y \xrightarrow[u]{e} \surd} \quad \frac{x \xrightarrow[u]{e} x'}{x + y \xrightarrow[u]{e} x'} \quad \frac{y \xrightarrow[u]{e} \surd}{x + y \xrightarrow[u]{e} \surd} \quad \frac{y \xrightarrow[u]{e} y'}{x + y \xrightarrow[u]{e} y'}$$

$$\frac{x \xrightarrow[u]{e} \surd}{x \cdot y \xrightarrow[u]{e} y} \quad \frac{x \xrightarrow[u]{e} x'}{x \cdot y \xrightarrow[u]{e} x' \cdot y}$$

1. $\mathbb{E} \subset \mathcal{B}(BATC^{sl})$;
2. if $u \in Loc^*$, $t \in \mathcal{B}(BATC^{sl})$ then $u :: t \in \mathcal{B}(BATC^{sl})$;
3. if $e \in \mathbb{E}$, $t \in \mathcal{B}(BATC^{sl})$ then $e \cdot t \in \mathcal{B}(BATC^{sl})$;
4. if $t, s \in \mathcal{B}(BATC^{sl})$ then $t + s \in \mathcal{B}(BATC^{sl})$.

Theorem 5.11 (Elimination theorem of BATC with static localities). *Let p be a closed BATC with static localities term. Then there is a basic BATC with static localities term q such that $BATC^{sl} \vdash p = q$.*

In this subsection, we will define a term-deduction system which gives the operational semantics of BATC with static localities. We give the operational transition rules for operators $\cdot$ and $+$ as Table 5.2 shows. And the predicate $\xrightarrow[u]{e} \surd$ represents successful termination after execution of the event e at the location u.

Theorem 5.12 (Congruence of BATC with static localities with respect to static location pomset bisimulation equivalence). *Static location pomset bisimulation equivalence $\sim_p^{sl}$ is a congruence with respect to BATC with static localities.*

Theorem 5.13 (Soundness of BATC with static localities modulo static location pomset bisimulation equivalence). *Let x and y be BATC with static localities terms. If $BATC^{sl} \vdash x = y$, then $x \sim_p^{sl} y$.*

Theorem 5.14 (Completeness of BATC with static localities modulo static location pomset bisimulation equivalence). *Let p and q be closed BATC with static localities terms, if $p \sim_p^{sl} q$ then $p = q$.*

Theorem 5.15 (Congruence of BATC with static localities with respect to static location step bisimulation equivalence). *Static location step bisimulation equivalence $\sim_s^{sl}$ is a congruence with respect to BATC with static localities.*

Theorem 5.16 (Soundness of BATC with static localities modulo static location step bisimulation equivalence). *Let x and y be BATC with static localities terms. If $BATC^{sl} \vdash x = y$, then $x \sim_s^{sl} y$.*

Theorem 5.17 (Completeness of BATC with static localities modulo static location step bisimulation equivalence). *Let p and q be closed BATC with static localities terms, if $p \sim_s^{sl} q$ then $p = q$.*

Theorem 5.18 (Congruence of BATC with static localities with respect to static location hp-bisimulation equivalence). *Static location hp-bisimulation equivalence $\sim_{hp}^{sl}$ is a congruence with respect to BATC with static localities.*

Theorem 5.19 (Soundness of BATC with static localities modulo static location hp-bisimulation equivalence). *Let x and y be BATC with static localities terms. If $BATC^{sl} \vdash x = y$, then $x \sim_{hp}^{sl} y$.*

Theorem 5.20 (Completeness of BATC with static localities modulo static location hp-bisimulation equivalence). *Let p and q be closed BATC with static localities terms, if $p \sim_{hp}^{sl} q$ then $p = q$.*

Theorem 5.21 (Congruence of BATC with static localities with respect to static location hhp-bisimulation equivalence). *Static location hhp-bisimulation equivalence $\sim_{hhp}^{sl}$ is a congruence with respect to BATC with static localities.*

Theorem 5.22 (Soundness of BATC with static localities modulo static location hhp-bisimulation equivalence). *Let x and y be BATC with static localities terms. If $BATC^{sl} \vdash x = y$, then $x \sim_{hhp}^{sl} y$.*

Theorem 5.23 (Completeness of BATC with static localities modulo static location hhp-bisimulation equivalence). *Let p and q be closed BATC with static localities terms, if $p \sim_{hhp}^{sl} q$ then $p = q$.*

5.3 APTC with static localities

We give the transition rules of APTC with static localities as Table 5.3 shows.

We define the basic terms for APTC with static localities.

Definition 5.24 (Basic terms of APTC with static localities). The set of basic terms of APTC with static localities, $\mathcal{B}(APTC^{sl})$, is inductively defined as follows:

1. $\mathbb{E} \subset \mathcal{B}(APTC^{sl})$;
2. if $u \in Loc^*, t \in \mathcal{B}(APTC^{sl})$ then $u :: t \in \mathcal{B}(APTC^{sl})$;
3. if $e \in \mathbb{E}, t \in \mathcal{B}(APTC^{sl})$ then $e \cdot t \in \mathcal{B}(APTC^{sl})$;
4. if $t, s \in \mathcal{B}(APTC^{sl})$ then $t + s \in \mathcal{B}(APTC^{sl})$;
5. if $t, s \in \mathcal{B}(APTC^{sl})$ then $t \between s \in \mathcal{B}(APTC^{sl})$.

Table 5.3 Transition rules of APTC with static localities.

$$\frac{x \xrightarrow[u]{e_1} \surd \quad y \xrightarrow[v]{e_2} \surd}{x \parallel y \xrightarrow[u\diamond v]{\{e_1,e_2\}} \surd} \qquad \frac{x \xrightarrow[u]{e_1} x' \quad y \xrightarrow[v]{e_2} \surd}{x \parallel y \xrightarrow[u\diamond v]{\{e_1,e_2\}} x'}$$

$$\frac{x \xrightarrow[u]{e_1} \surd \quad y \xrightarrow[v]{e_2} y'}{x \parallel y \xrightarrow[u\diamond v]{\{e_1,e_2\}} y'} \qquad \frac{x \xrightarrow[u]{e_1} x' \quad y \xrightarrow[v]{e_2} y'}{x \parallel y \xrightarrow[u\diamond v]{\{e_1,e_2\}} x' \between y'}$$

$$\frac{x \xrightarrow[u]{e_1} \surd \quad y \xrightarrow[v]{e_2} \surd \quad (e_1 \leq e_2)}{x \leftmerge y \xrightarrow[u\diamond v]{\{e_1,e_2\}} \surd} \qquad \frac{x \xrightarrow[u]{e_1} x' \quad y \xrightarrow[v]{e_2} \surd \quad (e_1 \leq e_2)}{x \leftmerge y \xrightarrow[u\diamond v]{\{e_1,e_2\}} x'}$$

$$\frac{x \xrightarrow[u]{e_1} \surd \quad y \xrightarrow[v]{e_2} y' \quad (e_1 \leq e_2)}{x \leftmerge y \xrightarrow[u\diamond v]{\{e_1,e_2\}} y'} \qquad \frac{x \xrightarrow[u]{e_1} x' \quad y \xrightarrow[v]{e_2} y' \quad (e_1 \leq e_2)}{x \leftmerge y \xrightarrow[u\diamond v]{\{e_1,e_2\}} x' \between y'}$$

$$\frac{x \xrightarrow[u]{e_1} \surd \quad y \xrightarrow[v]{e_2} \surd}{x \mid y \xrightarrow[u\diamond v]{\gamma(e_1,e_2)} \surd} \qquad \frac{x \xrightarrow[u]{e_1} x' \quad y \xrightarrow[v]{e_2} \surd}{x \mid y \xrightarrow[u\diamond v]{\gamma(e_1,e_2)} x'}$$

$$\frac{x \xrightarrow[u]{e_1} \surd \quad y \xrightarrow[v]{e_2} y'}{x \mid y \xrightarrow[u\diamond v]{\gamma(e_1,e_2)} y'} \qquad \frac{x \xrightarrow[u]{e_1} x' \quad y \xrightarrow[v]{e_2} y'}{x \mid y \xrightarrow[u\diamond v]{\gamma(e_1,e_2)} x' \between y'}$$

$$\frac{x \xrightarrow[u]{e_1} \surd \quad (\sharp(e_1,e_2))}{\Theta(x) \xrightarrow[u]{e_1} \surd} \qquad \frac{x \xrightarrow[u]{e_2} \surd \quad (\sharp(e_1,e_2))}{\Theta(x) \xrightarrow[u]{e_2} \surd}$$

$$\frac{x \xrightarrow[u]{e_1} x' \quad (\sharp(e_1,e_2))}{\Theta(x) \xrightarrow[u]{e_1} \Theta(x')} \qquad \frac{x \xrightarrow[u]{e_2} x' \quad (\sharp(e_1,e_2))}{\Theta(x) \xrightarrow[u]{e_2} \Theta(x')}$$

$$\frac{x \xrightarrow[u]{e_1} \surd \quad y \nrightarrow^{e_2} \quad (\sharp(e_1,e_2))}{x \triangleleft y \xrightarrow[u]{\tau} \surd} \qquad \frac{x \xrightarrow[u]{e_1} x' \quad y \nrightarrow^{e_2} \quad (\sharp(e_1,e_2))}{x \triangleleft y \xrightarrow[u]{\tau} x'}$$

$$\frac{x \xrightarrow[u]{e_1} \surd \quad y \nrightarrow^{e_3} \quad (\sharp(e_1,e_2), e_2 \leq e_3)}{x \triangleleft y \xrightarrow[u]{\tau} \surd} \qquad \frac{x \xrightarrow[u]{e_1} x' \quad y \nrightarrow^{e_3} \quad (\sharp(e_1,e_2), e_2 \leq e_3)}{x \triangleleft y \xrightarrow[u]{\tau} x'}$$

$$\frac{x \xrightarrow[u]{e_3} \surd \quad y \nrightarrow^{e_2} \quad (\sharp(e_1,e_2), e_1 \leq e_3)}{x \triangleleft y \xrightarrow[u]{\tau} \surd} \qquad \frac{x \xrightarrow[u]{e_3} x' \quad y \nrightarrow^{e_2} \quad (\sharp(e_1,e_2), e_1 \leq e_3)}{x \triangleleft y \xrightarrow[u]{\tau} x'}$$

Theorem 5.25 (Congruence theorem of APTC with static localities). *Static location truly concurrent bisimulation equivalences* $\sim_p^{sl}$, $\sim_s^{sl}$, $\sim_{hp}^{sl}$, *and* $\sim_{hhp}^{sl}$ *are all congruences with respect to APTC with static localities.*

So, we design the axioms of parallelism in Table 5.4, including algebraic laws for parallel operator $\parallel$, communication operator $\mid$, conflict elimination operator Θ, and unless operator $\triangleleft$, and also the whole parallel operator $\between$. Since the communication between two communicating events in different parallel branches may cause deadlock (a state of inactivity), which is caused by mismatch of two communicating events or the imperfectness of the communication channel. We introduce a new constant δ to denote the deadlock, and let the atomic event $e \in \mathbb{E} \cup \{\delta\}$.

Based on the definition of basic terms for APTC with static localities (see Definition 5.24) and axioms of parallelism (see Table 5.4), we can prove the elimination theorem of parallelism.

Theorem 5.26 (Elimination theorem of parallelism). *Let p be a closed APTC with static localities term. Then there is a basic APTC with static localities term q such that $APTC^{sl} \vdash p = q$.*

Theorem 5.27 (Generalization of APTC with static localities with respect to BATC with static localities). *APTC with static localities is a generalization of BATC with static localities.*

Theorem 5.28 (Soundness of APTC with static localities modulo static location pomset bisimulation equivalence). *Let x and y be APTC with static localities terms. If $APTC^{sl} \vdash x = y$, then $x \sim_p^{sl} y$.*

Theorem 5.29 (Completeness of APTC with static localities modulo static location pomset bisimulation equivalence). *Let p and q be closed APTC with static localities terms, if $p \sim_p^{sl} q$ then $p = q$.*

Theorem 5.30 (Soundness of APTC with static localities modulo static location step bisimulation equivalence). *Let x and y be APTC with static localities terms. If $APTC^{sl} \vdash x = y$, then $x \sim_s^{sl} y$.*

Theorem 5.31 (Completeness of APTC with static localities modulo static location step bisimulation equivalence). *Let p and q be closed APTC with static localities terms, if $p \sim_s^{sl} q$ then $p = q$.*

Theorem 5.32 (Soundness of APTC with static localities modulo static location hp-bisimulation equivalence). *Let x and y be APTC with static localities terms. If $APTC^{sl} \vdash x = y$, then $x \sim_{hp}^{sl} y$.*

Theorem 5.33 (Completeness of APTC with static localities modulo static location hp-bisimulation equivalence). *Let p and q be closed APTC with static localities terms, if $p \sim_{hp}^{sl} q$ then $p = q$.*

Theorem 5.34 (Soundness of APTC with static localities modulo static location hhp-bisimulation equivalence). *Let x and y be APTC with static localities terms. If $APTC^{sl} \vdash x = y$, then $x \sim_{hhp}^{sl} y$.*

Theorem 5.35 (Completeness of APTC with static localities modulo static location hhp-bisimulation equivalence). *Let p and q be closed APTC with static localities terms, if $p \sim_{hhp}^{sl} q$ then $p = q$.*

Table 5.4 Axioms of parallelism.

No.	Axiom
$A6$	$x + \delta = x$
$A7$	$\delta \cdot x = \delta$
$P1$	$x \between y = x \parallel y + x \mid y$
$P2$	$x \parallel y = y \parallel x$
$P3$	$(x \parallel y) \parallel z = x \parallel (y \parallel z)$
$P4$	$x \parallel y = x \leftmerge y + y \leftmerge x$
$P5$	$(e_1 \leq e_2) \quad e_1 \leftmerge (e_2 \cdot y) = (e_1 \leftmerge e_2) \cdot y$
$P6$	$(e_1 \leq e_2) \quad (e_1 \cdot x) \leftmerge e_2 = (e_1 \leftmerge e_2) \cdot x$
$P7$	$(e_1 \leq e_2) \quad (e_1 \cdot x) \leftmerge (e_2 \cdot y) = (e_1 \leftmerge e_2) \cdot (x \between y)$
$P8$	$(x + y) \leftmerge z = (x \leftmerge z) + (y \leftmerge z)$
$P9$	$\delta \leftmerge x = \delta$
$C1$	$e_1 \mid e_2 = \gamma(e_1, e_2)$
$C2$	$e_1 \mid (e_2 \cdot y) = \gamma(e_1, e_2) \cdot y$
$C3$	$(e_1 \cdot x) \mid e_2 = \gamma(e_1, e_2) \cdot x$
$C4$	$(e_1 \cdot x) \mid (e_2 \cdot y) = \gamma(e_1, e_2) \cdot (x \between y)$
$C5$	$(x + y) \mid z = (x \mid z) + (y \mid z)$
$C6$	$x \mid (y + z) = (x \mid y) + (x \mid z)$
$C7$	$\delta \mid x = \delta$
$C8$	$x \mid \delta = \delta$
$CE1$	$\Theta(e) = e$
$CE2$	$\Theta(\delta) = \delta$
$CE3$	$\Theta(x + y) = \Theta(x) + \Theta(y)$
$CE4$	$\Theta(x \cdot y) = \Theta(x) \cdot \Theta(y)$
$CE5$	$\Theta(x \parallel y) = ((\Theta(x) \triangleleft y) \parallel y) + ((\Theta(y) \triangleleft x) \parallel x)$
$CE6$	$\Theta(x \mid y) = ((\Theta(x) \triangleleft y) \mid y) + ((\Theta(y) \triangleleft x) \mid x)$
$U1$	$(\sharp(e_1, e_2)) \quad e_1 \triangleleft e_2 = \tau$
$U2$	$(\sharp(e_1, e_2), e_2 \leq e_3) \quad e_1 \triangleleft e_3 = \tau$
$U3$	$(\sharp(e_1, e_2), e_2 \leq e_3) \quad e3 \triangleleft e_1 = \tau$
$U4$	$e \triangleleft \delta = e$
$U5$	$\delta \triangleleft e = \delta$
$U6$	$(x + y) \triangleleft z = (x \triangleleft z) + (y \triangleleft z)$
$U7$	$(x \cdot y) \triangleleft z = (x \triangleleft z) \cdot (y \triangleleft z)$
$U8$	$(x \leftmerge y) \triangleleft z = (x \triangleleft z) \leftmerge (y \triangleleft z)$
$U9$	$(x \mid y) \triangleleft z = (x \triangleleft z) \mid (y \triangleleft z)$
$U10$	$x \triangleleft (y + z) = (x \triangleleft y) \triangleleft z$
$U11$	$x \triangleleft (y \cdot z) = (x \triangleleft y) \triangleleft z$
$U12$	$x \triangleleft (y \leftmerge z) = (x \triangleleft y) \triangleleft z$
$U13$	$x \triangleleft (y \mid z) = (x \triangleleft y) \triangleleft z$
$L5$	$u :: (x \between y) = u :: x \between u :: y$
$L6$	$u :: (x \parallel y) = u :: x \parallel u :: y$
$L7$	$u :: (x \mid y) = u :: x \mid u :: y$
$L8$	$u :: (\Theta(x)) = \Theta(u :: x)$
$L9$	$u :: (x \triangleleft y) = u :: x \triangleleft u :: y$
$L10$	$u :: \delta = \delta$

Table 5.5 Transition rules of encapsulation operator ∂_H.

$$\frac{x \xrightarrow[u]{e} \surd}{\partial_H(x) \xrightarrow[u]{e} \surd} \quad (e \notin H) \qquad \frac{x \xrightarrow[u]{e} x'}{\partial_H(x) \xrightarrow[u]{e} \partial_H(x')} \quad (e \notin H)$$

Table 5.6 Axioms of encapsulation operator.

No.	Axiom
$D1$	$e \notin H \quad \partial_H(e) = e$
$D2$	$e \in H \quad \partial_H(e) = \delta$
$D3$	$\partial_H(\delta) = \delta$
$D4$	$\partial_H(x + y) = \partial_H(x) + \partial_H(y)$
$D5$	$\partial_H(x \cdot y) = \partial_H(x) \cdot \partial_H(y)$
$D6$	$\partial_H(x \between y) = \partial_H(x) \between \partial_H(y)$
$L11$	$u :: \partial_H(x) = \partial_H(u :: x)$

The transition rules of encapsulation operator ∂_H are shown in Table 5.5.

Based on the transition rules for encapsulation operator ∂_H in Table 5.5, we design the axioms as Table 5.6 shows.

Theorem 5.36 (Congruence theorem of encapsulation operator ∂_H). *Static location truly concurrent bisimulation equivalences $\sim_p^{sl}$, $\sim_s^{sl}$, $\sim_{hp}^{sl}$, and $\sim_{hhp}^{sl}$ are all congruences with respect to encapsulation operator ∂_H.*

Theorem 5.37 (Elimination theorem of APTC with static localities). *Let p be a closed APTC with static localities term including the encapsulation operator ∂_H. Then there is a basic APTC with static localities term q such that $APTC \vdash p = q$.*

Theorem 5.38 (Soundness of APTC with static localities modulo static location pomset bisimulation equivalence). *Let x and y be APTC with static localities terms including encapsulation operator ∂_H. If $APTC^{sl} \vdash x = y$, then $x \sim_p^{sl} y$.*

Theorem 5.39 (Completeness of APTC with static localities modulo static location pomset bisimulation equivalence). *Let p and q be closed APTC with static localities terms including encapsulation operator ∂_H, if $p \sim_p^{sl} q$ then $p = q$.*

Theorem 5.40 (Soundness of APTC with static localities modulo static location step bisimulation equivalence). *Let x and y be APTC with static localities terms including encapsulation operator ∂_H. If $APTC^{sl} \vdash x = y$, then $x \sim_s^{sl} y$.*

Theorem 5.41 (Completeness of APTC with static localities modulo static location step bisimulation equivalence). *Let p and q be closed APTC with static localities terms including encapsulation operator ∂_H, if $p \sim_s^{sl} q$ then $p = q$.*

Theorem 5.42 (Soundness of APTC with static localities modulo static location hp-bisimulation equivalence). *Let x and y be APTC with static localities terms including encapsulation operator ∂_H. If $APTC^{sl} \vdash x = y$, then $x \sim_{hp}^{sl} y$.*

Theorem 5.43 (Completeness of APTC with static localities modulo static location hp-bisimulation equivalence). *Let p and q be closed APTC with static localities terms including encapsulation operator ∂_H, if $p \sim_{hp}^{sl} q$ then $p = q$.*

Theorem 5.44 (Soundness of APTC with static localities modulo static location hhp-bisimulation equivalence). *Let x and y be APTC with static localities terms including encapsulation operator ∂_H. If $APTC^{sl} \vdash x = y$, then $x \sim_{hhp}^{sl} y$.*

Theorem 5.45 (Completeness of APTC with static localities modulo static location hhp-bisimulation equivalence). *Let p and q be closed APTC with static localities terms including encapsulation operator ∂_H, if $p \sim_{hhp}^{sl} q$ then $p = q$.*

5.4 Recursion

In this section, we introduce recursion to capture infinite processes based on APTC with static localities. Since in APTC with static localities, there are four basic operators $::$, $\cdot$, $+$, and $\between$, the recursion must be adapted this situation to include $\between$.

In the following, E, F, G are recursion specifications, X, Y, Z are recursive variables.

Definition 5.46 (Recursive specification). A recursive specification is a finite set of recursive equations

$$X_1 = t_1(X_1, \cdots, X_n)$$
$$\cdots$$
$$X_n = t_n(X_1, \cdots, X_n)$$

where the left-hand sides of X_i are called recursion variables, and the right-hand sides $t_i(X_1, \cdots, X_n)$ are process terms in APTC with static localities with possible occurrences of the recursion variables $X_1, \cdots, X_n$.

Definition 5.47 (Solution). Processes $p_1, \cdots, p_n$ are a solution for a recursive specification $\{X_i = t_i(X_1, \cdots, X_n) | i \in \{1, \cdots, n\}\}$ (with respect to static location truly concurrent bisimulation equivalences $\sim_s^{sl}(\sim_p^{sl}, \sim_{hp}^{sl}, \sim_{hhp}^{sl})$) if $p_i \sim_s^{sl} (\sim_p^{sl}, \sim_{hp}^{sl}, \sim_{hhp}^{sl}) t_i(p_1, \cdots, p_n)$ for $i \in \{1, \cdots, n\}$.

Definition 5.48 (Guarded recursive specification). A recursive specification

$$X_1 = t_1(X_1, \cdots, X_n)$$
$$\cdots$$
$$X_n = t_n(X_1, \cdots, X_n)$$

Table 5.7 Transition rules of guarded recursion.

$$\frac{t_i(\langle X_1|E\rangle,\cdots,\langle X_n|E\rangle)\xrightarrow[u]{\{e_1,\cdots,e_k\}}\surd}{\langle X_i|E\rangle\xrightarrow[u]{\{e_1,\cdots,e_k\}}\surd}$$

$$\frac{t_i(\langle X_1|E\rangle,\cdots,\langle X_n|E\rangle)\xrightarrow[u]{\{e_1,\cdots,e_k\}}y}{\langle X_i|E\rangle\xrightarrow[u]{\{e_1,\cdots,e_k\}}y}$$

is guarded if the right-hand sides of its recursive equations can be adapted to the form by applications of the axioms in APTC with static localities and replacing recursion variables by the right-hand sides of their recursive equations,

$$(u_{11}::a_{11}\between\cdots\between u_{1i_1}::a_{1i_1})\cdot s_1(X_1,\cdots,X_n)+\cdots+(u_{k1}::a_{k1}\between\cdots\between u_{ki_k}::a_{ki_k})\cdot s_k(X_1,\cdots,X_n)$$
$$+(v_{11}::b_{11}\between\cdots\between v_{1j_1}::b_{1j_1})+\cdots+(v_{1j_1}::b_{1j_1}\between\cdots\between v_{1j_l}::b_{lj_l})$$

where $a_{11},\cdots,a_{1i_1},a_{k1},\cdots,a_{ki_k},b_{11},\cdots,b_{1j_1},b_{1j_1},\cdots,b_{lj_l}\in\mathbb{E}$, and the sum above is allowed to be empty, in which case it represents the deadlock δ.

Definition 5.49 (Linear recursive specification). A recursive specification is linear if its recursive equations are of the form

$$(u_{11}::a_{11}\between\cdots\between u_{1i_1}::a_{1i_1})X_1+\cdots+(u_{k1}::a_{k1}\between\cdots\between u_{ki_k}::a_{ki_k})X_k$$
$$+(v_{11}::b_{11}\between\cdots\between v_{1j_1}::b_{1j_1})+\cdots+(v_{1j_1}::b_{1j_1}\between\cdots\between v_{1j_l}::b_{lj_l})$$

where $a_{11},\cdots,a_{1i_1},a_{k1},\cdots,a_{ki_k},b_{11},\cdots,b_{1j_1},b_{1j_1},\cdots,b_{lj_l}\in\mathbb{E}$, and the sum above is allowed to be empty, in which case it represents the deadlock δ.

For a guarded recursive specifications E with the form

$$X_1=t_1(X_1,\cdots,X_n)$$
$$\cdots$$
$$X_n=t_n(X_1,\cdots,X_n)$$

the behavior of the solution $\langle X_i|E\rangle$ for the recursion variable X_i in E, where $i\in\{1,\cdots,n\}$, is exactly the behavior of their right-hand sides $t_i(X_1,\cdots,X_n)$, which is captured by the two transition rules in Table 5.7.

Theorem 5.50 (Conservativity of APTC with static localities and guarded recursion). *APTC with static localities and guarded recursion is a conservative extension of APTC with static localities.*

Table 5.8 Recursive definition and specification principle.

No.	Axiom
RDP	$\langle X_i\|E\rangle = t_i(\langle X_1\|E\rangle, \cdots, \langle X_n\|E\rangle) \quad (i \in \{1, \cdots, n\})$
RSP	if $y_i = t_i(y_1, \cdots, y_n)$ for $i \in \{1, \cdots, n\}$, then $y_i = \langle X_i\|E\rangle \quad (i \in \{1, \cdots, n\})$

Theorem 5.51 (Congruence theorem of APTC with static localities and guarded recursion). *Static location truly concurrent bisimulation equivalences $\sim_p^{sl}$, $\sim_s^{sl}$, $\sim_{hp}^{sl}$, and $\sim_{hhp}^{sl}$ are all congruences with respect to APTC with static localities and guarded recursion.*

The RDP (Recursive Definition Principle) and the RSP (Recursive Specification Principle) are shown in Table 5.8.

Theorem 5.52 (Elimination theorem of APTC with static localities and linear recursion). *Each process term in APTC with static localities and linear recursion is equal to a process term $\langle X_1|E\rangle$ with E a linear recursive specification.*

Theorem 5.53 (Soundness of APTC with static localities and guarded recursion). *Let x and y be APTC with static localities and guarded recursion terms. If $APTC$ with guarded recursion $\vdash x = y$, then*

1. $x \sim_s^{sl} y$;
2. $x \sim_p^{sl} y$;
3. $x \sim_{hp}^{sl} y$;
4. $x \sim_{hhp}^{sl} y$.

Theorem 5.54 (Completeness of APTC with static localities and linear recursion). *Let p and q be closed APTC with static localities and linear recursion terms, then,*

1. *if $p \sim_s^{sl} q$ then $p = q$;*
2. *if $p \sim_p^{sl} q$ then $p = q$;*
3. *if $p \sim_{hp}^{sl} q$ then $p = q$;*
4. *if $p \sim_{hhp}^{sl} q$ then $p = q$.*

5.5 Abstraction

To abstract away from the internal implementations of a program, and verify that the program exhibits the desired external behaviors, the silent step τ (and making τ distinct by τ^e), and abstraction operator τ_I are introduced, where $I \subseteq \mathbb{E}$ denotes the internal events. The silent step τ represents the internal events, when we consider the external behaviors of a process, τ events can be removed, that is, τ events must keep silent. The transition rule of τ is shown in Table 5.9. In the following, let the atomic event e range over $\mathbb{E} \cup \{\delta\} \cup \{\tau\}$, and let the communication function $\gamma : \mathbb{E} \cup \{\tau\} \times \mathbb{E} \cup \{\tau\} \rightarrow \mathbb{E} \cup \{\delta\}$, with each communication involved τ resulting into δ.

Table 5.9 Transition rule of the silent step.

$\overline{\tau \xrightarrow{\tau} \surd}$

Table 5.10 Axioms of silent step.

No.	Axiom
$B1$	$e \cdot \tau = e$
$B2$	$e \cdot (\tau \cdot (x + y) + x) = e \cdot (x + y)$
$B3$	$x \between \tau = x$
$L13$	$u :: \tau = \tau$

The silent step τ as an atomic event, is introduced into E. Considering the recursive specification $X = \tau X$, τs, $\tau\tau s$, and $\tau \cdots s$ are all its solutions, that is, the solutions make the existence of τ-loops which cause unfairness. To prevent τ-loops, we extend the definition of linear recursive specification (Definition 5.49) to the guarded one.

Definition 5.55 (Guarded linear recursive specification). A recursive specification is linear if its recursive equations are of the form

$$\begin{aligned}(u_{11} :: a_{11} \between \cdots \between u_{1i_1} :: a_{1i_1})X_1 + \cdots + (u_{k1} :: a_{k1} \between \cdots \between u_{ki_k} :: a_{ki_k})X_k \\ + (v_{11} :: b_{11} \between \cdots \between v_{1j_1} :: b_{1j_1}) + \cdots + (v_{1j_1} :: b_{1j_1} \between \cdots \between v_{1j_l} :: b_{lj_l})\end{aligned}$$

where $a_{11}, \cdots, a_{1i_1}, a_{k1}, \cdots, a_{ki_k}, b_{11}, \cdots, b_{1j_1}, b_{1j_1}, \cdots, b_{lj_l} \in \mathbb{E} \cup \{\tau\}$, and the sum above is allowed to be empty, in which case it represents the deadlock δ.

A linear recursive specification E is guarded if there does not exist an infinite sequence of τ-transitions $\langle X|E\rangle \xrightarrow{\tau} \langle X'|E\rangle \xrightarrow{\tau} \langle X''|E\rangle \xrightarrow{\tau} \cdots$.

Theorem 5.56 (Conservativity of APTC with static localities and silent step and guarded linear recursion). *APTC with static localities and silent step and guarded linear recursion is a conservative extension of APTC with static localities and linear recursion.*

Theorem 5.57 (Congruence theorem of APTC with static localities and silent step and guarded linear recursion). *Rooted branching static location truly concurrent bisimulation equivalences $\approx^{sl}_{rbp}$, $\approx^{sl}_{rbs}$ and $\approx^{sl}_{rbhp}$ are all congruences with respect to APTC with static localities and silent step and guarded linear recursion.*

We design the axioms for the silent step τ in Table 5.10.

Theorem 5.58 (Elimination theorem of APTC with static localities and silent step and guarded linear recursion). *Each process term in APTC with static localities and silent step and guarded linear recursion is equal to a process term $\langle X_1|E\rangle$ with E a guarded linear recursive specification.*

Table 5.11 Transition rule of the abstraction operator.

$\frac{x \xrightarrow[u]{e} \surd}{\tau_I(x) \xrightarrow[u]{e} \surd} \quad e \notin I$	$\frac{x \xrightarrow[u]{e} x'}{\tau_I(x) \xrightarrow[u]{e} \tau_I(x')} \quad e \notin I$
$\frac{x \xrightarrow[u]{e} \surd}{\tau_I(x) \xrightarrow{\tau} \surd} \quad e \in I$	$\frac{x \xrightarrow[u]{e} x'}{\tau_I(x) \xrightarrow{\tau} \tau_I(x')} \quad e \in I$

Theorem 5.59 (Soundness of APTC with static localities and silent step and guarded linear recursion). *Let x and y be APTC with static localities and silent step and guarded linear recursion terms. If APTC with static localities and silent step and guarded linear recursion $\vdash x = y$, then*

1. $x \approx^{sl}_{rbs} y$;
2. $x \approx^{sl}_{rbp} y$;
3. $x \approx^{sl}_{rbhp} y$;
4. $x \approx^{sl}_{rbhhp} y$.

Theorem 5.60 (Completeness of APTC with static localities and silent step and guarded linear recursion). *Let p and q be closed APTC with static localities and silent step and guarded linear recursion terms, then,*

1. *if* $p \approx^{sl}_{rbs} q$ *then* $p = q$;
2. *if* $p \approx^{sl}_{rbp} q$ *then* $p = q$;
3. *if* $p \approx^{sl}_{rbhp} q$ *then* $p = q$;
4. *if* $p \approx^{sl}_{rbhhp} q$ *then* $p = q$.

The unary abstraction operator τ_I ($I \subseteq \mathbb{E}$) renames all atomic events in I into τ. APTC with static localities and silent step and abstraction operator is called $APTC_\tau$ with static localities. The transition rules of operator τ_I are shown in Table 5.11.

Theorem 5.61 (Conservativity of $APTC_\tau$ with static localities and guarded linear recursion). *$APTC_\tau$ with static localities and guarded linear recursion is a conservative extension of APTC with static localities and silent step and guarded linear recursion.*

Theorem 5.62 (Congruence theorem of $APTC_\tau$ with static localities and guarded linear recursion). *Rooted branching static location truly concurrent bisimulation equivalences $\approx^{sl}_{rbp}$, $\approx^{sl}_{rbs}$, $\approx^{sl}_{rbhp}$, and $\approx^{sl}_{rbhhp}$ are all congruences with respect to $APTC_\tau$ with static localities and guarded linear recursion.*

We design the axioms for the abstraction operator τ_I in Table 5.12.

Theorem 5.63 (Soundness of $APTC_\tau$ with static localities and guarded linear recursion). *Let x and y be $APTC_\tau$ with static localities and guarded linear recursion terms. If $APTC_\tau$ with static localities and guarded linear recursion $\vdash x = y$, then*

Table 5.12 Axioms of abstraction operator.

No.	Axiom
$TI1$	$e \notin I \quad \tau_I(e) = e$
$TI2$	$e \in I \quad \tau_I(e) = \tau$
$TI3$	$\tau_I(\delta) = \delta$
$TI4$	$\tau_I(x + y) = \tau_I(x) + \tau_I(y)$
$TI5$	$\tau_I(x \cdot y) = \tau_I(x) \cdot \tau_I(y)$
$TI6$	$\tau_I(x \between y) = \tau_I(x) \between \tau_I(y)$
$L14$	$u :: \tau_I(x) = \tau_I(u :: x)$
$L15$	$e \notin I \quad \tau_I(u :: e) = u :: e$
$L16$	$e \in I \quad \tau_I(u :: e) = \tau$

Table 5.13 Cluster fair abstraction rule.

No.	Axiom
$CFAR$	If X is in a cluster for I with exits $\{(u_{11} :: a_{11} \between \cdots \between u_{1i} :: a_{1i})Y_1, \cdots, (u_{m1} :: a_{m1} \between \cdots \between u_{mi} :: a_{mi})Y_m,$ $v_{11} :: b_{11} \between \cdots \between v_{1j} :: b_{1j}, \cdots, v_{n1} :: b_{n1} \between \cdots \between v_{nj} :: b_{nj}\}$, then $\tau \cdot \tau_I(\langle X\|E\rangle) =$ $\tau \cdot \tau_I((u_{11} :: a_{11} \between \cdots \between u_{1i} :: a_{1i})\langle Y_1\|E\rangle + \cdots + (u_{m1} :: a_{m1} \between \cdots \between u_{mi} :: a_{mi})\langle Y_m\|E\rangle$ $+ v_{11} :: b_{11} \between \cdots \between v_{1j} :: b_{1j} + \cdots + v_{n1} :: b_{n1} \between \cdots \between v_{nj} :: b_{nj})$

1. $x \approx^{sl}_{rbs} y$;
2. $x \approx^{sl}_{rbp} y$;
3. $x \approx^{sl}_{rbhp} y$;
4. $x \approx^{sl}_{rbhhp} y$.

Though τ-loops are prohibited in guarded linear recursive specifications (see Definition 5.55) in a specifiable way, they can be constructed using the abstraction operator, for example, there exist τ-loops in the process term $\tau_{\{a\}}(\langle X|X = aX\rangle)$. To avoid τ-loops caused by τ_I and ensure fairness, the concept of cluster and $CFAR$ (Cluster Fair Abstraction Rule) [25] are still valid in true concurrency, we introduce them below. (See Table 5.13.)

Definition 5.64 (Cluster). Let E be a guarded linear recursive specification, and $I \subseteq \mathbb{E}$. Two recursion variable X and Y in E are in the same cluster for I iff there exist sequences of transitions $\langle X|E\rangle \xrightarrow[u]{\{b_{11},\cdots,b_{1i}\}} \cdots [u] \xrightarrow{\{b_{m1},\cdots,b_{mi}\}} \langle Y|E\rangle$ and $\langle Y|E\rangle \xrightarrow[v]{\{c_{11},\cdots,c_{1j}\}} \cdots \xrightarrow[v]{\{c_{n1},\cdots,c_{nj}\}} \langle X|E\rangle$, where $b_{11},\cdots,b_{mi},c_{11},\cdots,c_{nj} \in I \cup \{\tau\}$.

$u_1 :: a_1 \between \cdots \between u_k :: a_k$ or $(u_1 :: a_1 \between \cdots \between u_k :: a_k)X$ is an exit for the cluster C iff: (1) $u_1 :: a_1 \between \cdots \between u_k :: a_k$ or $(u_1 :: a_1 \between \cdots \between u_k :: a_k)X$ is a summand at the right-hand side of the recursive equation for a recursion variable in C, and (2) in the case of $(u_1 :: a_1 \between \cdots \between u_k :: a_k)X$, either $a_l \notin I \cup \{\tau\} (l \in \{1, 2, \cdots, k\})$ or $X \notin C$.

Theorem 5.65 (Soundness of $CFAR$). *$CFAR$ is sound modulo rooted branching truly concurrent bisimulation equivalences $\approx_{rbs}^{sl}$, $\approx_{rbp}^{sl}$, $\approx_{rbhp}^{sl}$, and $\approx_{rbhhp}^{sl}$.*

Theorem 5.66 (Completeness of $APTC_\tau$ with static localities and guarded linear recursion and $CFAR$). *Let p and q be closed $APTC_\tau$ with static localities and guarded linear recursion and $CFAR$ terms, then,*

1. *if $p \approx_{rbs}^{sl} q$ then $p = q$;*
2. *if $p \approx_{rbp}^{sl} q$ then $p = q$;*
3. *if $p \approx_{rbhp}^{sl} q$ then $p = q$;*
4. *if $p \approx_{rbhhp}^{sl} q$ then $p = q$.*

6

Building blocks based structured parallel programming

We will discuss the usual usage case in parallel programming, then introduce the so-called building block and building blocks based parallel programming.

6.1 Orchestration and choreography

In Chapter 2, we have discussed the structured and unstructured parallelism in true concurrency. The usual usage case in parallel computing is illustrated in Fig. 6.1. There are two aspects in this case: orchestration and choreography. Orchestration contains a control flow of atomic actions, including ordinary atomic actions and communicating actions, and interacts with outside through the communicating actions. While choreography defines the interactions among the involved parties.

Usually, the orchestration is encapsulated as an object, or a thread, or an application process, or a remote process, or a distributed object, or a distributed application, as the two smaller dashed squares in Fig. 6.1 illustrate.

The choreography defines the communications among the orchestrations, and corresponding communications are object call, communication among threads, communica-

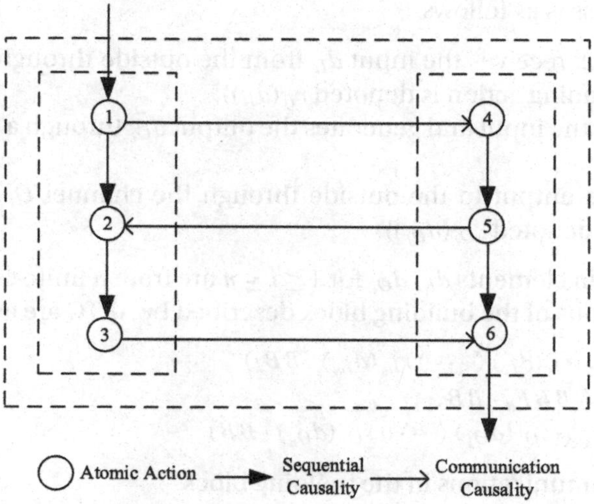

FIGURE 6.1 Orchestration and choreography.

Theory of Structured Parallel Programming. https://doi.org/10.1016/B978-0-44-324814-6.00010-1

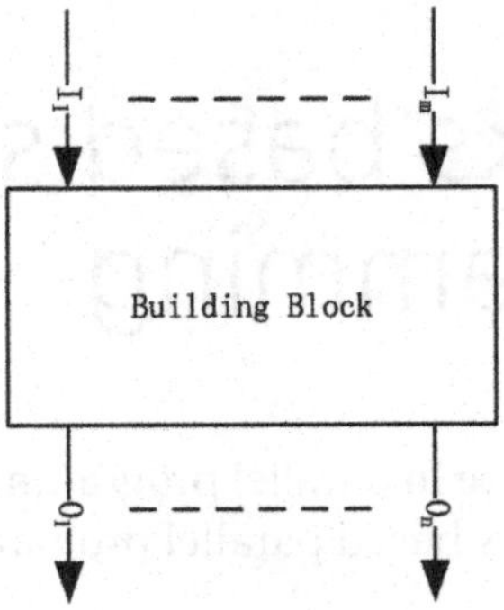

FIGURE 6.2 The building block.

tion among processes, remote process call, distributed object call, and distributed communications (may be synchronous or asynchronous). And also the choreography can be encapsulated as an entity, such as an object, a thread, a process, a remote process, a distributed object, and a distributed application, as the biggest dashed square in Fig. 6.1 illustrates.

6.2 The building block in parallel programming

According to the above analyses, both the orchestration and the choreography can be encapsulated as an entity which is called building block in parallel programming, as Fig. 6.2 illustrates. The building block interacts with the outside through m inputs and n outputs, and encapsulates a control flow inside.

The typical process is as follows.

1. The building block receives the input d_{I_i} from the outside through the channel I_i (the corresponding reading action is denoted $r_{I_i}(d_{I_i})$);
2. Then it processes the input and generates the output d_{O_i} through a processing function BBF_i;
3. Then it sends the output to the outside through the channel O_i (the corresponding sending action is denoted $s_{O_i}(d_{O_i})$).

We assume all data elements d_{I_i}, d_{O_i} for $1 \leq i \leq n$ are from a finite set Δ.

The state transitions of the building block described by APTC are as follows.

$BB = \sum_{d_{I_1},\cdots,d_{I_n}\in\Delta}(r_{I_1}(d_{I_1}) \between \cdots \between r_{I_m}(d_{I_m}) \cdot BB_2)$

$BB_2 = BBF_1 \between \cdots \between BBF_n \cdot BB_3$

$BB_3 = \sum_{d_{O_1},\cdots,d_{O_n}\in\Delta}(s_{O_1}(d_{O_1}) \between \cdots \between s_{O_n}(d_{O_n}) \cdot BB)$

There are no communications in the building block.

Let all modules be in parallel, then the building block BB can be presented by the following process term.

$$\tau_I(\partial_H(\Theta(BB))) = \tau_I(\partial_H(BB))$$

where $H = \emptyset$, $I = \{BBF_i\}$ for $1 \leq i \leq n$.

Then we get the following conclusion on the building block.

Theorem 6.1 (Correctness of the building block). *The building block $\tau_I(\partial_H(BB))$ can exhibit desired external behaviors.*

Proof. Based on the above state transitions of the above modules, by use of the algebraic laws of APTC, we can prove that

$\tau_I(\partial_H(BB)) = \sum_{d_{I_1},d_{O_1},\cdots,d_{I_m},d_{O_n}\in\Delta}(r_{I_1}(d_{I_1}) \parallel \cdots \parallel r_{I_m}(d_{I_m}) \cdot s_{O_1}(d_{O_1}) \parallel \cdots \parallel s_{O_n}(d_{O_n})) \cdot \tau_I(\partial_H(BB))$,

that is, the building block $\tau_I(\partial_H(BB))$ can exhibit desired external behaviors.

For the details of proof, please refer to Section 3.10, and we omit it. □

6.3 Building blocks based parallel programming

After the building blocks (may be encapsulated orchestrations or encapsulated choreographies) are defined, the parallel programming becomes choreography among these building blocks, and then the integrated choreography maybe encapsulated as a new bigger building block. As Fig. 6.1 illustrates, the left orchestration is encapsulated as a building block (BB1), the right orchestration is encapsulated as another building block (BB2), and the choreography between BB1 and BB2 is encapsulated as the third building block (BB3).

Without loss of generality, we explain the building block based parallel programming through the example in Fig. 6.1. The process of Fig. 6.1 is as follows.

1. The building block BB1 receives the input d_{I_1} from the outside through the channel I_1 (the corresponding reading action is denoted $r_{I_1}(d_{I_1})$), then after an inner processing function $BB1F_1$, generates the output data d_{O_1}, and sends it to BB2 through the channel O_1 (the corresponding sending action is denoted $s_{O_1}(d_{O_1})$);
2. The building block BB2 receives the input d_{O_1} from BB1 through the channel O_1 (the corresponding reading action is denoted $r_{O_1}(d_{O_1})$), then after an inner processing function $BB2F_1$, generates the output data d_{O_5}, and sends it to BB1 through the channel O_5 (the corresponding sending action is denoted $s_{O_5}(d_{O_5})$);
3. BB1 receives the input d_{O_5} from BB2 through the channel O_5 (the corresponding reading action is denoted $r_{O_5}(d_{O_5})$), then after an inner processing function $BB1F_2$, generates the output data d_{O_3}, and sends it to BB2 through the channel O_3 (the corresponding sending action is denoted $s_{O_3}(d_{O_3})$);
4. BB2 receives the input d_{O_3} from BB1 through the channel O_3 (the corresponding reading action is denoted $r_{O_3}(d_{O_3})$), then after an inner processing function $BB2F_2$, generates the output data d_{O_6}, and sends it to the outside through the channel O_6 (the corresponding sending action is denoted $s_{O_6}(d_{O_6})$).

We assume all data elements d_{I_i}, d_{O_i} for $1 \leq i \leq 6$ are from a finite set Δ.

The state transitions of the building block BB1 described by APTC are as follows.

$BB1 = \sum_{d_{I_1} \in \Delta} r_{I_1}(d_{I_1}) \cdot BB1_2$

$BB1_2 = BB1F_1 \cdot BB1_3$

$BB1_3 = \sum_{d_{O_1} \in \Delta} s_{O_1}(d_{O_1}) \cdot BB1_4$

$BB1_4 = r_{O_5}(d_{O_5}) \cdot BB1_5)$

$BB1_5 = BB1F_2 \cdot BB1_6$

$BB1_6 = s_{O_3}(d_{O_3}) \cdot BB1$

There is no communications in the building block BB1.

Let all modules be in parallel, then the building block BB1 can be presented by the following process term.

$$\tau_I(\partial_H(\Theta(BB1))) = \tau_I(\partial_H(BB1))$$

where $H_1 = \emptyset$, $I_1 = \{BB1F_i\}$ for $1 \leq i \leq 2$.

Then we get the following conclusion on the building block BB1.

Theorem 6.2 (Correctness of the building block BB1). *The building block BB1 $\tau_{I_1}(\partial_{H_1}(BB1))$ can exhibit desired external behaviors.*

Proof. Based on the above state transitions of the above modules, by use of the algebraic laws of APTC, we can prove that

$$\tau_{I_1}(\partial_{H_1}(BB1)) = \sum_{d_{I_1}, d_{O_1}, d_{O_5}, d_{O_3} \in \Delta}(r_{I_1}(d_{I_1}) \cdot s_{O_1}(d_{O_1}) \cdot r_{O_5}(d_{O_5}) \cdot s_{O_3}(d_{O_3})) \cdot \tau_{I_1}(\partial_{H_1}(BB1)),$$

that is, the building block BB1 $\tau_{I_1}(\partial_{H_1}(BB1))$ can exhibit desired external behaviors.

For the details of proof, please refer to Section 3.10, and we omit it. □

The state transitions of the building block BB2 described by APTC are as follows.

$BB2 = \sum_{d_{O_1} \in \Delta} r_{O_1}(d_{O_1}) \cdot BB2_2$

$BB2_2 = BB2F_1 \cdot BB2_3$

$BB2_3 = \sum_{d_{O_5} \in \Delta} s_{O_5}(d_{O_5}) \cdot BB2_4$

$BB2_4 = r_{O_3}(d_{O_3}) \cdot BB2_5)$

$BB2_5 = BB2F_2 \cdot BB2_6$

$BB2_6 = s_{O_6}(d_{O_6}) \cdot BB2$

There is no communications in the building block BB2.

Let all modules be in parallel, then the building block BB2 can be presented by the following process term.

$$\tau_I(\partial_H(\Theta(BB2))) = \tau_I(\partial_H(BB2))$$

where $H_2 = \emptyset$, $I_2 = \{BB2F_i\}$ for $1 \leq i \leq 2$.

Then we get the following conclusion on the building block BB2.

Theorem 6.3 (Correctness of the building block BB2). *The building block BB2 $\tau_{I_2}(\partial_{H_2}(BB2))$ can exhibit desired external behaviors.*

Proof. Based on the above state transitions of the above modules, by use of the algebraic laws of APTC, we can prove that

$$\tau_{I_2}(\partial_{H_2}(BB2)) = \sum_{d_{O_1},d_{O_5},d_{O_3},d_{O_6}\in\Delta}(r_{O_1}(d_{O_1})\cdot s_{O_5}(d_{O_5})\cdot r_{O_3}(d_{O_3})\cdot s_{O_6}(d_{O_6}))\cdot\tau_{I_2}(\partial_{H_2}(BB1)),$$

that is, the building block BB2 $\tau_{I_2}(\partial_{H_2}(BB2))$ can exhibit desired external behaviors.

For the details of proof, please refer to Section 3.10, and we omit it. □

There are three communication functions between BB1 and BB2.

$$\gamma(r_{O_1}(d_{O_1}), s_{O_1}(d_{O_1})) \triangleq c_{O_1}(d_{O_1})$$
$$\gamma(r_{O_5}(d_{O_5}), s_{O_5}(d_{O_5})) \triangleq c_{O_5}(d_{O_5})$$
$$\gamma(r_{O_3}(d_{O_3}), s_{O_3}(d_{O_3})) \triangleq c_{O_3}(d_{O_3})$$

Let all modules be in parallel, then the building block BB3 can be presented by the following process term.

$$\tau_{I_3}(\partial_{H_3}(\Theta(BB1 \between BB2))) = \tau_{I_3}(\partial_{H_3}(BB1 \between BB2))$$

where $H_3 = \{r_{O_1}(d_{O_1}), s_{O_1}(d_{O_1}), r_{O_5}(d_{O_5}), s_{O_5}(d_{O_5}), r_{O_3}(d_{O_3}), s_{O_3}(d_{O_3})\}$,
$I_3 = \{BB1F_1, BB1F_2, BB2F_1, BB2F_2, c_{O_1}(d_{O_1}), c_{O_5}(d_{O_5}), c_{O_3}(d_{O_3})\}$.

Then we get the following conclusion on the building block.

Theorem 6.4 (Correctness of the building block BB3). *The building block BB3 $\tau_{I_3}(\partial_{H_3}(BB3))$ can exhibit desired external behaviors.*

Proof. Based on the above state transitions of the above modules, by use of the algebraic laws of APTC, we can prove that

$$\tau_{I_3}(\partial_{H_3}(BB3)) = \sum_{d_{I_1},d_{O_6}\in\Delta}(r_{I_1}(d_{I_1})\cdot s_{O_6}(d_{O_6}))\cdot\tau_{I_3}(\partial_{H_3}(BB3)),$$

that is, the building block BB3 $\tau_{I_3}(\partial_{H_3}(BB3))$ can exhibit desired external behaviors.

For the details of proof, please refer to Section 3.10, and we omit it. □

7 Modeling and verification of parallel programming languages

In this chapter, we will show the modeling of parallel programming language. For an imperative language (for details, please see Appendix A), the syntactic sets are as follows.

- Numbers set **N**, with positive, negative integers, and zero, and $n, m \in \mathbf{N}$;
- Truth values set **T**, with values {**true**, **false**};
- Storage locations **Loc**, and $X, Y \in \mathbf{Loc}$;
- Arithmetic expressions **Aexp**, and $a \in \mathbf{Aexp}$;
- Boolean expressions **Bexp**, and $b \in \mathbf{Bexp}$;
- Commands **Com**, and $c \in \mathbf{Com}$.

The formation rules of PPL are:
For **Aexp**:

$$a ::= n \quad | \quad X \quad | \quad a_0 + a_1 \quad | \quad a_0 - a_1 \quad | \quad a_0 \times a_1$$

For **Bexp**:

$$b ::= \mathbf{true} \quad | \quad \mathbf{false} \quad | \quad a_0 = a_1 \quad | \quad a_0 \leq a_1 \quad | \quad \neg b \quad | \quad b_0 \wedge b_1 \quad | \quad b_0 \vee b_1$$

For **Com**:

$$c ::= \mathbf{skip} \quad | \quad X := a \quad | \quad c_0; c_1 \quad | \quad \mathbf{if}\ b\ \mathbf{then}\ c_0\ \mathbf{else}\ c_1 \quad | \quad \mathbf{while}\ b\ \mathbf{do}\ c \quad | \quad c_0 \parallel c_1$$

In the following section, we will discuss the modeling of such language by APTC and its guarded extensions.

7.1 Numbers and arithmetic expressions

Numbers and arithmetic expressions are the data and data related manipulation, after evaluation, the data may be stored through the assign command, composed into a Boolean expression, or exchanged through communication channels (shared memory, wired or wireless channels).

APTC and guarded APTC do not support data manipulation, but Boolean expressions and communications, and also atomic actions manipulating data.

Theory of Structured Parallel Programming. https://doi.org/10.1016/B978-0-44-324814-6.00011-3

7.2 Truth values and Boolean expressions

Truth value and Boolean expressions can be modeled as guards in guarded APTC, **ture** as ϵ and **false** as δ and Boolean expressions as guards. And the axioms of guarded APTC lead to a Boolean Algebra.

7.3 Storage locations and assign command

Since data are hidden behind of the atomic actions, storage location, and assign command are modeled as a kind of atomic actions.

7.4 Commands

The assign command is modeled as a kind of atomic actions, **skip** is modeled as the empty action ϵ in APTC and guarded APTC. ; is modeled as the sequential composition $\cdot$ in APTC.

if b **then** c_0 **else** c_1, can be modeled as $\{b = \textbf{true}\} \cdot c_0 + \{b = \textbf{false}\} \cdot c_1$.

while b **do** c, can be captured by the following recursive specification:

$$X = \{b = \textbf{true}\} \cdot c \cdot X + \{b = \textbf{false}\} \cdot Y$$

The command $c_0 \parallel c_1$ can be modeled by $\between$, $\parallel$, $\mathbin{|\!\!\lfloor}$, and $|$ in APTC and guarded APTC.

7.5 Verification of parallel programs

By use of the axiom systems of APTC and guarded APTC, putting the program segments into parallel, abstracting internal actions, we can verify if the program is correct, that is, if the program exhibits desired behaviors (please see the example in Section 3.10).

8

Modeling and verification of parallel programming patterns

In this chapter, we will introduce the modeling of parallel programming patterns [15] by use of APTC and guarded APTC.

8.1 Parallel control patterns

8.1.1 Fork-Join

The Fork-Join pattern forks the control flow into several ones, and rejoins later, as Fig. 8.1 shows. In Fig. 8.1, the clause e_0 forks into e_1, e_2, and e_3, and later joins as e_4.

The program segment in Fig. 8.1 can be modeled by APTC as follows.

$$e_0 \cdot (e_1 \parallel e_2 \parallel e_3) \cdot e_4$$

8.1.2 Map

The Map pattern maps every element of the data set through a function and then outputs, as Fig. 8.2 shows. In Fig. 8.2, the data element d_i is processed through the clause e_i, and then sends the result data outside.

The program segment in Fig. 8.2 can be modeled by APTC as follows.

$$(receive_1(d_1) \cdot e_1 \cdot send_1(d_1')) \parallel (receive_2(d_2) \cdot e_2 \cdot send_2(d_2')) \parallel (receive_3(d_3) \cdot e_3 \cdot send_3(d_3'))$$

8.1.3 Stencil

The Stencil pattern is a generalization of the Map pattern with the input data can come from the "neighbors", as Fig. 8.3 shows. In Fig. 8.3, the clause inputs of e_1 are coming from the neighbors d_{11}, d_{12}, d_{13}, and d_{14}, the e_1 executes and generates the output.

The program segment in Fig. 8.3 can be modeled by APTC as follows.

$$(receive_{11}(d_{11}) \parallel receive_{12}(d_{12}) \parallel receive_{13}(d_{13}) \parallel receive_{14}(d_{14})) \cdot e_1 \cdot send_1(d')$$

8.1.4 Reduction

The Reduction pattern combines every data element into a single data element through associative functions, as Fig. 8.4 shows. In Fig. 8.4, the data elements d_1 and d_2 are com-

Theory of Structured Parallel Programming. https://doi.org/10.1016/B978-0-44-324814-6.00012-5

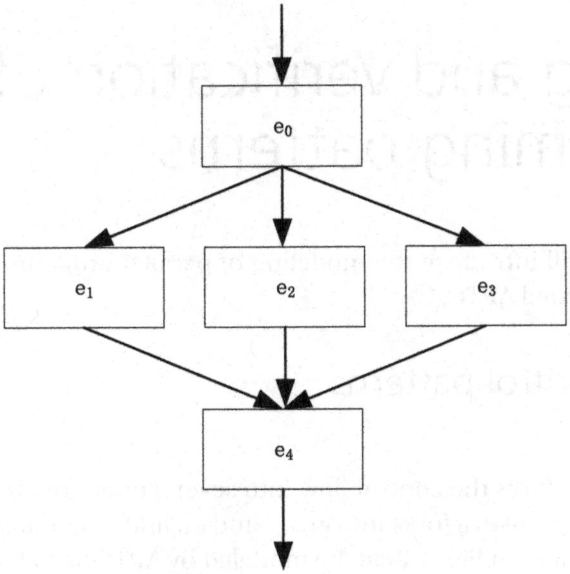

FIGURE 8.1 Fork-Join pattern.

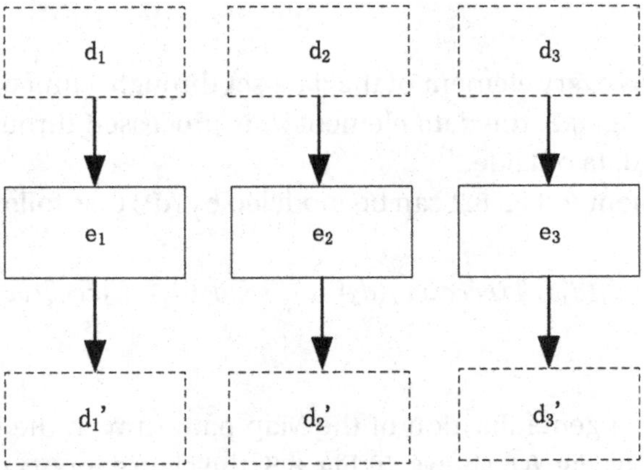

FIGURE 8.2 Map pattern.

bined by e_1, d_3 and d_4 are combined by e_2, and then combined by e_3 and generates the data element d'.

The program segment in Fig. 8.4 can be modeled by APTC as follows.

$$(((receive_1(d_1) \parallel receive_2(d_2)) \cdot e_1) \parallel ((receive_3(d_3) \parallel receive_4(d_4)) \cdot e_2)) \cdot e_3 \cdot send(d')$$

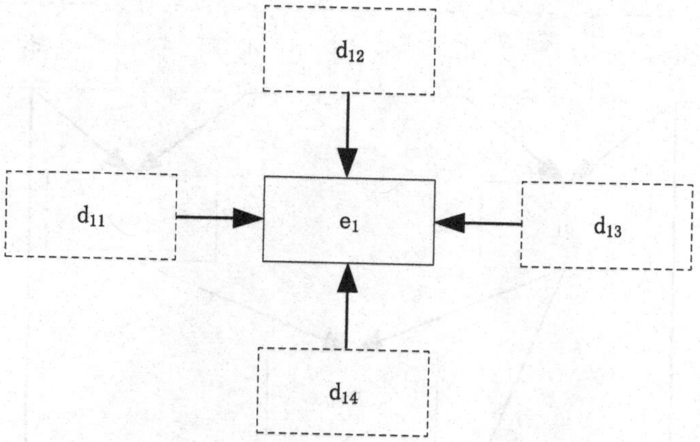

FIGURE 8.3 Stencil pattern.

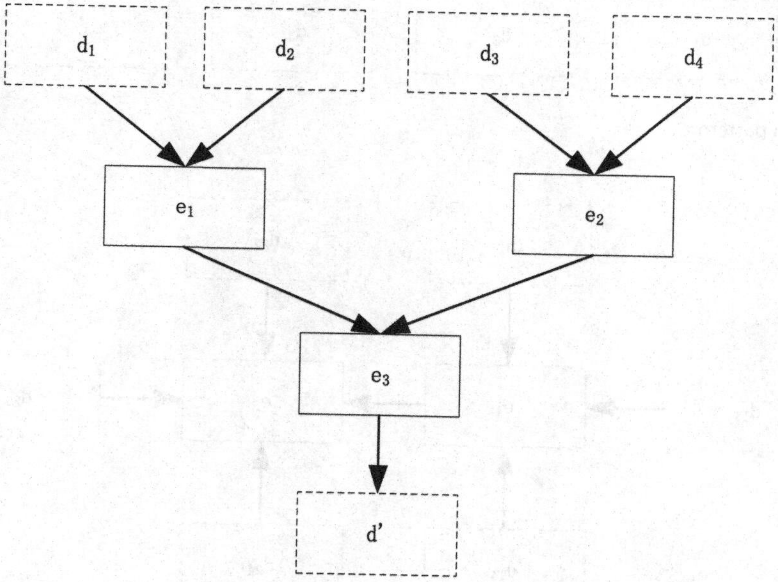

FIGURE 8.4 Reduction pattern.

8.1.5 Scan

The Scan pattern computes all partial reductions, as Fig. 8.5 shows. In Fig. 8.5, the data element may be sent out directly or may be processed by reductions.

The program segment in Fig. 8.5 can be modeled by APTC as follows.

$(receive_1(d_1)\cdot send_1(d_1')) \parallel ((receive_1(d_1) \parallel receive_2(d_2))\cdot e_1 \cdot send_2(d_2')) \parallel ((((receive_1(d_1) \parallel receive_2(d_2))\cdot e_1) \parallel ((receive_3(d_3) \parallel receive_4(d_4))\cdot e_2))\cdot e_3 \cdot send(d_3')) \parallel (receive_4(d_4)\cdot send_4(d_4'))$

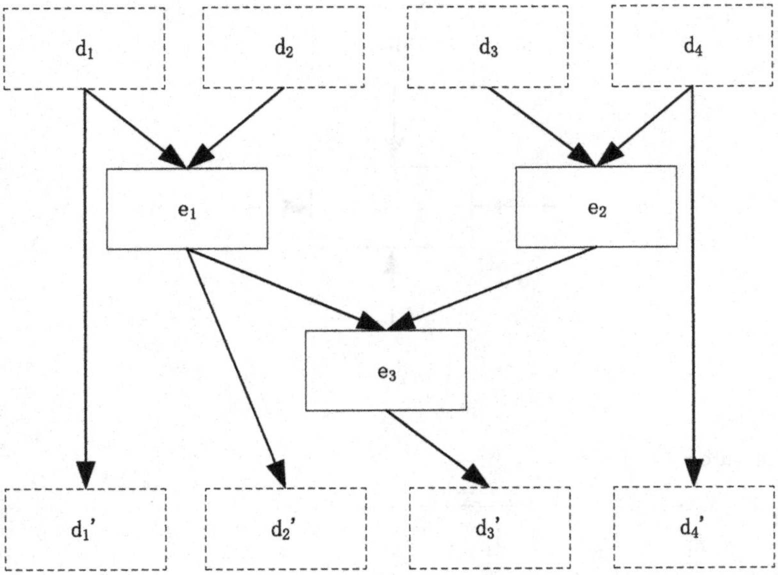

FIGURE 8.5 Scan pattern.

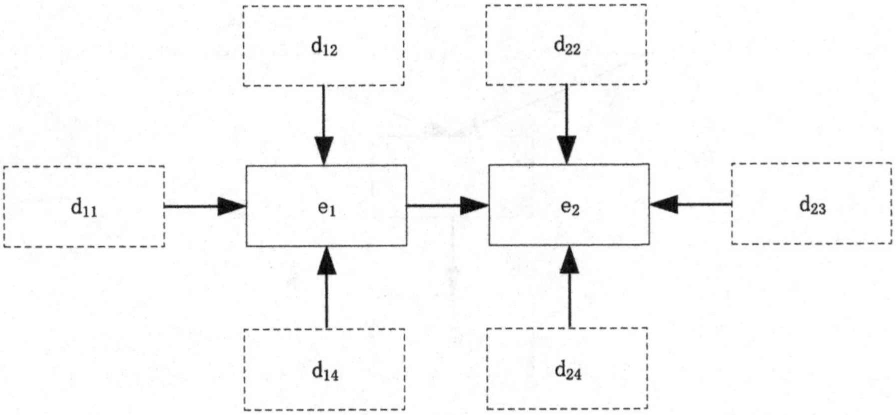

FIGURE 8.6 Recurrence pattern.

8.1.6 Recurrence

The Recurrence pattern is a generalization of iteration with the input data can come from the output of "neighbors", as Fig. 8.6 shows. In Fig. 8.6, the clause inputs of e_2 are coming from the neighbors e_1, d_{22}, d_{23}, and d_{24}, the e_2 executes and generates the output.

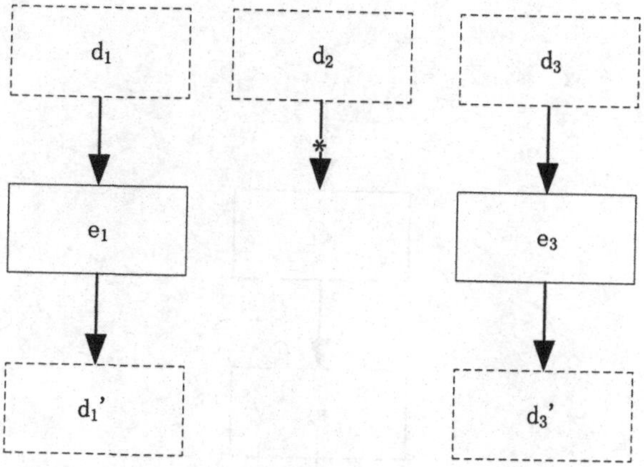

FIGURE 8.7 Pack pattern.

The program segment in Fig. 8.3 can be modeled by APTC as follows.

$$((receive_{11}(d_{11}) \parallel receive_{12}(d_{12}) \parallel receive_{14}(d_{14})) \cdot e_1 \cdot send_1(d_1')) \between ((receive_{21}(d_1') \parallel receive_{22}(d_{22}) \parallel receive_{23}(d_{23}) \parallel receive_{24}(d_{24})) \cdot e_2 \cdot send_2(d_2'))$$

8.2 Parallel data management patterns

8.2.1 Pack

The Pack pattern can be used to eliminate the unused data element in a data collection, as Fig. 8.7 shows. In Fig. 8.7, the data element d_2 is unused and eliminated.

The program segment in Fig. 8.7 can be modeled by APTC as follows.

$$(receive_1(d_1) \cdot e_1 \cdot send_1(d_1')) \parallel (receive_3(d_3) \cdot e_3 \cdot send_3(d_3'))$$

8.2.2 Pipeline

The Pipeline pattern connects data-processing tasks one step by another, as Fig. 8.8 shows. In Fig. 8.8, there are two steps e_1 and e_2 in the pipeline.

The program segment in Fig. 8.8 can be modeled by APTC as follows.

$$receive(d) \cdot e_1 \cdot e_2 \cdot send(d')$$

8.2.3 Geometric decomposition

The Geometric decomposition pattern breaks data into a set of sub-collections, as Fig. 8.9 shows. In Fig. 8.9, the data set $d_1 - d_4$ is broken into two data collections: $d_1 - d_2$ and $d_3 - d_4$.

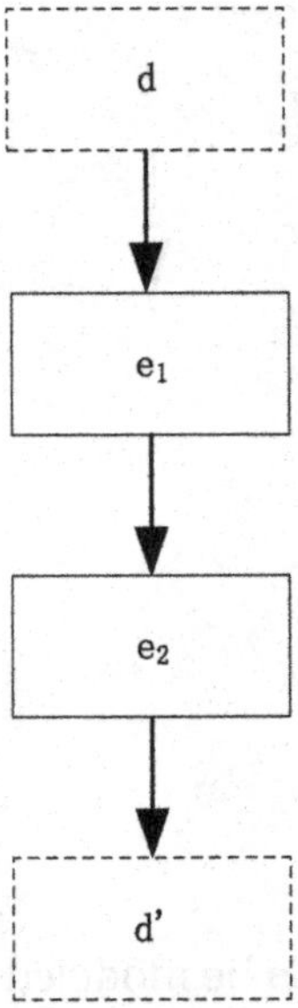

FIGURE 8.8 Pipeline pattern.

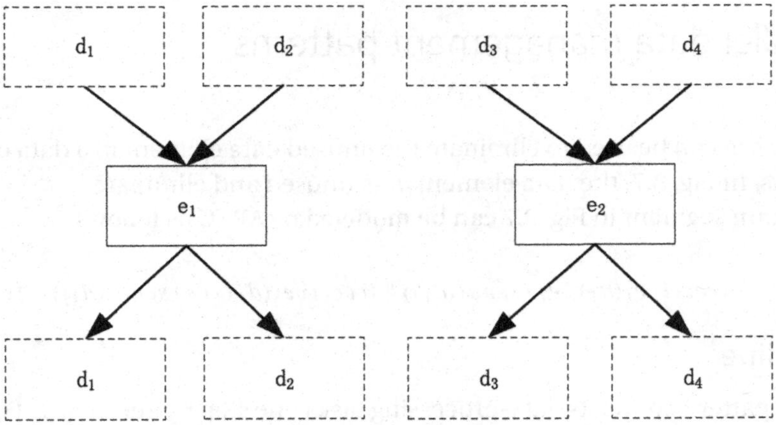

FIGURE 8.9 Geometric decomposition pattern.

The program segment in Fig. 8.9 can be modeled by APTC as follows.

$((receive_1(d_1) \parallel receive_2(d_2)) \cdot e_1 \cdot (send_1(d_1) \parallel send_2(d_2))) \parallel ((receive_3(d_3) \parallel receive_4(d_4)) \cdot e_2 \cdot (send_3(d_3) \parallel send_4(d_4)))$

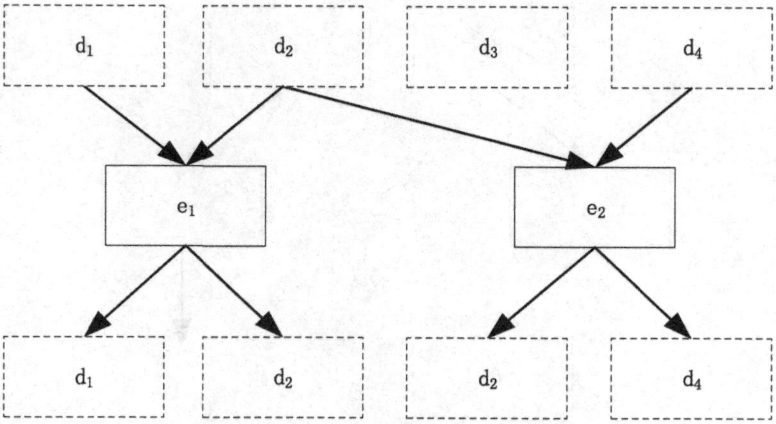

FIGURE 8.10 Gather pattern.

8.2.4 Gather

The Gather pattern reads a set of data collections according to a set of indices, as Fig. 8.10 shows. In Fig. 8.10, the indices are [0, 1, 1, 3].

The program segment in Fig. 8.10 can be modeled by APTC as follows.

$((receive_1(d_1) \parallel receive_2(d_2)) \cdot e_1 \cdot (send_1(d_1) \parallel send_2(d_2))) \parallel ((receive_2(d_2) \parallel receive_4(d_4)) \cdot e_2 \cdot (send_2(d_2) \parallel send_4(d_4)))$

8.2.5 Scatter

The Scatter pattern is the inverse of the Gather pattern, it writes a set of data collections according to a set of indices, as Fig. 8.11 shows. In Fig. 8.11, the indices are [0, 1, 2, 2].

The program segment in Fig. 8.11 can be modeled by APTC as follows.

$(receive_1(d_1) \parallel receive_2(d_2)) \cdot e_1 \cdot (send_1(d_1) \parallel send_2(d_2))$

8.3 Other parallel patterns

8.3.1 Superscalar sequences

The Superscalar sequence pattern operates according to the data dependencies, as Fig. 8.12 shows. In Fig. 8.12, the data dependencies are defined respectively.

The program segment in Fig. 8.12 can be modeled by APTC as follows.

$(receive_1(d_1) \cdot e_1 \cdot send_1(d_1')) \between (receive_3(d_3) \cdot e_3 \cdot send_3(d_3')) \between ((receive_2(d_2) \parallel receive_1(d_1') \parallel receive_3(d_3')) \cdot e_2 \cdot send(d'))$

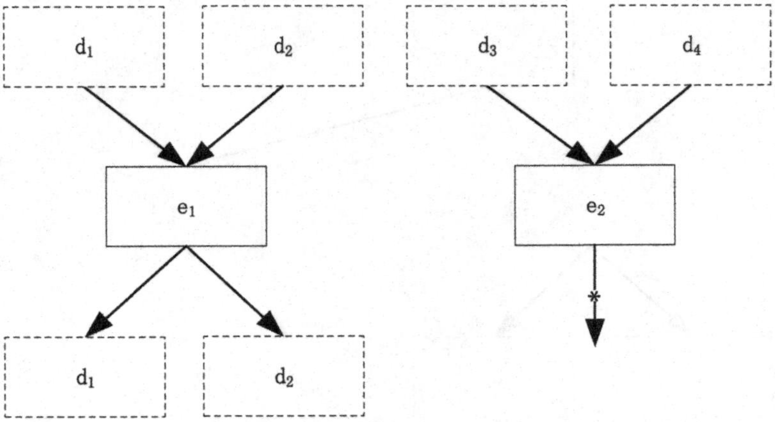

FIGURE 8.11 Scatter pattern.

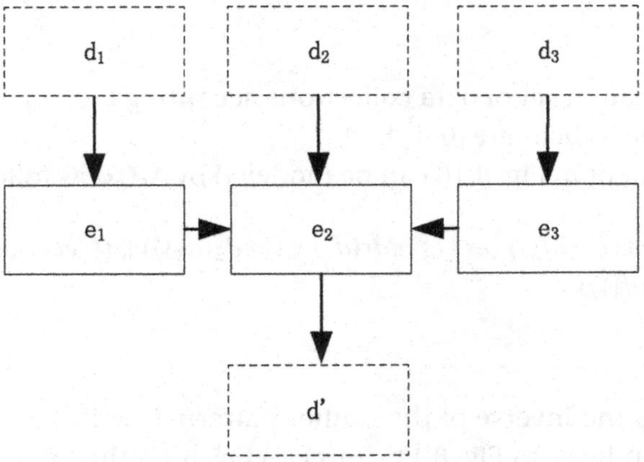

FIGURE 8.12 Superscalar sequence pattern.

8.3.2 Speculative selection

The Speculative selection pattern generalizes the selection to make the condition and both branches can run in parallel, as Fig. 8.13 shows. In Fig. 8.13, both the condition and the two branches can execute in parallel.

The program segment in Fig. 8.13 can be modeled by guarded APTC as follows.

$$(\{b = \mathbf{true}\} \cdot e_1) \parallel (\{b = \mathbf{false}\} \cdot e_2)$$

Note that, $\{b = \mathbf{true}\}$ and $\{b = \mathbf{false}\}$ are guards.

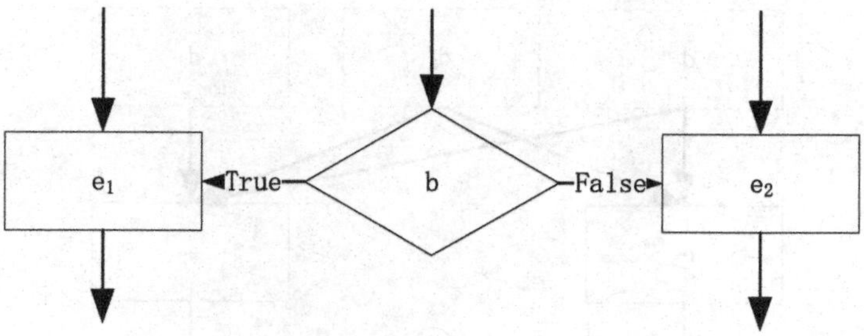

FIGURE 8.13 Speculative selection pattern.

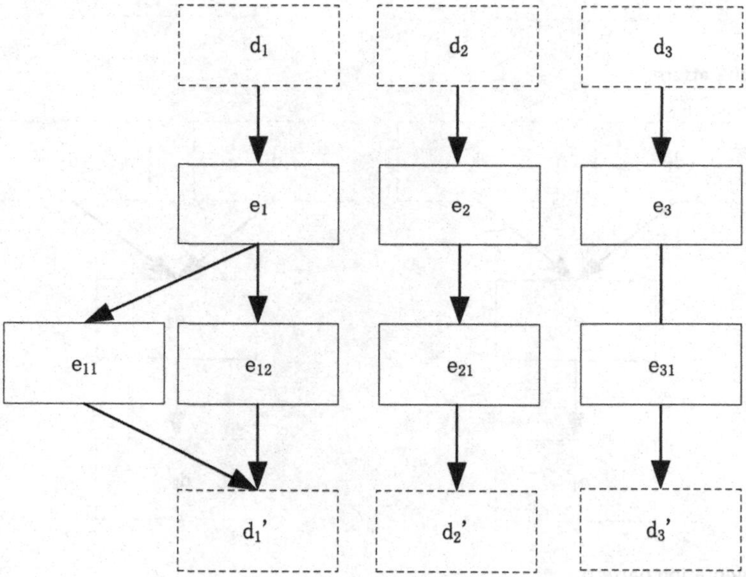

FIGURE 8.14 Workpile pattern.

8.3.3 Workpile

The Workpile pattern generalizes the Map pattern with each function can generate one or more instances, as Fig. 8.14 shows. In Fig. 8.14, e_1 generates e_{11} and e_{12}, e_2 generates e_{21}, and e_3 generates e_{31}.

The program segment in Fig. 8.14 can be modeled by APTC as follows.

$$(receive_1(d_1)\cdot e_1\cdot(e_{11}\parallel e_{12})\cdot send_1(d_1'))\parallel(receive_2(d_2)\cdot e_2\cdot e_{21}\cdot send_2(d_2'))\parallel(receive_3(d_3)\cdot e_3\cdot e_{31}\cdot send_3(d_3'))$$

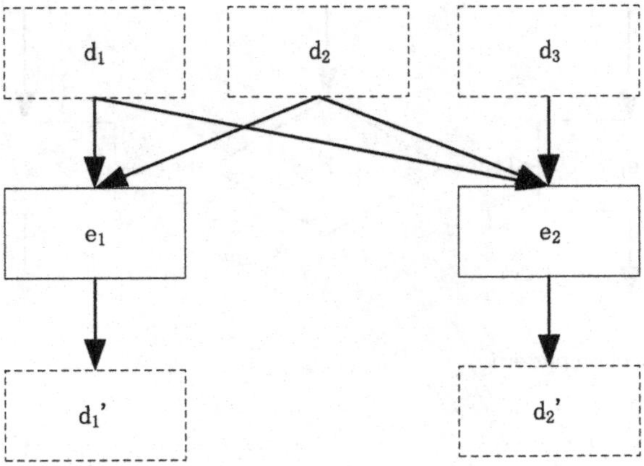

FIGURE 8.15 Search pattern.

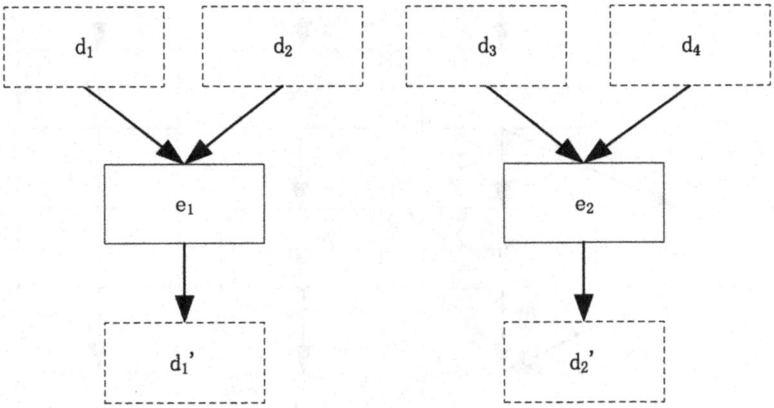

FIGURE 8.16 Segmentation pattern.

8.3.4 Search

The Search pattern finds the required data from the data collections, as Fig. 8.15 shows. In Fig. 8.15, e_1 finds d_1 and d_2, and e_2 finds d_1, d_2, and d_3.

The program segment in Fig. 8.15 can be modeled by APTC as follows.

$((receive_1(d_1) \parallel receive_2(d_2)) \cdot e_1 \cdot send_1(d_1')) \parallel ((receive_1(d_1) \parallel receive_2(d_2) \parallel receive_3(d_3)) \cdot e_2 \cdot send_2(d_2'))$

8.3.5 Segmentation

The Segmentation pattern operates on the segmented data collections, as Fig. 8.16 shows. In Fig. 8.16, d_1 and d_2 are one segment, and d_3 and d_4 are another.

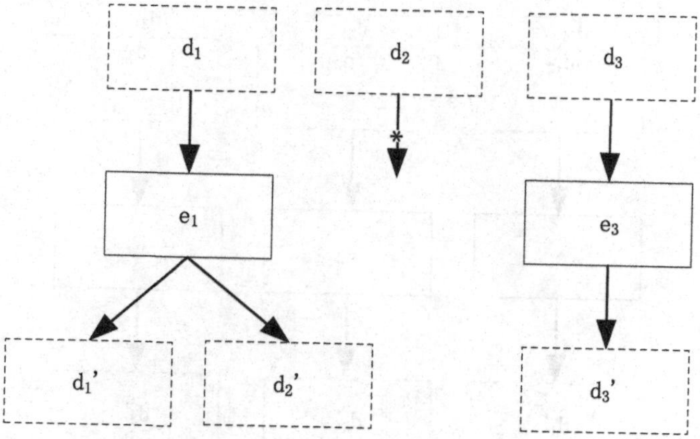

FIGURE 8.17 Expand pattern.

The program segment in Fig. 8.16 can be modeled by APTC as follows.

$$((receive_1(d_1) \parallel receive_2(d_2)) \cdot e_1 \cdot send_1(d_1')) \parallel ((receive_3(d_3) \parallel receive_4(d_4)) \cdot e_2 \cdot send_2(d_2'))$$

8.3.6 Expand

The Expand pattern can be deemed as a mixture of the Pack pattern and the Map pattern, as Fig. 8.17 shows. In Fig. 8.17, d_1 is split in d_1' and d_2', and d_2 is unused.

The program segment in Fig. 8.17 can be modeled by APTC as follows.

$$(receive_1(d_1) \cdot e_1 \cdot (send_1(d_1') \parallel send_1(d_2'))) \parallel (receive_3(d_3) \cdot e_3 \cdot send_3(d_3'))$$

8.3.7 Category reduction

The Category reduction pattern finds the data elements in the same category and reduces them to one element, as Fig. 8.18 shows. In Fig. 8.18, the data d_{11} and d_{12} are in the same category, and d_{21} and d_{22}, and d_{31} and d_{32} are in the same category.

The program segment in Fig. 8.18 can be modeled by APTC as follows.

$$((receive_1(d_{11}) \parallel receive_1(d_{12})) \cdot e_1 \cdot send_1(d_1')) \parallel ((receive_2(d_{21}) \parallel receive_2(d_{22})) \cdot e_2 \cdot send_2(d_2')) \parallel ((receive_3(d_{31}) \parallel receive_3(d_{32})) \cdot e_3 \cdot send_3(d_3'))$$

8.3.8 Term graph rewriting

The Term graph rewriting pattern provides a graph-like concurrency, as Fig. 8.19 shows. In Fig. 8.19, this style concurrency is only defined by causalities among atomic actions, and is the so-called true concurrency.

In Chapter 2 and APTC in Chapter 3, we have already proven that Fig. 8.19 is equivalent to Fig. 8.20 and can be structured.

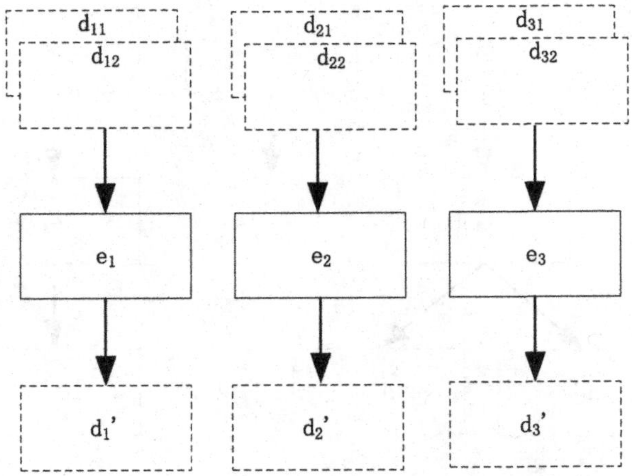

FIGURE 8.18 Category Reduction pattern.

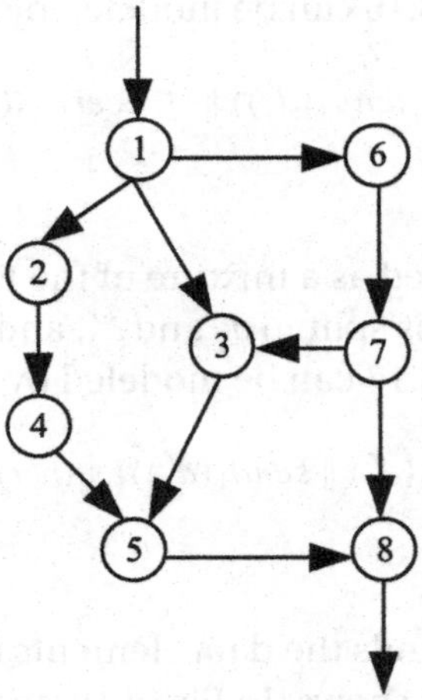

FIGURE 8.19 Term graph rewriting pattern 1.

8.4 Verification of parallel programming patterns

By use of the axiom systems of APTC and guarded APTC, putting the parallel programming patterns based program segments into parallel, abstracting internal actions, we can verify if the program is correct, that is, if the program exhibits desired behaviors (please see the example in Section 3.10).

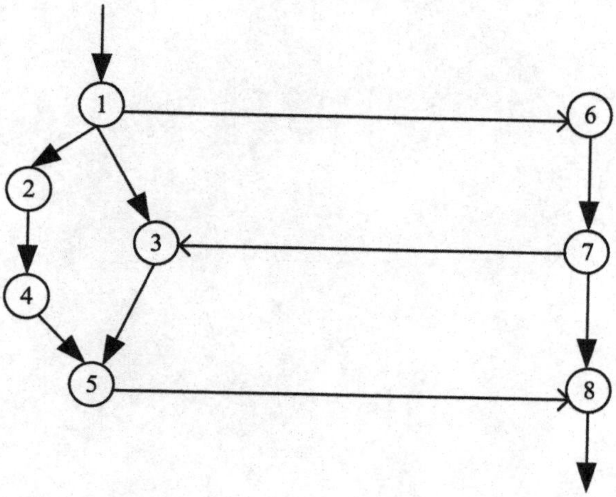

FIGURE 8.20 Term graph rewriting pattern 2.

9 Modeling and verification of distributed systems

In this chapter, we will introduce the modeling of distributed systems [16] by use of APTC, guarded APTC, and distributed APTC.

9.1 A model of distributed computations

A distributed system consists of a set of processors and a set of channels among the processors, as Fig. 9.1 shows. Each processor may be a shared memories based multi-cores or multi-processors system. The whole distributed computational task is defined by atomic actions and causal relations among them. And there exist two kinds of causalities: one is executional order defined causality, and the other is communication defined causality. Note that: (1) In each processor, there also exists causality defined concurrency (two actions without causal relations between them will be executed concurrently); (2) Communications will always occur between two different parallel branches, it may occur between two different processors through communication channels, or in the same processor, or occur between two cores through the shared memories.

A distributed system is a set of autonomous processors with communications among them through the communication channels, it can be modeled by APTC, guarded APTC, and distributed APTC with the following distinct features.

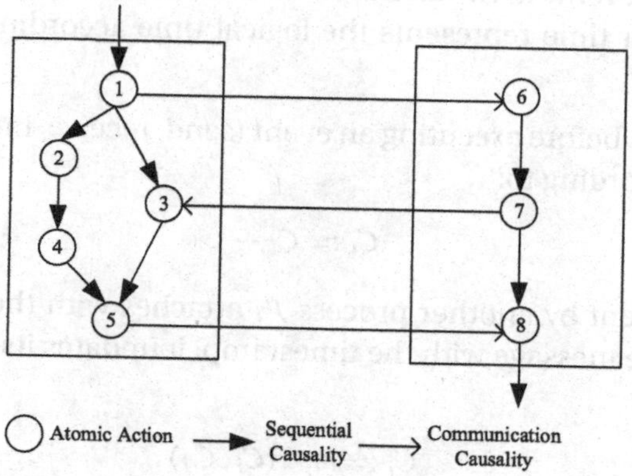

FIGURE 9.1 A model of distributed computations.

Theory of Structured Parallel Programming. https://doi.org/10.1016/B978-0-44-324814-6.00013-7

- No common physical clock. There is not a common physical clock in the distributed systems. This feature means that the asynchronous cooperation nature among different processors. APTC and its extensions can model the asynchronous cooperations among processors by use of the placeholder extension in the following way: (1) describe each processor's behaviors by the language elements including send and receive messages through some channels and the appropriate placeholder; (2) put each processor in parallel.
- No shared memories. There are not shared memories among different processors. This feature means that communications always occur as message exchanges through some communication channels. APTC and its extensions support the definition of the communication functions, through which synchronous or asynchronous communications can be defined.
- Geographical separation. The processors in the distributed systems are geographical separated. This feature means the same function actions performed on different processors should be distinguished. Distributed APTC can be used to model the distribution of the different processors in the distributed systems.
- Autonomy and heterogeneity. Each processor is executed autonomously and implemented heterogeneously. The autonomy is assured by the abstraction mechanism of APTC and its extensions, each processor is encapsulated and abstracted away from its internal computations. And the heterogeneity is assured by the neutrality of APTC and its extensions, APTC and its extensions are neutral languages independent to any concrete implementation and just capture the computations and concurrency.

Since the lack of global physical time, the logical time is determined by the causalities among actions defined in the distributed systems. The clock consistency condition says:

$$e_i \leq e_i \Rightarrow C(e_i) < C(e_j)$$

where e_i and e_j are two events in the distributed systems, $C(e)$ is the logical time of event e.

The Lamport's scalar time represents the logical time according to the following two time updating rules:

1. R1: In the process P_i, before executing an event (send, receive, internal), the logical time C_i of P_i updates according to:

$$C_i := C_i + 1$$

2. R2: Each message sent by another process P_j attaches with the logical time C_j of P_j, when P_i receives the message with the timestamp, it updates its logical time C_i according to:

$$C_i := max(C_i, C_j)$$

then P_i executes the rule R1 and processes the message.

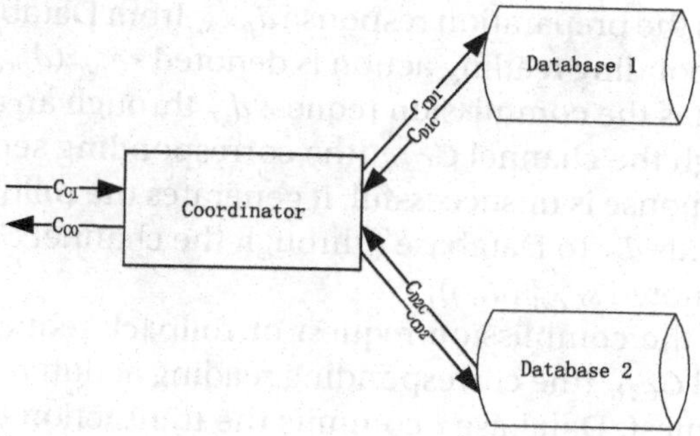

FIGURE 9.2 Two-phase commit protocol.

APTC and its extensions have the natural advantages to analyze the logical time, for their explicit definition of causal relation $\leq$, sequential composition $\cdot$, communication merge $\mid$, and communication function γ.

9.2 Distributed transactions

Traditional transaction has ACID (Atomicity, Consistency, Isolation, and Durability) properties, while distributed transaction implements transactions in distributed system and consists of a set of local transactions. In this section, we will discuss the modeling and verification of several classical distributed transaction protocols, including the so-called Two-Phase Commit protocol (2PC), and Three-Phase Commit protocol (3PC).

9.2.1 Two-phase commit protocol

The 2PC protocol introduces a transaction coordinator to coordinate and manage the distributed transactions, and it includes two phases: the preparation phase and the commission phase, as Fig. 9.2 illustrates.

The process of 2PC protocol is following.

1. Coordinator receives the transaction request d from the outside through the channel C_{CI} (the corresponding reading action is denoted $r_{C_{CI}}(d)$), the Coordinator generates the preparation request d_{pr_i} for the Database i through the internal action $prepare$, and sends d_{pr_i} to the corresponding Database i through the channel C_{CDi} (the corresponding sending action is denoted $s_{C_{CDi}}(d_{preq_i})$);
2. Database i receives the preparation request d_{preq_i} from Coordinator through the channel C_{CDi} (the corresponding reading action is denoted $r_{C_{CDi}}(d_{preq_i})$), then after an internal processing pr_i, generates the preparation response d_{pres_i}, and sends d_{pres_i} to Coordinator through the channel C_{DiC} (the corresponding sending action is denoted $s_{C_{DiC}}(d_{pres_i})$);

3. Coordinator receives the preparation response d_{pres_i} from Database i through the channel C_{DiC} (the corresponding reading action is denoted $r_{C_{DiC}}(d_{pres_i})$), if all responses are successful, it generates the commission request d_{cr} through an action cr, and sends d_{cr} to Database i through the channel C_{CDi} (the corresponding sending action is denoted $s_{C_{CDi}}(d_{cr})$); if one response is unsuccessful, it generates the rollback request d_{rr} through an action rr, and sends d_{rr} to Database i through the channel C_{CDi} (the corresponding sending action is denoted $s_{C_{CDi}}(d_{rr})$);
4. Database i receives the commission request or rollback request d_r from Coordinator through the channel C_{CDi} (the corresponding reading action is denoted $r_{C_{CDi}}(d_r)$), if d_r is a commission request, Database i commits the transaction through an action com_i, and sends the commission response d_{cres} to Coordinator through the channel C_{DiC} (the corresponding sending action is denoted $s_{C_{DiC}}(d_{cres})$); if d_r is a rollback request, Database i rollbacks the transaction through an action $roll_i$, and sends the rollback response d_{rres} to Coordinator through the channel C_{DiC} (the corresponding sending action is denoted $s_{C_{DiC}}(d_{rres})$);
5. Coordinator receives the response d_{res} from Database i through the channel C_{DiC} (the corresponding reading action is denoted $r_{C_{DiC}}(d_{res})$), if the response d_{res} is a commission response, Coordinator sends the transaction success response d_s to the outside through the channel C_{CO} (the corresponding sending action is denoted $s_{C_{CO}}(d_s)$); if the response d_{res} is a rollback response, Coordinator sends the transaction failure response d_f to the outside through the channel C_{CO} (the corresponding sending action is denoted $s_{C_{CO}}(d_f)$).

Where $d \in \Delta$, Δ is the set of data.

Coordinator's state transitions described by $APTC_G$ are following.

$C = Loc_C :: \sum_{d\in\Delta} r_{C_{CI}}(d) \cdot C_2$

$C_2 = prepare \cdot C_3$

$C_3 = (s_{C_{CD1}}(d_{preq_1}) \parallel \cdots \parallel s_{C_{CDn}}(d_{preq_n})) \cdot C_4$

$C_4 = (r_{C_{D1C}}(d_{pres_1}) \parallel \cdots \parallel r_{C_{DnC}}(d_{pres_n})) \cdot C_5$

$C_5 = \{d_{pres_1} = SUCCESS \parallel \cdots \parallel d_{pres_n} = SUCCESS\} \cdot cr \cdot (s_{C_{CD1}}(d_{cr}) \parallel \cdots \parallel s_{C_{CDn}}(d_{cr})) \cdot C_6 + \{d_{pres_1} = FAILURE + \cdots + d_{pres_n} = FAILURE\} \cdot rr \cdot (s_{C_{CD1}}(d_{rr}) \parallel \cdots \parallel s_{C_{CDn}}(d_{rr})) \cdot C_6$

$C_6 = (r_{C_{D1C}}(d_{res}) \parallel \cdots \parallel r_{C_{DnC}}(d_{res})) \cdot C_7$

$C_7 = \{d_{res} = COMMIT\} \cdot s_{C_{CO}}(d_s) \cdot C + \{d_{res} = ROLLBACK\} \cdot s_{C_{CO}}(d_f) \cdot C$

The state transitions of Database i described by $APTC_G$ are following.

$D_i = Loc_{D_i} :: r_{C_{DiC}}(d_{preq_i}) \cdot D_{i_2}$

$D_{i_2} = pr_i \cdot D_{i_3}$

$D_{i_3} = s_{C_{DiC}}(d_{pres_i}) \cdot D_{i_4}$

$D_{i_4} = r_{C_{CDi}}(d_r) \cdot D_{i_5}$

$D_{i_5} = \{d_r = d_{cr}\} \cdot com_i \cdot s_{C_{DiC}}(d_{cres}) \cdot D_i + \{d_r = d_{rr}\} \cdot roll_i \cdot s_{C_{DiC}}(d_{rres}) \cdot D_i$

The sending action and the reading action of the same type data through the same channel can communicate with each other, otherwise, will cause a deadlock δ. We define the following communication functions.

$$\gamma(r_{C_{CDi}}(d_{preq_i}), s_{C_{CDi}}(d_{preq_i})) \triangleq c_{C_{CDi}}(d_{preq_i})$$
$$\gamma(r_{C_{DiC}}(d_{pres_i}), s_{C_{DiC}}(d_{pres_i})) \triangleq c_{C_{DiC}}(d_{pres_i})$$
$$\gamma(r_{C_{CDi}}(d_{cr}), s_{C_{CDi}}(d_{cr})) \triangleq c_{C_{CDi}}(d_{cr})$$
$$\gamma(r_{C_{CDi}}(d_{rr}), s_{C_{CDi}}(d_{rr})) \triangleq c_{C_{CDi}}(d_{rr})$$
$$\gamma(r_{C_{DiC}}(d_{cres}), s_{C_{DiC}}(d_{cres})) \triangleq c_{C_{DiC}}(d_{cres})$$
$$\gamma(r_{C_{DiC}}(d_{rres}), s_{C_{DiC}}(d_{rres})) \triangleq c_{C_{DiC}}(d_{rres})$$

Let all modules be in parallel, then the protocol $C \quad D_1 \quad \cdots \quad D_n$ can be presented by the following process term.

$$\tau_I(\partial_H(\Theta(C \between D_1 \between \cdot \between D_n))) = \tau_I(\partial_H(C \between D_1 \between \cdot \between D_n))$$

where $H = \{r_{C_{CDi}}(d_{preq_i}), s_{C_{CDi}}(d_{preq_i}), r_{C_{DiC}}(d_{pres_i}), s_{C_{DiC}}(d_{pres_i}),$
$r_{C_{CDi}}(d_{cr}), s_{C_{CDi}}(d_{cr}), r_{C_{CDi}}(d_{rr}), s_{C_{CDi}}(d_{rr}),$
$r_{C_{DiC}}(d_{cres}), s_{C_{DiC}}(d_{cres}), r_{C_{DiC}}(d_{rres}), s_{C_{DiC}}(d_{rres}) | d \in \Delta\}$ for $1 \leq i \leq n$,

$I = \{c_{C_{CDi}}(d_{preq_i}), c_{C_{DiC}}(d_{pres_i}), c_{C_{CDi}}(d_{cr}), c_{C_{CDi}}(d_{rr}),$
$c_{C_{DiC}}(d_{cres}), c_{C_{DiC}}(d_{rres}), prepare, \{d_{pres_i} = SUCCESS\}, \{d_{pres_i} = FAILURE\},$
$cr, rr, \{d_{res} = COMMIT\}, \{d_{res} = ROLLBACK\}, pr_i, com_i, roll_i \{d_r = d_{cr}\}, \{d_r = d_{rr}\} | D \in \Delta\}$ for $1 \leq i \leq n$.

Then we get the following conclusion on the protocol.

Theorem 9.1. *The 2PC protocol in Fig. 9.2 is correct.*

Proof. Based on the above state transitions of the above modules, by use of the algebraic laws of $APTC_G$, we can prove that

$$\tau_I(\partial_H(C \between D_1 \between \cdot \between D_n)) = \sum_{d \in \Delta}(Loc_C :: r_{C_{CI}}(d) \cdot (Loc_C :: s_{C_{CO}}(d_c) + Loc_C :: s_{C_{CO}}(d_f)) \cdot \tau_I(\partial_H(C \between D_1 \between \cdot \between D_n)).$$

For the details of proof, please refer to Section 3.10, and we omit it. □

9.2.2 Three-phase commit protocol

The 3PC protocol introduces a transaction coordinator to coordinate and manage the distributed transactions, and it includes three phases: the preparation phase, the pre-commission phase, and the commission phase, as Fig. 9.3 illustrates.

The process of 3PC protocol is following.

1. Coordinator receives the transaction request d from the outside through the channel C_{CI} (the corresponding reading action is denoted $r_{C_{CI}}(d)$), the Coordinator generates the preparation request d_{pr_i} for the Database i through the internal action $prepare$, and sends d_{pr_i} to the corresponding Database i through the channel C_{CDi} (the corresponding sending action is denoted $s_{C_{CDi}}(d_{preq_i})$);
2. Database i receives the preparation request d_{preq_i} from Coordinator through the channel C_{CDi} (the corresponding reading action is denoted $r_{C_{CDi}}(d_{preq_i})$), then after an internal processing pr_i, generates the preparation response d_{pres_i}, and sends d_{pres_i} to

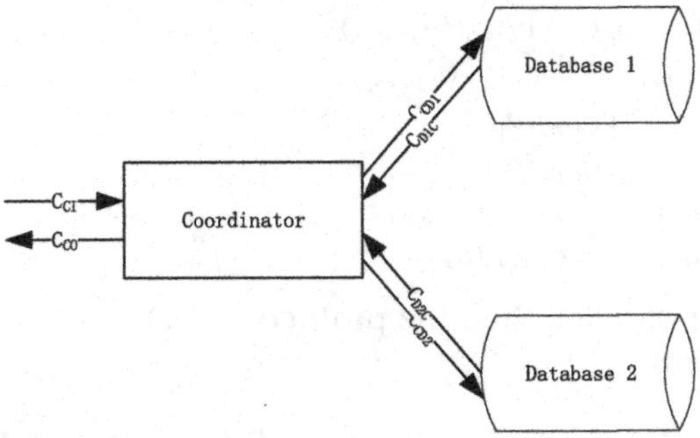

FIGURE 9.3 Three-phase commit protocol.

Coordinator through the channel C_{DiC} (the corresponding sending action is denoted $s_{C_{DiC}}(d_{pres_i})$);

3. Coordinator receives the preparation response d_{pres_i} from Database i through the channel C_{DiC} (the corresponding reading action is denoted $r_{C_{DiC}}(d_{pres_i})$), if all responses are successful, it generates the pre-commission request d_{pcr} through an action pcr, and sends d_{pcr} to Database i through the channel C_{CDi} (the corresponding sending action is denoted $s_{C_{CDi}}(d_{pcr})$); if one response is unsuccessful, it sends the transaction failure response in d_{pcr} to Database i through the channel C_{CDi} (the corresponding sending action is denoted $s_{C_{CDi}}(d_{pcr})$);
4. Database i receives the pre-commission request d_{pcr} from Coordinator through the channel C_{CDi} (the corresponding reading action is denoted $r_{C_{CDi}}(d_{pcr})$), Database i pre-commits the transaction through an action pc_i, and generates and sends the response d_{pcres} to Coordinator through the channel C_{DiC} (the corresponding sending action is denoted $s_{C_{DiC}}(d_{pcres})$);
5. Coordinator receives the pre-commission response d_{pcres_i} from Database i through the channel C_{DiC} (the corresponding reading action is denoted $r_{C_{DiC}}(d_{pcres_i})$), if all responses are successful, it generates the commission request d_{cr} through an action cr, and sends d_{cr} to Database i through the channel C_{CDi} (the corresponding sending action is denoted $s_{C_{CDi}}(d_{cr})$); if one response is unsuccessful, it sends the rollback request d_{rr} to Database i through the channel C_{CDi} (the corresponding sending action is denoted $s_{C_{CDi}}(d_{rr})$);
6. Database i receives the commission request or the rollback request d_r from Coordinator through the channel C_{CDi} (the corresponding reading action is denoted $r_{C_{CDi}}(d_r)$), if d_r is a commission request, Database i commits the transaction through an action com_i, and sends the commission response d_{cres} to Coordinator through the channel C_{DiC} (the corresponding sending action is denoted $s_{C_{DiC}}(d_{cres})$); if d_r is a rollback request, Database i rollbacks the transaction through an action $roll_i$, and sends the rollback response d_{rres} to Coordinator through the channel C_{DiC} (the corresponding sending action is denoted $s_{C_{DiC}}(d_{rres})$);

7. Coordinator receives the response d_{res} from Database i through the channel C_{DiC} (the corresponding reading action is denoted $r_{C_{DiC}}(d_{res})$), if the response d_{res} is a commission response, Coordinator sends the transaction success response d_s to the outside through the channel C_{CO} (the corresponding sending action is denoted $s_{C_{CO}}(d_s)$); if the response d_{res} is a rollback response, Coordinator sends the transaction failure response d_f to the outside through the channel C_{CO} (the corresponding sending action is denoted $s_{C_{CO}}(d_f)$).

Where $d \in \Delta$, Δ is the set of data.
Coordinator's state transitions described by $APTC_G$ are following.

$C = Loc_C :: \sum_{d\in\Delta} r_{C_{CI}}(d) \cdot C_2$
$C_2 = prepare \cdot C_3$
$C_3 = (s_{C_{CD1}}(d_{preq_1}) \parallel \cdots \parallel s_{C_{CDn}}(d_{preq_n})) \cdot C_4$
$C_4 = (r_{C_{D1C}}(d_{pres_1}) \parallel \cdots \parallel r_{C_{DnC}}(d_{pres_n})) \cdot C_5$
$C_5 = \{d_{pres_1} = SUCCESS \parallel \cdots \parallel d_{pres_n} = SUCCESS\} \cdot pcr \cdot (s_{C_{CD1}}(d_{pcr}) \parallel \cdots \parallel s_{C_{CDn}}(d_{pcr})) \cdot C_6 + \{d_{pres_1} = FAILURE + \cdots + d_{pres_n} = FAILURE\} \cdot s_{C_{CO}}(d_f) \cdot C_6$
$C_6 = (r_{C_{D1C}}(d_{pcres}) \parallel \cdots \parallel r_{C_{DnC}}(d_{pcres})) \cdot C_7$
$C_7 = \{d_{pcres_1} = SUCCESS \parallel \cdots \parallel d_{pcres_n} = SUCCESS\} \cdot cr \cdot (s_{C_{CD1}}(d_{cr}) \parallel \cdots \parallel s_{C_{CDn}}(d_{cr})) \cdot C_8 + \{d_{pcres_1} = FAILURE + \cdots + d_{pcres_n} = FAILURE\} \cdot s_{C_{CO}}(d_f) \cdot C_8$
$C_8 = (r_{C_{D1C}}(d_{res}) \parallel \cdots \parallel r_{C_{DnC}}(d_{res})) \cdot C_9$
$C_9 = \{d_{res} = COMMIT\} \cdot s_{C_{CO}}(d_s) \cdot C + \{d_{res} = ROLLBACK\} \cdot s_{C_{CO}}(d_f) \cdot C$

The state transitions of Database i described by $APTC_G$ are following.

$D_i = Loc_{D_i} :: r_{C_{DiC}}(d_{pres_i}) \cdot D_{i_2}$
$D_{i_2} = pr_i \cdot D_{i_3}$
$D_{i_3} = s_{C_{DiC}}(d_{pres_i}) \cdot D_{i_4}$
$D_{i_4} = r_{C_{CDi}}(d_{pcr}) \cdot D_{i_5}$
$D_{i_5} = pc_i \cdot D_{i_6}$
$D_{i_6} = s_{C_{DiC}}(d_{pcres_i}) \cdot D_{i_7}$
$D_{i_7} = r_{C_{CDi}}(d_r) \cdot D_{i_8}$
$D_{i_8} = \{d_r = d_{cr}\} \cdot com_i \cdot s_{C_{DiC}}(d_{cres}) \cdot D_i + \{d_r = d_{rr}\} \cdot roll_i \cdot s_{C_{DiC}}(d_{rres}) \cdot D_i$

The sending action and the reading action of the same type data through the same channel can communicate with each other, otherwise, will cause a deadlock δ. We define the following communication functions.

$\gamma(r_{C_{CDi}}(d_{preq_i}), s_{C_{CDi}}(d_{preq_i})) \triangleq c_{C_{CDi}}(d_{preq_i})$
$\gamma(r_{C_{DiC}}(d_{pres_i}), s_{C_{DiC}}(d_{pres_i})) \triangleq c_{C_{DiC}}(d_{pres_i})$
$\gamma(r_{C_{CDi}}(d_{pcr}), s_{C_{CDi}}(d_{pcr})) \triangleq c_{C_{CDi}}(d_{pcr})$
$\gamma(r_{C_{CDi}}(d_{cr}), s_{C_{CDi}}(d_{cr})) \triangleq c_{C_{CDi}}(d_{cr})$
$\gamma(r_{C_{CDi}}(d_{rr}), s_{C_{CDi}}(d_{rr})) \triangleq c_{C_{CDi}}(d_{rr})$
$\gamma(r_{C_{DiC}}(d_{cres}), s_{C_{DiC}}(d_{cres})) \triangleq c_{C_{DiC}}(d_{cres})$
$\gamma(r_{C_{DiC}}(d_{pcres}), s_{C_{DiC}}(d_{pcres})) \triangleq c_{C_{DiC}}(d_{pcres})$

Let all modules be in parallel, then the protocol $C \quad D_1 \quad \cdots \quad D_n$ can be presented by the following process term.

$$\tau_I(\partial_H(\Theta(C \between D_1 \between \cdot \between D_n))) = \tau_I(\partial_H(C \between D_1 \between \cdot \between D_n))$$

where $H = \{r_{CCDi}(d_{preq_i}), s_{CCDi}(d_{preq_i}), r_{CDiC}(d_{pres_i}), s_{CDiC}(d_{pres_i}),$
$r_{CCDi}(d_{pcr}), s_{CCDi}(d_{pcr}),$
$r_{CCDi}(d_{cr}), s_{CCDi}(d_{cr}), r_{CCDi}(d_{rr}), s_{CCDi}(d_{rr}),$
$r_{CDiC}(d_{cres}), s_{CDiC}(d_{cres}), r_{CDiC}(d_{pcres}), s_{CDiC}(d_{pcres})|d \in \Delta\}$ for $1 \leq i \leq n$,
$I = \{c_{CCDi}(d_{preq_i}), c_{CDiC}(d_{pres_i}), c_{CCDi}(d_{pcr}), c_{CCDi}(d_{cr}), c_{CCDi}(d_{rr}),$
$c_{CDiC}(d_{cres}), c_{CDiC}(d_{pcres}), prepare, \{d_{pres_i} = SUCCESS\}, \{d_{pres_i} = FAILURE\},$
$\{d_{pcres_i} = SUCCESS\}, \{d_{pcres_i} = FAILURE\}, pcr, cr, rr, \{d_{res} = COMMIT\}, \{d_{res} = ROLLBACK\},$
$pr_i, pc_i, com_i, roll_i, \{d_r = d_{cr}\}, \{d_r = d_{rr}\}|D \in \Delta\}$ for $1 \leq i \leq n$.

Then we get the following conclusion on the protocol.

Theorem 9.2. *The 3PC protocol in Fig. 9.3 is correct.*

Proof. Based on the above state transitions of the above modules, by use of the algebraic laws of $APTC_G$, we can prove that

$$\tau_I(\partial_H(C \between D_1 \between \cdot \between D_n)) = \sum_{d\in\Delta}(Loc_C :: r_{CCI}(d) \cdot (Loc_C :: s_{CCO}(d_c) + Loc_C :: s_{CCO}(d_f)) \cdot \tau_I(\partial_H(C \between D_1 \between \cdot \between D_n)).$$

For the details of proof, please refer to Section 3.10, and we omit it. □

9.3 Authentication in distributed systems

In the symmetric encryption and decryption, they use only one key k. The inputs of symmetric encryption are the key k and the plaintext D and the output is the ciphertext, so we treat the symmetric encryption as an atomic action denoted $enc_k(D)$. We also use $ENC_k(D)$ to denote the ciphertext output. The inputs of symmetric decryption are the same key k and the ciphertext $ENC_k(D)$ and output is the plaintext D, we also treat the symmetric decryption as an atomic action $dec_k(ENC_k(D))$. And we also use $DEC_k(ENC_k(D))$ to denote the output of the corresponding decryption.

For D is plaintext, it is obvious that $DEC_k(ENC_k(D)) = D$ and $enc_k(D) \leq dec_k(ENC_k(D))$, where $\leq$ is the causal relation; and for D is the ciphertext, $ENC_k(DEC_k(D)) = D$ and $dec_k(D) \leq enc_k(DEC_k(D))$ hold.

In the asymmetric encryption and decryption, they use two keys: the public key pk_s and the private key sk_s generated from the same seed s. The inputs of asymmetric encryption are the key pk_s or sk_s and the plaintext D and the output is the ciphertext, so we treat the asymmetric encryption as an atomic action denoted $enc_{pk_s}(D)$ or $enc_{sk_s}(D)$. We also use $ENC_{pk_s}(D)$ and $ENC_{sk_s}(D)$ to denote the ciphertext outputs. The inputs of asymmetric decryption are the corresponding key sk_s or pk_s and the ciphertext $ENC_{pk_s}(D)$ or $ENC_{sk_s}(D)$, and output is the plaintext D, we also treat the asymmetric decryption as an atomic action $dec_{sk_s}(ENC_{pk_s}(D))$ and $dec_{pk_s}(ENC_{sk_s}(D))$. And we also use $DEC_{sk_s}(ENC_{pk_s}(D))$ and $DEC_{pk_s}(ENC_{sk_s}(D))$ to denote the corresponding decryption outputs.

For D is plaintext, it is obvious that $DEC_{sk_s}(ENC_{pk_s}(D)) = D$ and $DEC_{pk_s}(ENC_{sk_s}(D)) = D$, and $enc_{pk_s}(D) \leq dec_{sk_s}(ENC_{pk_s}(D))$ and $enc_{sk_s}(D) \leq dec_{pk_s}(ENC_{sk_s}(D))$, where $\leq$ is the causal relation; and for D is the ciphertext, $ENC_{sk_s}(DEC_{pk_s}(D)) = D$ and $ENC_{pk_s}(DEC_{sk_s}(D)) = D$, and $dec_{pk_s}(D) \leq enc_{sk_s}(DEC_{pk_s}(D))$ and $dec_{sk_s}(D) \leq enc_{pk_s}(DEC_{sk_s}(D))$.

The hash function is used to generate the digest of the data. The input of the hash function $hash$ is the data D and the output is the digest of the data. We treat the hash function as an atomic action denoted $hash(D)$, and we also use $HASH(D)$ to denote the output digest.

For $D_1 = D_2$, it is obvious that $HASH(D_1) = HASH(D_2)$.

Digital signature uses the private key sk_s to encrypt some data and the public key pk_s to decrypt the encrypted data to implement the so-called non-repudiation. The inputs of sigh function are some data D and the private key sk_s and the output is the signature. We treat the signing function as an atomic action $sign_{sk_s}(D)$, and also use $SIGN_{sk_s}(D)$ to denote the signature. The inputs of the de-sign function are the public key pk_s and the signature $SIGN_{sk_s}(D)$, and the output is the original data D. We also treat the de-sign function as an atomic action $de\text{-}sign_{pk_s}(SIGN_{sk_s}(D))$, and also we use $DE\text{-}SIGN_{pk_s}(SIGN_{sk_s}(D))$ to denote the output of the de-sign action.

It is obvious that $DE\text{-}SIGN_{pk_s}(SIGN_{sk_s}(D)) = D$.

MAC (Message Authentication Code) is used to authenticate data by symmetric keys k and often assumed that k is privately shared only between two principals A and B. The inputs of the MAC function are the key k and some data D, and the output is the MACs. We treat the MAC function as an atomic action $mac_k(D)$, and use $MAC_k(D)$ to denote the output MACs.

The MACs $MAC_k(D)$ are generated by one principal A and with D together sent to the other principal B. The other principal B regenerate the MACs $MAC_k(D)'$, if $MAC_k(D) = MAC_k(D)'$, then the data D are from A.

Random sequence generation is used to generate a random sequence, which may be a symmetric key k, a pair of public key pk_s and sk_s, or a nonce $nonce$ (usually used to resist replay attacks). We treat the random sequence generation function as an atomic action rsg_k for symmetric key generation, rsg_{pk_s,sk_s} for asymmetric key pair generation, and rsg_N for nonce generation, and the corresponding outputs are k, pk_s and sk_s, N respectively.

9.3.1 Protocols based on symmetric cryptosystems

The Wide-Mouth Frog protocol shown in Fig. 9.4 uses symmetric keys for secure communication, that is, the key k_{AB} between Alice and Bob is privately shared to Alice and Bob, Alice, Bob have shared keys with Trent k_{AT} and k_{BT} already.

The process of the protocol is as follows.

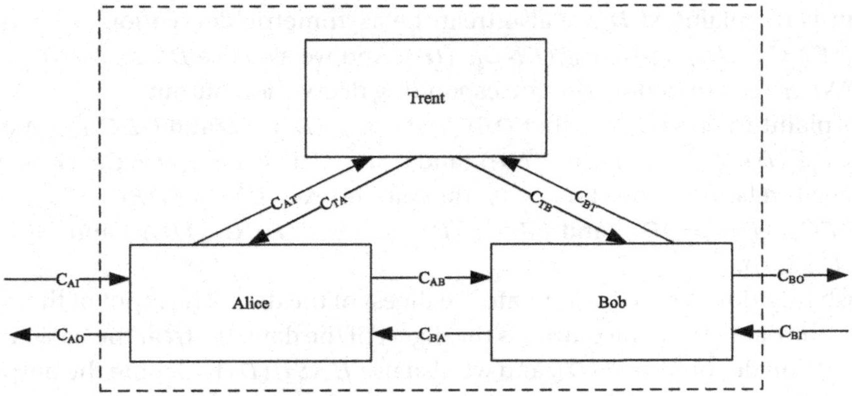

FIGURE 9.4 Wide-Mouth Frog protocol.

1. Alice receives some messages D from the outside through the channel C_{AI} (the corresponding reading action is denoted $r_{C_{AI}}(D)$), if k_{AB} is not established, she generates a random session key k_{AB} through an action $rsg_{k_{AB}}$, encrypts the key request message T_A, B, k_{AB} with k_{AT} through an action $enc_{k_{AT}}(T_A, B, k_{AB})$ where T_A Alice's time stamp, and sends $A, ENC_{k_{AT}}(T_A, B, k_{AB})$ to Trent through the channel C_{AT} (the corresponding sending action is denoted $s_{C_{AT}}(A, ENC_{k_{AT}}(T_A, B, k_{AB})))$;
2. Trent receives the message $A, ENC_{k_{AT}}(T_A, B, k_{AB})$ through the channel C_{AT} (the corresponding reading action is denoted $r_{C_{AT}}(A, ENC_{k_{AT}}(T_A, B, k_{AB})))$, he decrypts the message through an action $dec_{k_{AT}}(ENC_{k_{AT}}(T_A, B, k_{AB}))$. If $isFresh(T_A) = TRUE$ where $isFresh$ is a function to deciding whether a time stamp is fresh, he encrypts T_B, A, k_{AB} with k_{BT} through an action $enc_{k_{BT}}(T_B, A, k_{AB})$, sends $\top$ to Alice through the channel C_{TA} (the corresponding sending action is denoted $s_{C_{TA}}(\top)$) and $ENC_{k_{BT}}(T_B, A, k_{AB})$ to Bob through the channel C_{TB} (the corresponding sending action is denoted $s_{C_{TB}}(ENC_{k_{BT}}(T_B, A, k_{AB})))$; else if $isFresh(T_A) = FLASE$, he sends $\perp$ to Alice and Bob (the corresponding sending actions are denoted $s_{C_{TA}}(\perp)$ and $s_{C_{TB}}(\perp)$ respectively);
3. Bob receives d_{TB} from Trent through the channel C_{TB} (the corresponding reading action is denoted $r_{C_{TB}}(d_{TB})$). If $d_{TB} = \perp$, he sends $\perp$ to Alice through the channel C_{BA} (the corresponding sending action is denoted $s_{C_{BA}}(\perp)$); if $d_{TB} \neq \perp$, he decrypts $ENC_{k_{BT}}(T_B, A, k_{AB})$ through an action $dec_{k_{BT}}(ENC_{k_{BT}}(T_B, A, k_{AB}))$. If $isFresh(T_B) = TRUE$, he gets k_{AB}, and sends $\top$ to Alice (the corresponding sending action is denoted $s_{C_{BA}}(\top)$); if $isFresh(T_B) = FALSE$, he sends $\perp$ to Alice through the channel C_{BA} (the corresponding sending action is denoted $s_{C_{BA}}(\perp)$);
4. Alice receives d_{TA} from Trent through the channel C_{TA} (the corresponding reading action is denoted $r_{C_{TA}}(d_{TA})$), receives d_{BA} from Bob through the channel C_{BA} (the corresponding reading action is denoted $r_{C_{BA}}(d_{BA})$). If $d_{TA} = \top \cdot d_{BA} = \top$, after an encryption processing $enc_{k_{AB}}(T_{A_D}, D)$, Alice sends $ENC_{k_{AB}}(T_{A_D}, D)$ to Bob through the channel C_{AB} (the corresponding sending action is denoted $s_{C_{AB}}(T_{A_D}, ENC_{k_{AB}}(D)))$; else

if $d_{TA} = \perp + d_{BA} = \perp$, Alice sends $\perp$ to the outside through the channel C_{AO} (the corresponding sending action is denoted $s_{C_{AO}}(\perp)$);

5. Bob receives the message $ENC_{k_{AB}}(T_{A_D}, D)$ through the channel C_{AB} (the corresponding reading action is denoted $r_{C_{AB}}(T_{A_D}, ENC_{k_{AB}}(D))$), after a decryption processing $dec_{k_{AB}}(ENC_{k_{AB}}(T_{A_D}, D))$, if $isFresh(T_{A_D}) = TRUE$, he sends D to the outside through the channel C_{BO} (the corresponding sending action is denoted $s_{C_{BO}}(D)$), if $isFresh(T_{A_D}) = FALSE$, he sends $\perp$ to the outside through the channel C_{BO} (the corresponding sending action is denoted $s_{C_{BO}}(\perp)$).

Where $D \in \Delta$, Δ is the set of data.

Alice's state transitions described by $APTC_G$ are as follows.

$A = Loc_A :: \sum_{D\in\Delta} r_{C_{AI}}(D) \cdot A_2$
$A_2 = \{k_{AB} = NULL\} \cdot rsg_{k_{AB}} \cdot A_3 + \{k_{AB} \neq NULL\} \cdot A_7$
$A_3 = enc_{k_{AT}}(T_A, B, k_{AB}) \cdot A_4$
$A_4 = s_{C_{AT}}(A, ENC_{k_{AT}}(T_A, B, k_{AB})) \cdot A_5$
$A_5 = (r_{C_{TA}}(d_{TA}) \parallel r_{C_{BA}}(d_{BA})) \cdot A_6$
$A_6 = \{d_{TA} = \top \cdot d_{BA} = \top\} \cdot A_7 + \{d_{TA} = \perp + d_{BA} = \perp\} \cdot A_9$
$A_7 = enc_{k_{AB}}(T_{A_D}, D) \cdot A_8$
$A_8 = s_{C_{AB}}(T_{A_D}, ENC_{k_{AB}}(D)) \cdot A$
$A_9 = s_{C_{AO}}(\perp) \cdot A$

Bob's state transitions described by $APTC_G$ are as follows.

$B = Loc_B :: \{k_{AB} = NULL\} \cdot B_1 + \{k_{AB} \neq NULL\} \cdot B_5$
$B_1 = r_{C_{TB}}(d_{TB}) \cdot B_2$
$B_2 = \{d_{TB} \neq \perp\} \cdot B_3 + \{d_{TB} = \perp\} \cdot s_{C_{BA}}(\perp) \cdot B_5$
$B_3 = dec_{k_{BT}}(ENC_{k_{BT}}(T_B, A, k_{AB})) \cdot B_4$
$B_4 = \{isFresh(T_B) = TRUE\} \cdot s_{C_{BA}}(\top) \cdot B_5 + \{isFresh(T_B) = FALSE\} \cdot s_{C_{BA}}(\perp) \cdot B_5$
$B_5 = r_{C_{AB}}(T_{A_D}, ENC_{k_{AB}}(D)) \cdot B_6$
$B_6 = dec_{k_{AB}}(ENC_{k_{AB}}(T_{A_D}, D)) \cdot B_7$
$B_7 = \{isFresh(T_{A_D}) = TRUE\} \cdot s_{C_{BO}}(D) \cdot B + \{isFresh(T_{A_D}) = FALSE\} \cdot s_{C_{BO}}(\perp) \cdot B$

Trent's state transitions described by $APTC_G$ are as follows.

$T = Loc_T :: r_{C_{AT}}(A, ENC_{k_{AT}}(T_A, B, k_{AB})) \cdot T_2$
$T_2 = dec_{k_{AT}}(ENC_{k_{AT}}(T_A, B, k_{AB})) \cdot T_3$
$T_3 = \{isFresh(T_A) = TRUE\} \cdot enc_{k_{BT}}(T_B, A, k_{AB}) \cdot (s_{C_{TA}}(\top) \parallel s_{C_{TB}}(ENC_{k_{BT}}(T_B, A, k_{AB})))T$
$+ \{isFresh(T_A) = FALSE\} \cdot (s_{C_{TA}}(\perp) \parallel s_{C_{TB}}(\perp)) \cdot T$

The sending action and the reading action of the same type data through the same channel can communicate with each other, otherwise, will cause a deadlock δ. We define the following communication functions.

$\gamma(r_{C_{AT}}(A, ENC_{k_{AT}}(T_A, B, k_{AB})), s_{C_{AT}}(A, ENC_{k_{AT}}(T_A, B, k_{AB}))) \triangleq c_{C_{AT}}(A, ENC_{k_{AT}}(T_A, B, k_{AB}))$

$\gamma(r_{C_{TA}}(d_{TA}), s_{C_{TA}}(d_{TA})) \triangleq c_{C_{TA}}(d_{TA})$
$\gamma(r_{C_{BA}}(d_{BA}), s_{C_{BA}}(d_{BA})) \triangleq c_{C_{BA}}(d_{BA})$
$\gamma(r_{C_{AB}}(T_{A_D}, ENC_{k_{AB}}(D)), s_{C_{AB}}(T_{A_D}, ENC_{k_{AB}}(D))) \triangleq c_{C_{AB}}(T_{A_D}, ENC_{k_{AB}}(D))$
$\gamma(r_{C_{TB}}(d_{TB}), s_{C_{TB}}(d_{TB})) \triangleq c_{C_{TB}}(d_{TB})$

Let all modules be in parallel, then the protocol $A \quad B \quad T$ can be presented by the following process term.

$$\tau_I(\partial_H(\Theta(A \between B \between T))) = \tau_I(\partial_H(A \between B \between T))$$

where $H = \{r_{C_{AT}}(A, ENC_{k_{AT}}(T_A, B, k_{AB})), s_{C_{AT}}(A, ENC_{k_{AT}}(T_A, B, k_{AB})),$
$r_{C_{TA}}(d_{TA}), s_{C_{TA}}(d_{TA}), r_{C_{BA}}(d_{BA}), s_{C_{BA}}(d_{BA}),$
$r_{C_{AB}}(T_{A_D}, ENC_{k_{AB}}(D)), s_{C_{AB}}(T_{A_D}, ENC_{k_{AB}}(D)), r_{C_{TB}}(d_{TB}), s_{C_{TB}}(d_{TB})|D \in \Delta\},$
$I = \{c_{C_{AT}}(A, ENC_{k_{AT}}(T_A, B, k_{AB})), c_{C_{TA}}(d_{TA}), c_{C_{BA}}(d_{BA}),$
$c_{C_{AB}}(T_{A_D}, ENC_{k_{AB}}(D)), c_{C_{TB}}(d_{TB}), \{k_{AB} = NULL\}, rsg_{k_{AB}},$
$\{k_{AB} \neq NULL\}, enc_{k_{AT}}(T_A, B, k_{AB}), \{d_{TA} = \top \cdot d_{BA} = \top\}, \{d_{TA} = \bot + d_{BA} = \bot\},$
$enc_{k_{AB}}(T_{A_D}, D), \{d_{TB} \neq \bot\}, \{d_{TB} = \bot\}, dec_{k_{BT}}(ENC_{k_{BT}}(T_B, A, k_{AB})),$
$\{isFresh(T_B) = TRUE\}, \{isFresh(T_B) = FALSE\}, dec_{k_{AB}}(ENC_{k_{AB}}(T_{A_D}, D)),$
$\{isFresh(T_{A_D}) = TRUE\}, \{isFresh(T_{A_D}) = FALSE\}, dec_{k_{AT}}(ENC_{k_{AT}}(T_A, B, k_{AB})),$
$\{isFresh(T_A) = TRUE\}, enc_{k_{BT}}(T_B, A, k_{AB}), \{isFresh(T_A) = FALSE\}|D \in \Delta\}.$

Then we get the following conclusion on the protocol.

Theorem 9.3. *The Wide-Mouth Frog protocol in Fig. 9.4 is secure.*

Proof. Based on the above state transitions of the above modules, by use of the algebraic laws of $APTC_G$, we can prove that

$\tau_I(\partial_H(A \between B \between T)) = \sum_{D\in\Delta}(Loc_A :: r_{C_{AI}}(D) \cdot ((Loc_A :: s_{C_{AO}}(\bot) \parallel Loc_B :: s_{C_{BO}}(\bot)) + Loc_B :: s_{C_{BO}}(D))) \cdot \tau_I(\partial_H(A \between B \between T)).$

For the details of proof, please refer to Section 3.10, and we omit it.

That is, the Wide-Mouth Frog protocol in Fig. 9.4 $\tau_I(\partial_H(A \between B \between T))$ can exhibit desired external behaviors:

1. For information leakage, because k_{AT} is privately shared only between Alice and Trent, k_{BT} is privately shared only between Bob and Trent, k_{AB} is privately shared only among Trent;
2. For replay attack, the using of time stamps T_A, T_B, and T_{A_D}, makes that $\tau_I(\partial_H(A \between B \between T)) = \sum_{D\in\Delta}(r_{C_{AI}}(D) \cdot (s_{C_{AO}}(\bot) \parallel s_{C_{BO}}(\bot))) \cdot \tau_I(\partial_H(A \between B \between T))$, it is desired;
3. Without replay attack, the protocol would be $\tau_I(\partial_H(A \between B \between T)) = \sum_{D\in\Delta}(r_{C_{AI}}(D) \cdot s_{C_{BO}}(D)) \cdot \tau_I(\partial_H(A \between B \between T))$, it is desired;
4. For the man-in-the-middle attack, because k_{AT} is privately shared only between Alice and Trent, k_{BT} is privately shared only between Bob and Trent, k_{AB} is privately shared only among Trent, Alice, and Bob. For the modeling of the man-in-the-middle attack, the Wide-Mouth Frog protocol can be against the man-in-the-middle attack;

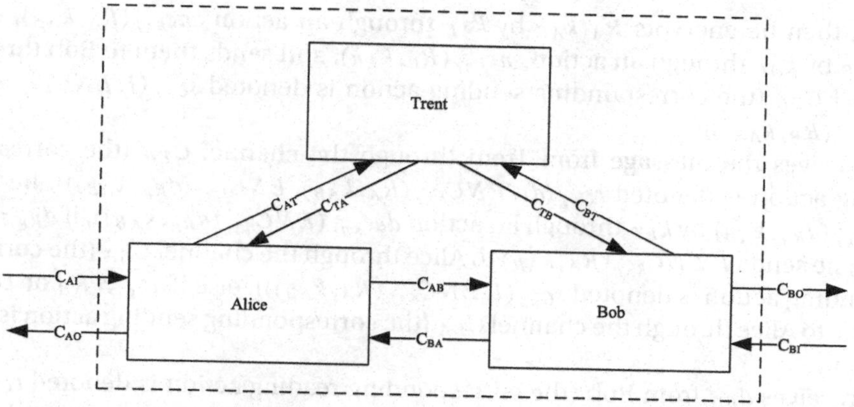

FIGURE 9.5 Otway-Rees protocol.

5. For the unexpected and non-technical leaking of k_{AT}, k_{BT}, k_{AB}, or they being not strong enough, or Trent being dishonest, they are out of the scope of analyses of security protocols;
6. For malicious tampering and transmission errors, they are out of the scope of analyses of security protocols. □

The Otway-Rees protocol shown in Fig. 9.5 uses symmetric keys for secure communication, that is, the key k_{AB} between Alice and Bob is privately shared to Alice and Bob, Alice, Bob have shared keys with Trent k_{AT} and k_{BT} already.

The process of the protocol is as follows.

1. Alice receives some messages D from the outside through the channel C_{AI} (the corresponding reading action is denoted $r_{C_{AI}}(D)$), if k_{AB} is not established, she generates the random numbers I, R_A through the actions rsg_I and rsg_{R_A}, encrypts R_A, I, A, B by k_{AT} through an action $enc_{k_{AT}}(R_A, I, A, B)$, and sends $I, A, B, ENC_{k_{AT}}(R_A, I, A, B)$ to Bob through the channel C_{AB} (the corresponding sending action is denoted $s_{C_{AB}}(I, A, B, ENC_{k_{AT}}(R_A, I, A, B)))$;
2. Bob receives $I, A, B, ENC_{k_{AT}}(R_A, I, A, B)$ from Alice through the channel C_{AB} (the corresponding reading action is denoted $r_{C_{AB}}(I, A, B, ENC_{k_{AT}}(R_A, I, A, B)))$, he generates a random number R_B through an action rsg_{R_B}, encrypts R_B, I, A, B by k_{BT} through an action $enc_{k_{BT}}(R_B, I, A, B)$, and sends $I, A, B, ENC_{k_{AT}}(R_A, I, A, B), ENC_{k_{BT}}(R_B, I, A, B)$ to Trent through the channel C_{BT} (the corresponding sending action is denoted $s_{C_{BT}}(I, A, B, ENC_{k_{AT}}(R_A, I, A, B), ENC_{k_{BT}}(R_B, I, A, B)))$;
3. Trent receives $I, A, B, ENC_{k_{AT}}(R_A, I, A, B), ENC_{k_{BT}}(R_B, I, A, B)$ through the channel C_{BT} (the corresponding reading action is denoted $r_{C_{BT}}(I, A, B, ENC_{k_{AT}}(R_A, I, A, B), ENC_{k_{BT}}(R_B, I, A, B)))$, he decrypts the message $ENC_{k_{AT}}(R_A, I, A, B)$ through an action $dec_{k_{AT}}(ENC_{k_{AT}}(R_A, I, A, B))$ and the message $ENC_{k_{BT}}(R_B, I, A, B)$ through an action $dec_{k_{BT}}(ENC_{k_{BT}}(R_B, I, A, B))$, generates a random session key k_{AB} through an action

$rsg_{k_{AB}}$, then he encrypts R_A, k_{AB} by k_{AT} through an action $enc_{k_{AT}}(R_A, k_{AB})$, encrypts R_B, k_{AB} by k_{BT} through an action $enc_{k_{BT}}(R_B, k_{AB})$, and sends them to Bob through the channel C_{TB} (the corresponding sending action is denoted $s_{C_{TB}}(I, ENC_{k_{AT}}(R_A, k_{AB}), ENC_{k_{BT}}(R_B, k_{AB})))$;

4. Bob receives the message from Trent through the channel C_{TB} (the corresponding reading action is denoted $r_{C_{TB}}(d_I, ENC_{k_{AT}}(R_A, k_{AB}), ENC_{k_{BT}}(d_{R_B}, k_{AB})))$, he decrypts $ENC_{k_{BT}}(d_{R_B}, k_{AB})$ by k_{BT} through an action $dec_{k_{BT}}(ENC_{k_{BT}}(d_{R_B}, k_{AB}))$, if $d_{R_B} = R_B$ and $d_I = I$, he sends $I, ENC_{k_{AT}}(R_A, k_{AB})$ to Alice through the channel C_{BA} (the corresponding sending action is denoted $s_{C_{BA}}(I, ENC_{k_{AB}}(R_A, k_{AB})))$; else if $d_{R_B} \neq R_B$ or $D_I \neq I$, he sends $\perp$ to Alice through the channel C_{BA} (the corresponding sending action is denoted $s_{C_{BA}}(\perp)$);
5. Alice receives d_{BA} from Bob (the corresponding reading action is denoted $r_{C_{BA}}(d_{BA})$), if $d_{BA} = \perp$, she sends $\perp$ to Bob through the channel C_{AB} (the corresponding sending action is denoted $s_{C_{AB}}(\perp)$); else if $d_{BA} \neq \perp$, she decrypts $ENC_{k_{AT}}(R_A, k_{AB})$ by k_{AT} through an action $dec_{k_{AT}}(ENC_{k_{AT}}(R_A, k_{AB}))$, if $d_{R_A} = R_A$ and $d_I = I$, she generates a random number R_D through an action rsg_{R_D}, encrypts R_D, D by k_{AB} through an action $enc_{k_{AB}}(R_D, D)$, and sends it to Bob through the channel C_{AB} (the corresponding sending action is denoted $s_{C_{AB}}(ENC_{k_{AB}}(R_D, D)))$, else if $d_{R_A} \neq R_A$ or $d_I \neq I$, she sends $\perp$ to Bob through the channel C_{AB} (the corresponding sending action is denoted $s_{C_{AB}}(\perp)$);
6. Bob receives d_{AB} from Alice (the corresponding reading action is denoted $r_{C_{AB}}(d_{AB})$), if $d_{AB} = \perp$, he sends $\perp$ to the outside through the channel C_{BO} (the corresponding sending action is denoted $s_{C_{BO}}(\perp)$); else if $d_{AB} \neq \perp$, she decrypts $ENC_{k_{AB}}(R_D, D)$ by k_{AB} through an action $dec_{k_{AB}}(ENC_{k_{AB}}(R_D, D))$, if $isFresh(R_D) = TRUE$, she sends D to the outside through the channel C_{BO} (the corresponding sending action is denoted $s_{C_{BO}}(D)$), else if $isFresh(d_{R_D}) = FALSE$, he sends $\perp$ to the outside through the channel C_{BO} (the corresponding sending action is denoted $s_{C_{BO}}(\perp)$).

Where $D \in \Delta$, Δ is the set of data.

Alice's state transitions described by $APTC_G$ are as follows.

$A = Loc_A :: \sum_{D\in\Delta} r_{C_{AI}}(D) \cdot A_2$

$A_2 = \{k_{AB} = NULL\} \cdot rsg_I \cdot rsg_{R_A} \cdot A_3 + \{k_{AB} \neq NULL\} \cdot A_9$

$A_3 = enc_{k_{AT}}(R_A, I, A, B) \cdot A_4$

$A_4 = s_{C_{AB}}(I, A, B, ENC_{k_{AT}}(R_A, I, A, B)) \cdot A_5$

$A_5 = r_{C_{BA}}(d_{BA}) \cdot A_6$

$A_6 = \{d_{BA} \neq \perp\} \cdot A_7 + \{d_{BA} = \perp\} \cdot s_{C_{AB}}(\perp) \cdot A$

$A_7 = dec_{k_{AT}}(ENC_{k_{AT}}(R_A, k_{AB})) \cdot A_8$

$A_8 = \{d_{R_A} = R_A \cdot d_I = I\} \cdot A_9 + \{d_{R_A} \neq R_A + d_I \neq I\} \cdot A_{12}$

$A_9 = rsg_{R_D} \cdot A_{10}$

$A_{10} = enc_{k_{AB}}(R_D, D) \cdot A_{11}$

$A_{11} = s_{C_{AB}}(ENC_{k_{AB}}(R_D, D)) \cdot A$

$A_{12} = s_{C_{AB}}(\perp) \cdot A$

Bob's state transitions described by $APTC_G$ are as follows.

$$B = Loc_B :: \{k_{AB} = NULL\} \cdot B_1 + \{k_{AB} \neq NULL\} \cdot B_8$$
$$B_1 = r_{C_{AB}}(I, A, B, ENC_{k_{AT}}(R_A, I, A, B)) \cdot B_2$$
$$B_2 = rsg_{R_B} \cdot B_3$$
$$B_3 = enc_{k_{BT}}(R_B, I, A, B) \cdot B_4$$
$$B_4 = s_{C_{BT}}(I, A, B, ENC_{k_{AT}}(R_A, I, A, B), ENC_{k_{BT}}(R_B, I, A, B)) \cdot B_5$$
$$B_5 = r_{C_{TB}}(d_I, ENC_{k_{AT}}(R_A, k_{AB}), ENC_{k_{BT}}(d_{R_B}, k_{AB})) \cdot B_6$$
$$B_6 = dec_{k_{BT}}(ENC_{k_{BT}}(d_{R_B}, k_{AB})) \cdot B_7$$
$$B_7 = \{d_{R_B} = R_B \cdot d_I = I\} \cdot s_{C_{BA}}(I, ENC_{k_{AB}}(R_A, k_{AB})) \cdot B_8 + \{d_{R_B} \neq R_B + d_I \neq I\} \cdot s_{C_{AB}}(\perp) \cdot B_8$$
$$B_8 = r_{C_{AB}}(d_{AB}) \cdot B_9$$
$$B_9 = \{d_{AB} = \perp\} \cdot s_{C_{BO}}(\perp) \cdot B + \{d_{AB} \neq \perp\} \cdot B_{10}$$
$$B_{10} = dec_{k_{AB}}(ENC_{k_{AB}}(R_D, D)) \cdot B_{11}$$
$$B_{11} = \{isFresh(R_D) = TRUE\} \cdot B_{12} + \{isFresh(R_D) = FLASE\} \cdot s_{C_{BO}}(\perp) \cdot B$$
$$B_{12} = s_{C_{BO}}(D) \cdot B$$

Trent's state transitions described by $APTC_G$ are as follows.

$$T = Loc_T :: r_{C_{BT}}(I, A, B, ENC_{k_{AT}}(R_A, I, A, B), ENC_{k_{BT}}(R_B, I, A, B)) \cdot T_2$$
$$T_2 = dec_{k_{AT}}(ENC_{k_{AT}}(R_A, I, A, B)) \cdot T_3$$
$$T_3 = dec_{k_{BT}}(ENC_{k_{BT}}(R_B, I, A, B)) \cdot T_4$$
$$T_4 = rsg_{k_{AB}} \cdot T_5$$
$$T_5 = enc_{k_{AT}}(R_A, k_{AB}) \cdot T_6$$
$$T_6 = enc_{k_{BT}}(R_B, k_{AB}) \cdot T_7$$
$$T_7 = s_{C_{TB}}(I, ENC_{k_{AT}}(R_A, k_{AB}), ENC_{k_{BT}}(R_B, k_{AB})) \cdot T$$

The sending action and the reading action of the same type data through the same channel can communicate with each other, otherwise, will cause a deadlock δ. We define the following communication functions.

$$\gamma(r_{C_{AB}}(I, A, B, ENC_{k_{AT}}(R_A, I, A, B)), s_{C_{AB}}(I, A, B, ENC_{k_{AT}}(R_A, I, A, B)))$$
$$\triangleq c_{C_{AB}}(I, A, B, ENC_{k_{AT}}(R_A, I, A, B))$$
$$\gamma(r_{C_{BA}}(d_{BA}), s_{C_{BA}}(d_{BA})) \triangleq c_{C_{BA}}(d_{BA})$$
$$\gamma(r_{C_{BT}}(I, A, B, ENC_{k_{AT}}(R_A, I, A, B), ENC_{k_{BT}}(R_B, I, A, B)),$$
$$s_{C_{BT}}(I, A, B, ENC_{k_{AT}}(R_A, I, A, B), ENC_{k_{BT}}(R_B, I, A, B)))$$
$$\triangleq c_{C_{BT}}(I, A, B, ENC_{k_{AT}}(R_A, I, A, B), ENC_{k_{BT}}(R_B, I, A, B))$$
$$\gamma(r_{C_{TB}}(d_I, ENC_{k_{AT}}(R_A, k_{AB}), ENC_{k_{BT}}(d_{R_B}, k_{AB})),$$
$$s_{C_{TB}}(d_I, ENC_{k_{AT}}(R_A, k_{AB}), ENC_{k_{BT}}(d_{R_B}, k_{AB})))$$
$$\triangleq c_{C_{TB}}(d_I, ENC_{k_{AT}}(R_A, k_{AB}), ENC_{k_{BT}}(d_{R_B}, k_{AB}))$$
$$\gamma(r_{C_{AB}}(d_{AB}), s_{C_{AB}}(d_{AB})) \triangleq c_{C_{AB}}(d_{AB})$$

Let all modules be in parallel, then the protocol $A \quad B \quad T$ can be presented by the following process term.

$$\tau_I(\partial_H(\Theta(A \between B \between T))) = \tau_I(\partial_H(A \between B \between T))$$

where $H = \{r_{C_{AB}}(I, A, B, ENC_{k_{AT}}(R_A, I, A, B)), s_{C_{AB}}(I, A, B, ENC_{k_{AT}}(R_A, I, A, B)),$ $r_{C_{BA}}(d_{BA}), s_{C_{BA}}(d_{BA}), r_{C_{AB}}(d_{AB}), s_{C_{AB}}(d_{AB}),$

$r_{C_{BT}}(I, A, B, ENC_{k_{AT}}(R_A, I, A, B), ENC_{k_{BT}}(R_B, I, A, B)),$
$s_{C_{BT}}(I, A, B, ENC_{k_{AT}}(R_A, I, A, B), ENC_{k_{BT}}(R_B, I, A, B)),$
$r_{C_{TB}}(d_I, ENC_{k_{AT}}(R_A, k_{AB}), ENC_{k_{BT}}(d_{R_B}, k_{AB})),$
$s_{C_{TB}}(d_I, ENC_{k_{AT}}(R_A, k_{AB}), ENC_{k_{BT}}(d_{R_B}, k_{AB}))|D \in \Delta\},$
$I = \{c_{C_{AB}}(I, A, B, ENC_{k_{AT}}(R_A, I, A, B)), c_{C_{BA}}(d_{BA}), c_{C_{AB}}(d_{AB}),$
$c_{C_{BT}}(I, A, B, ENC_{k_{AT}}(R_A, I, A, B), ENC_{k_{BT}}(R_B, I, A, B)),$
$c_{C_{TB}}(d_I, ENC_{k_{AT}}(R_A, k_{AB}), ENC_{k_{BT}}(d_{R_B}, k_{AB})),$
$\{k_{AB} = NULL\}, rsg_I, rsg_{R_A}, \{k_{AB} \neq NULL\}, enc_{k_{AT}}(R_A, I, A, B),$
$\{d_{BA} \neq \perp\}, \{d_{BA} = \perp\}, dec_{k_{AT}}(ENC_{k_{AT}}(R_A, k_{AB})),$
$\{d_{R_A} = R_A \cdot d_I = I\}, \{d_{R_A} \neq R_A + d_I \neq I\}, rsg_{R_D},$
$enc_{k_{AB}}(R_D, D), rsg_{R_B}, enc_{k_{BT}}(R_B, I, A, B),$
$dec_{k_{BT}}(ENC_{k_{BT}}(d_{R_B}, k_{AB})), \{d_{R_B} = R_B \cdot d_I = I\},$
$\{d_{R_B} \neq R_B + d_I \neq I\}, \{d_{AB} = \perp\}, \{d_{AB} \neq \perp\},$
$dec_{k_{AB}}(ENC_{k_{AB}}(R_D, D)), \{isFresh(R_D) = TRUE\}, \{isFresh(R_D) = FALSE\},$
$dec_{k_{AT}}(ENC_{k_{AT}}(R_A, I, A, B)), dec_{k_{BT}}(ENC_{k_{BT}}(R_B, I, A, B)),$
$rsg_{k_{AB}}, enc_{k_{AT}}(R_A, k_{AB}), enc_{k_{BT}}(R_B, k_{AB})|D \in \Delta\}.$

Then we get the following conclusion on the protocol.

Theorem 9.4. *The Otway-Rees protocol in Fig. 9.5 is secure.*

Proof. Based on the above state transitions of the above modules, by use of the algebraic laws of $APTC_G$, we can prove that

$\tau_I(\partial_H(A \between B \between T)) = \sum_{D\in\Delta}(Loc_A :: r_{C_{AI}}(D) \cdot (Loc_B :: s_{C_{BO}}(\perp) + Loc_B :: s_{C_{BO}}(D))) \cdot \tau_I(\partial_H(A \between B \between T)).$

For the details of proof, please refer to Section 3.10, and we omit it.

That is, the Otway-Rees protocol in Fig. 9.5 $\tau_I(\partial_H(A \between B \between T))$ can exhibit desired external behaviors:

1. For information leakage, because k_{AT} is privately shared only between Alice and Trent, k_{BT} is privately shared only between Bob and Trent, k_{AB} is privately shared only among Trent, Alice, and Bob;
2. For the man-in-the-middle attack, because k_{AT} is privately shared only between Alice and Trent, k_{BT} is privately shared only between Bob and Trent, k_{AB} is privately shared only among Trent, Alice, and Bob, and the use of the random numbers I, R_A, and R_B, the protocol would be $\tau_I(\partial_H(A \between B \between T)) = \sum_{D\in\Delta}(r_{C_{AI}}(D) \cdot s_{C_{BO}}(\perp)) \cdot \tau_I(\partial_H(A \between B \between T))$, it is desired, the Otway-Rees protocol can be against the man-in-the-middle attack;
3. For replay attack, the using of the random numbers I, R_A, and R_B, makes that $\tau_I(\partial_H(A \between B \between T)) = \sum_{D\in\Delta}(r_{C_{AI}}(D) \cdot s_{C_{BO}}(\perp)) \cdot \tau_I(\partial_H(A \between B \between T))$, it is desired;
4. Without man-in-the-middle and replay attack, the protocol would be $\tau_I(\partial_H(A \between B \between T)) = \sum_{D\in\Delta}(r_{C_{AI}}(D) \cdot s_{C_{BO}}(D)) \cdot \tau_I(\partial_H(A \between B \between T))$, it is desired;
5. For the unexpected and non-technical leaking of k_{AT}, k_{BT}, k_{AB}, or they being not strong enough, or Trent being dishonest, they are out of the scope of analyses of security protocols;

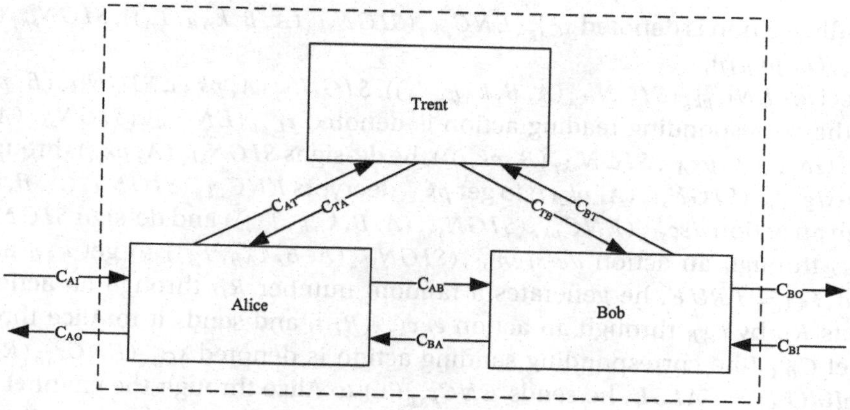

FIGURE 9.6 Denning-Sacco protocol.

6. For malicious tampering and transmission errors, they are out of the scope of analyses of security protocols. □

9.3.2 Protocols based on asymmetric cryptosystems

The Denning-Sacco protocol shown in Fig. 9.6 uses asymmetric keys and symmetric keys for secure communication, that is, the key k_{AB} between Alice and Bob is privately shared to Alice and Bob, Alice's, Bob's, and Trent's public keys pk_A, pk_B, and pk_T can be publicly gotten.

The process of the protocol is as follows.

1. Alice receives some messages D from the outside through the channel C_{AI} (the corresponding reading action is denoted $r_{C_{AI}}(D)$), if k_{AB} is not established, she sends A, B to Trent through the channel C_{AT} (the corresponding sending action is denoted $s_{C_{AT}}(A, B)$);
2. Trent receives A, B through the channel C_{AT} (the corresponding reading action is denoted $r_{C_{AT}}(A, B)$), he signs Alice's and Bob's public keys pk_A and pk_B through the actions $sign_{sk_T}(A, pk_A)$ and $sign_{sk_T}(B, pk_B)$, and sends the signatures to Alice through the channel C_{TA} (the corresponding sending action is denoted $s_{C_{TA}}(SIGN_{sk_T}(A, pk_A), SIGN_{sk_T}(B, pk_B)))$;
3. Alice receives the message from Trent through the channel C_{TA} (the corresponding reading action is denoted $r_{C_{TA}}(SIGN_{sk_T}(A, pk_A), SIGN_{sk_T}(B, pk_B)))$, she de-signs $SIGN_{sk_T}(B, pk_B)$ through an action $de\text{-}sign_{pk_T}(SIGN_{sk_T}(B, pk_B))$ to get pk_B, generates a random session key k_{AB} through an action $rsg_{k_{AB}}$, signs A, B, k_{AB}, T_A through an action $sign_{sk_A}(A, B, k_{AB}, T_A)$, and encrypts the signature by pk_B through an action $enc_{pk_B}(SIGN_{sk_A}(A, B, k_{AB}, T_A))$, then sends $ENC_{pk_B}(SIGN_{sk_A}(A, B, k_{AB}, T_A))$, $SIGN_{sk_T}(A, pk_A)$, $SIGN_{sk_T}(B, pk_B)$ to Bob through the channel C_{AB} (the correspond-

ing sending action is denoted $s_{C_{AB}}(ENC_{pk_B}(SIGN_{sk_A}(A, B, k_{AB}, T_A)), SIGN_{sk_T}(A, pk_A), SIGN_{sk_T}(B, pk_B)))$;

4. Bob receives $ENC_{pk_B}(SIGN_{sk_A}(A, B, k_{AB}, T_A)), SIGN_{sk_T}(A, pk_A), SIGN_{sk_T}(B, pk_B)$ from Alice (the corresponding reading action is denoted $r_{C_{AB}}(ENC_{pk_B}(SIGN_{sk_A}(A, B, k_{AB}, T_A)), SIGN_{sk_T}(A, pk_A), SIGN_{sk_T}(B, pk_B)))$, he de-signs $SIGN_{sk_T}(A, pk_A)$ through an action $de\text{-}sign_{pk_T}(SIGN_{sk_T}(A, pk_A))$ to get pk_A, decrypts $ENC_{pk_B}(SIGN_{sk_A}(A, B, k_{AB}, T_A))$ through an action $dec_{sk_B}(ENC_{pk_B}(SIGN_{sk_A}(A, B, k_{AB}, T_A)))$ and de-sign $SIGN_{sk_A}(A, B, k_{AB}, T_A)$ through an action $de\text{-}sign_{pk_A}(SIGN_{sk_A}(A, B, k_{AB}, T_A))$ to get k_{AB} and T_A, if $isValid(T_A) = TRUE$, he generates a random number R_D through an action rsg_{R_D}, encrypts R_D by k_{AB} through an action $enc_{k_{AB}}(R_D)$, and sends it to Alice through the channel C_{BA} (the corresponding sending action is denoted $s_{C_{BA}}(ENC_{k_{AB}}(R_D)))$, else if $isValid(T_A) = FALSE$, he sends $ENC_{k_{AB}}(\perp)$ to Alice through the channel C_{BA} (the corresponding sending action is denoted $s_{C_{BA}}(ENC_{k_{AB}}(\perp)))$;
5. Alice receives $ENC_{k_{AB}}(d_{BA})$ from Bob (the corresponding reading action is denoted $r_{C_{BA}}(ENC_{k_{AB}}(d_{BA})))$, if $d_{BA} = \perp$, she sends $ENC_{k_{AB}}(\perp)$ to Bob through the channel C_{AB} (the corresponding sending action is denoted $s_{C_{AB}}(ENC_{k_{AB}}(\perp)))$; else if $d_{BA} \neq \perp$, if $isFresh(d_{BA}) = TRUE$, she generates a random number R'_D through an action $rsg_{R'_D}$, encrypts R'_D, D by k_{AB} through an action $enc_{k_{AB}}(R'_D, D)$, and sends it to Bob through the channel C_{AB} (the corresponding sending action is denoted $s_{C_{AB}}(ENC_{k_{AB}}(R'_D, D)))$, else if $isFresh(d_{BA}) = FALSE$, he sends $ENC_{k_{AB}}(\perp)$ to Bob through the channel C_{AB} (the corresponding sending action is denoted $s_{C_{AB}}(ENC_{k_{AB}}(\perp)))$;
6. Bob receives $ENC_{k_{AB}}(d'_{AB})$ from Alice (the corresponding reading action is denoted $r_{C_{AB}}(ENC_{k_{AB}}(d'_{AB})))$, if $d'_{AB} = \perp$, he sends $\perp$ to the outside through the channel C_{BO} (the corresponding sending action is denoted $s_{C_{BO}}(\perp))$; else if $d'_{AB} \neq \perp$, if $isFresh(d_{R'_D}) = TRUE$, she sends D to the outside through the channel C_{BO} (the corresponding sending action is denoted $s_{C_{BO}}(D))$, else if $isFresh(d'_{R_D}) = FALSE$, he sends $\perp$ to the outside through the channel C_{BO} (the corresponding sending action is denoted $s_{C_{BO}}(\perp))$.

Where $D \in \Delta$, Δ is the set of data.

Alice's state transitions described by $APTC_G$ are as follows.

$$A = Loc_A :: \sum_{D\in\Delta} r_{C_{AI}}(D) \cdot A_2$$
$$A_2 = \{k_{AB} = NULL\} \cdot A_3 + \{k_{AB} \neq NULL\} \cdot A_{13}$$
$$A_3 = s_{C_{AT}}(A, B) \cdot A_4$$
$$A_4 = r_{C_{TA}}(SIGN_{sk_T}(A, pk_A), SIGN_{sk_T}(B, pk_B)) \cdot A_5$$
$$A_5 = de\text{-}sign_{pk_T}(SIGN_{sk_T}(B, pk_B)) \cdot A_6$$
$$A_6 = rsg_{k_{AB}} \cdot A_7$$
$$A_7 = sign_{sk_A}(A, B, k_{AB}, T_A) \cdot A_8$$
$$A_8 = enc_{pk_B}(SIGN_{sk_A}(A, B, k_{AB}, T_A)) \cdot A_9$$
$$A_9 = s_{C_{AB}}(ENC_{pk_B}(SIGN_{sk_A}(A, B, k_{AB}, T_A)), SIGN_{sk_T}(A, pk_A), SIGN_{sk_T}(B, pk_B)) \cdot A_{10}$$
$$A_{10} = r_{C_{BA}}(ENC_{k_{AB}}(d_{BA})) \cdot A_{11}$$
$$A_{11} = \{d_{BA} \neq \perp\} \cdot A_{12} + \{d_{BA} = \perp\} \cdot s_{C_{AB}}(ENC_{k_{AB}}(\perp)) \cdot A$$
$$A_{12} = \{isFresh(d_{BA}) = TRUE\} \cdot A_{13} + \{isFresh(d_{BA}) = FALSE\} \cdot s_{C_{AB}}(ENC_{k_{AB}}(\perp)) \cdot A$$

$$A_{13} = rsg_{R'_D} \cdot A_{14}$$
$$A_{14} = enc_{k_{AB}}(R'_D, D) \cdot A_{15}$$
$$A_{15} = s_{C_{AB}}(ENC_{k_{AB}}(R'_D, D)) \cdot A$$

Bob's state transitions described by $APTC_G$ are as follows.

$$B = Loc_B :: \{k_{AB} = NULL\} \cdot B_1 + \{k_{AB} \neq NULL\} \cdot B_9$$
$$B_1 = r_{C_{AB}}(ENC_{pk_B}(SIGN_{sk_A}(A, B, k_{AB}, T_A)), SIGN_{sk_T}(A, pk_A), SIGN_{sk_T}(B, pk_B)) \cdot B_2$$
$$B_2 = de\text{-}sign_{pk_T}(SIGN_{sk_T}(A, pk_A)) \cdot B_3$$
$$B_3 = dec_{sk_B}(ENC_{pk_B}(SIGN_{sk_A}(A, B, k_{AB}, T_A))) \cdot B_4$$
$$B_4 = de\text{-}sign_{pk_A}(SIGN_{sk_A}(A, B, k_{AB}, T_A)) \cdot B_5$$
$$B_5 = \{isValid(T_A) = TRUE\} \cdot B_6 + \{isValid(T_A) = FALSE\} \cdot s_{C_{BA}}(ENC_{k_{AB}}(\bot)) \cdot B_9$$
$$B_6 = rsg_{R_D} \cdot B_7$$
$$B_7 = enc_{k_{AB}}(R_D) \cdot B_8$$
$$B_8 = s_{C_{BA}}(ENC_{k_{AB}}(d_{BA})) \cdot B_9$$
$$B_9 = r_{C_{AB}}(ENC_{k_{AB}}(d'_{AB})) \cdot B_{10}$$
$$B_{10} = dec_{k_{AB}}(ENC_{k_{AB}}(d'_{AB})) \cdot B_{11}$$
$$B_{11} = \{d'_{AB} = \bot\} \cdot s_{C_{BO}}(\bot) \cdot B + \{d'_{AB} \neq \bot\} \cdot B_{12}$$
$$B_{12} = \{isFresh(d_{R'_D}) = FLASE\} \cdot s_{C_{BO}}(\bot)B + \{isFresh(d_{R'_D}) = TRUE\} \cdot B_{13}$$
$$B_{13} = s_{C_{BO}}(D) \cdot B$$

Trent's state transitions described by $APTC_G$ are as follows.

$$T = Loc_T :: r_{C_{AT}}(A, B) \cdot T_2$$
$$T_2 = sign_{sk_T}(A, pk_A) \cdot T_3$$
$$T_3 = sign_{sk_T}(B, pk_B) \cdot T_4$$
$$T_4 = s_{C_{TA}}(SIGN_{sk_T}(A, pk_A), SIGN_{sk_T}(B, pk_B)) \cdot T$$

The sending action and the reading action of the same type data through the same channel can communicate with each other, otherwise, will cause a deadlock δ. We define the following communication functions.

$$\gamma(r_{C_{AT}}(A, B), s_{C_{AT}}(A, B)) \triangleq c_{C_{AT}}(A, B)$$
$$\gamma(r_{C_{TA}}(SIGN_{sk_T}(A, pk_A), SIGN_{sk_T}(B, pk_B)), s_{C_{TA}}(SIGN_{sk_T}(A, pk_A), SIGN_{sk_T}(B, pk_B))) \triangleq c_{C_{TA}}(SIGN_{sk_T}(A, pk_A), SIGN_{sk_T}(B, pk_B))$$
$$\gamma(r_{C_{AB}}(ENC_{pk_B}(SIGN_{sk_A}(A, B, k_{AB}, T_A)), SIGN_{sk_T}(A, pk_A), SIGN_{sk_T}(B, pk_B)), s_{C_{AB}}(ENC_{pk_B}(SIGN_{sk_A}(A, B, k_{AB}, T_A)), SIGN_{sk_T}(A, pk_A), SIGN_{sk_T}(B, pk_B))) \triangleq c_{C_{AB}}(ENC_{pk_B}(SIGN_{sk_A}(A, B, k_{AB}, T_A)), SIGN_{sk_T}(A, pk_A), SIGN_{sk_T}(B, pk_B))$$
$$\gamma(r_{C_{BA}}(ENC_{k_{AB}}(d_{BA})), s_{C_{BA}}(ENC_{k_{AB}}(d_{BA}))) \triangleq c_{C_{BA}}(ENC_{k_{AB}}(d_{BA}))$$
$$\gamma(r_{C_{AB}}(ENC_{k_{AB}}(d'_{AB})), s_{C_{AB}}(ENC_{k_{AB}}(d'_{AB}))) \triangleq c_{C_{AB}}(ENC_{k_{AB}}(d'_{AB}))$$

Let all modules be in parallel, then the protocol $A \quad B \quad T$ can be presented by the following process term.

$$\tau_I(\partial_H(\Theta(A \between B \between T))) = \tau_I(\partial_H(A \between B \between T))$$

where $H=\{r_{C_{AT}}(A,B), s_{C_{AT}}(A,B), r_{C_{BA}}(ENC_{k_{AB}}(d_{BA})), s_{C_{BA}}(ENC_{k_{AB}}(d_{BA})),$
$r_{C_{AB}}(ENC_{k_{AB}}(d'_{AB})), s_{C_{AB}}(ENC_{k_{AB}}(d'_{AB})),$
$r_{C_{TA}}(SIGN_{sk_T}(A,pk_A), SIGN_{sk_T}(B,pk_B)), s_{C_{TA}}(SIGN_{sk_T}(A,pk_A), SIGN_{sk_T}(B,pk_B)),$
$r_{C_{AB}}(ENC_{pk_B}(SIGN_{sk_A}(A,B,k_{AB},T_A)), SIGN_{sk_T}(A,pk_A), SIGN_{sk_T}(B,pk_B)),$
$s_{C_{AB}}(ENC_{pk_B}(SIGN_{sk_A}(A,B,k_{AB},T_A)), SIGN_{sk_T}(A,pk_A), SIGN_{sk_T}(B,pk_B))|D\in\Delta\},$

$I=\{c_{C_{AT}}(A,B), c_{C_{BA}}(ENC_{k_{AB}}(d_{BA})), c_{C_{AB}}(ENC_{k_{AB}}(d'_{AB})),$
$c_{C_{TA}}(SIGN_{sk_T}(A,pk_A), SIGN_{sk_T}(B,pk_B)),$
$c_{C_{AB}}(ENC_{pk_B}(SIGN_{sk_A}(A,B,k_{AB},T_A)), SIGN_{sk_T}(A,pk_A), SIGN_{sk_T}(B,pk_B)),$
$\{k_{AB}=NULL\}, \{k_{AB}\neq NULL\}, de\text{-}sign_{pk_T}(SIGN_{sk_T}(B,pk_B)),$
$rsg_{k_{AB}}, sign_{sk_A}(A,B,k_{AB},T_A), enc_{pk_B}(SIGN_{sk_A}(A,B,k_{AB},T_A)),$
$\{isFresh(d_{BA})=TRUE\}, \{isFresh(d_{BA})=FALSE\}, \{d_{BA}\neq\bot\}, \{d_{BA}=\bot\},$
$rsg_{R'_D}, enc_{k_{AB}}(R'_D, D), de\text{-}sign_{pk_T}(SIGN_{sk_T}(A,pk_A)),$
$dec_{sk_B}(ENC_{pk_B}(SIGN_{sk_A}(A,B,k_{AB},T_A))), de\text{-}sign_{pk_A}(SIGN_{sk_A}(A,B,k_{AB},T_A)),$
$\{isValid(T_A)=TRUE\}, \{isValid(T_A)=FALSE\}, rsg_{R_D}, enc_{k_{AB}}(R_D),$
$dec_{k_{AB}}(ENC_{k_{AB}}(d'_{AB})), \{d'_{AB}=\bot\}, \{d'_{AB}\neq\bot\},$
$\{isFresh(d_{R'_D})=TRUE\}, \{isFresh(d_{R'_D})=FLASE\}, sign_{sk_T}(A,pk_A), sign_{sk_T}(B,pk_B)|D\in\Delta\}.$

Then we get the following conclusion on the protocol.

Theorem 9.5. *The Denning-Sacco protocol in Fig. 9.6 is secure.*

Proof. Based on the above state transitions of the above modules, by use of the algebraic laws of $APTC_G$, we can prove that

$$\tau_I(\partial_H(A\between B\between T))=\sum_{D\in\Delta}(Loc_A::r_{C_{AI}}(D)\cdot(Loc_B::s_{C_{BO}}(\bot)+Loc_B::s_{C_{BO}}(D)))\cdot\tau_I(\partial_H(A\between B\between T)).$$

For the details of proof, please refer to Section 3.10, and we omit it.

That is, the Denning-Sacco protocol in Fig. 9.6 $\tau_I(\partial_H(A\between B\between T))$ can exhibit desired external behaviors:

1. For the man-in-the-middle attack, because pk_A and pk_B are signed by Trent, the protocol would be $\tau_I(\partial_H(A\between B\between T))=\sum_{D\in\Delta}(r_{C_{AI}}(D)\cdot s_{C_{BO}}(\bot))\cdot\tau_I(\partial_H(A\between B\between T))$, it is desired, the Denning-Sacco protocol can be against the man-in-the-middle attack;
2. For replay attack, the using of the time stamp T_A, random numbers R_D and R'_D, makes that $\tau_I(\partial_H(A\between B\between T))=\sum_{D\in\Delta}(r_{C_{AI}}(D)\cdot s_{C_{BO}}(\bot))\cdot\tau_I(\partial_H(A\between B\between T))$, it is desired;
3. Without man-in-the-middle and replay attack, the protocol would be $\tau_I(\partial_H(A\between B\between T))=\sum_{D\in\Delta}(r_{C_{AI}}(D)\cdot s_{C_{BO}}(D))\cdot\tau_I(\partial_H(A\between B\between T))$, it is desired;
4. For the unexpected and non-technical leaking of sk_A, sk_B, k_{AB}, or they being not strong enough, or Trent being dishonest, they are out of the scope of analyses of security protocols;
5. For malicious tampering and transmission errors, they are out of the scope of analyses of security protocols. □

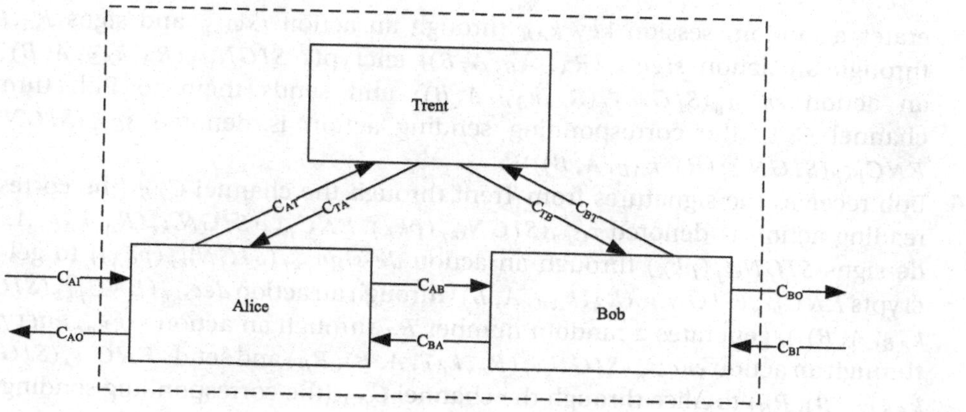

FIGURE 9.7 Woo-Lam protocol.

The Woo-Lam protocol shown in Fig. 9.7 uses asymmetric keys and symmetric keys for secure communication, that is, the key k_{AB} between Alice and Bob is privately shared to Alice and Bob, Alice's, Bob's, and Trent's public keys pk_A, pk_B, and pk_T can be publicly gotten.

The process of the protocol is as follows.

1. Alice receives some messages D from the outside through the channel C_{AI} (the corresponding reading action is denoted $r_{C_{AI}}(D)$), if k_{AB} is not established, she sends A, B to Trent through the channel C_{AT} (the corresponding sending action is denoted $s_{C_{AT}}(A, B)$);
2. Trent receives A, B through the channel C_{AT} (the corresponding reading action is denoted $r_{C_{AT}}(A, B)$), he signs Bob's public key pk_B through the action $sign_{sk_T}(pk_B)$, and sends the signature to Alice through the channel C_{TA} (the corresponding sending action is denoted $s_{C_{TA}}(SIGN_{sk_T}(pk_B))$);
3. Alice receives the message from Trent through the channel C_{TA} (the corresponding reading action is denoted $r_{C_{TA}}(SIGN_{sk_T}(pk_B))$), she de-signs $SIGN_{sk_T}(pk_B)$ through an action $de\text{-}sign_{pk_T}(SIGN_{sk_T}(pk_B))$ to get pk_B, generates a random number R_A through an action rsg_{R_A} and encrypts A, R_A by pk_B through an action $enc_{pk_B}(A, R_A)$, and sends $ENC_{pk_B}(A, R_A)$ to Bob through the channel C_{AB} (the corresponding sending action is denoted $s_{C_{AB}}(ENC_{pk_B}(A, R_A))$);
4. Bob receives $ENC_{pk_B}(A, R_A)$ from Alice (the corresponding reading action is denoted $r_{C_{AB}}(ENC_{pk_B}(A, R_A))$), he decrypts $ENC_{pk_B}(A, R_A)$ through an action $dec_{sk_B}(ENC_{pk_B}(A, R_A))$ to get A and R_A, encrypts R_A by pk_T through an action $enc_{pk_T}(R_A)$, then sends $A, B, ENC_{pk_T}(R_A)$ to Trent through the channel C_{BT} (the corresponding sending action is denoted $s_{C_{BT}}(A, B, ENC_{pk_T}(R_A))$);
5. Trent receives $A, B, ENC_{pk_T}(R_A)$ from Bob through the channel C_{BT} (the corresponding reading action is denoted $r_{C_{BT}}(A, B, ENC_{pk_T}(R_A))$), he decrypts the message through an action $dec_{sk_T}(ENC_{pk_T}(R_A))$, signs pk_A through an action $sign_{sk_T}(pk_A)$, gen-

erates a random session key k_{AB} through an action $rsg_{k_{AB}}$ and signs R_A, k_{AB}, A, B through an action $sign_{sk_T}(R_A, k_{AB}, A, B)$, encrypts $SIGN_{sk_T}(R_A, k_{AB}, A, B)$ through an action $enc_{pk_B}(SIGN_{sk_T}(R_A, k_{AB}, A, B))$ and sends them to Bob through the channel C_{TB} (the corresponding sending action is denoted $s_{C_{TB}}(SIGN_{sk_T}(pk_A), ENC_{pk_B}(SIGN_{sk_T}(R_A, k_{AB}, A, B))))$;

6. Bob receives the signatures from Trent through the channel C_{TB} (the corresponding reading action is denoted $r_{C_{TB}}(SIGN_{sk_T}(pk_A), ENC_{pk_B}(SIGN_{sk_T}(R_A, k_{AB}, A, B))))$, he de-signs $SIGN_{sk_T}(pk_A)$ through an action $de\text{-}sign_{pk_T}(SIGN_{sk_T}(pk_A))$ to get pk_A, decrypts $ENC_{pk_B}(SIGN_{sk_T}(R_A, k_{AB}, A, B))$ through an action $dec_{sk_B}(ENC_{pk_B}(SIGN_{sk_T}(R_A, k_{AB}, A, B)))$, generates a random number R_B through an action rsg_{R_B}, encrypts them through an action $enc_{pk_A}(SIGN_{sk_T}(R_A, k_{AB}, A, B), R_B)$ and sends $ENC_{pk_A}(SIGN_{sk_T}(R_A, k_{AB}, A, B), R_B)$ to Alice through the channel C_{BA} (the corresponding sending action is denoted $s_{C_{BA}}(ENC_{pk_A}(SIGN_{sk_T}(R_A, k_{AB}, A, B), R_B)))$;
7. Alice receives $ENC_{pk_A}(SIGN_{sk_T}(d_{R_A}, k_{AB}, A, B), R_B)$ from Bob (the corresponding reading action is denoted $r_{C_{BA}}(ENC_{pk_A}(SIGN_{sk_T}(d_{R_A}, k_{AB}, A, B), R_B)))$, she decrypts the message through an action $dec_{sk_A}(ENC_{pk_A}(SIGN_{sk_T}(R_A, k_{AB}, A, B), R_B))$, de-sign $SIGN_{sk_T}(R_A, k_{AB}, A, B)$ through an action $de\text{-}sign_{pk_T}(SIGN_{sk_T}(R_A, k_{AB}, A, B))$, if $d_{R_A} \neq R_A$, she sends $ENC_{k_{AB}}(\bot)$ to Bob through the channel C_{AB} (the corresponding sending action is denoted $s_{C_{AB}}(ENC_{k_{AB}}(\bot)))$; else if $d_{R_A} = R_A$, encrypts R_B, D by k_{AB} through an action $enc_{k_{AB}}(R_B, D)$, and sends it to Bob through the channel C_{AB} (the corresponding sending action is denoted $s_{C_{AB}}(ENC_{k_{AB}}(R_B, D)))$;
8. Bob receives $ENC_{k_{AB}}(d_{AB})$ from Alice (the corresponding reading action is denoted $r_{C_{AB}}(ENC_{k_{AB}}(d_{AB})))$, if $d_{AB} = \bot$, he sends $\bot$ to the outside through the channel C_{BO} (the corresponding sending action is denoted $s_{C_{BO}}(\bot)$); else if $d_{AB} \neq \bot$, if $d_{R_B} = R_B$, she sends D to the outside through the channel C_{BO} (the corresponding sending action is denoted $s_{C_{BO}}(D)$), else if $d_{R_B} \neq R_B$, he sends $\bot$ to the outside through the channel C_{BO} (the corresponding sending action is denoted $s_{C_{BO}}(\bot)$).

Where $D \in \Delta$, Δ is the set of data.

Alice's state transitions described by $APTC_G$ are as follows.

$$A = Loc_A :: \textstyle\sum_{D\in\Delta} r_{C_{AI}}(D) \cdot A_2$$
$$A_2 = \{k_{AB} = NULL\} \cdot A_3 + \{k_{AB} \neq NULL\} \cdot A_9$$
$$A_3 = s_{C_{AT}}(A, B) \cdot A_4$$
$$A_4 = r_{C_{TA}}(SIGN_{sk_T}(pk_B)) \cdot A_5$$
$$A_5 = de\text{-}sign_{pk_T}(SIGN_{sk_T}(pk_B)) \cdot A_6$$
$$A_6 = rsg_{R_A} \cdot A_7$$
$$A_7 = enc_{sk_P}(A, R_A) \cdot A_8$$
$$A_8 = s_{C_{AB}}(ENC_{sk_P}(A, R_A)) \cdot A_9$$
$$A_9 = r_{C_{BA}}(ENC_{pk_A}(SIGN_{sk_T}(d_{R_A}, k_{AB}, A, B), R_B)) \cdot A_{10}$$
$$A_{10} = \{d_{R_A} = R_A\} \cdot A_{11} + \{d_{R_A} \neq R_A\} \cdot s_{C_{AB}}(ENC_{k_{AB}}(\bot)) \cdot A$$
$$A_{11} = enc_{k_{AB}}(R_B, D) \cdot A_{12}$$
$$A_{12} = s_{C_{AB}}(ENC_{k_{AB}}(R_B, D)) \cdot A$$

Bob's state transitions described by $APTC_G$ are as follows.

$B = Loc_B :: \{k_{AB} = NULL\} \cdot B_1 + \{k_{AB} \neq NULL\} \cdot B_{10}$
$B_1 = r_{C_{AB}}(ENC_{sk_P}(A, R_A)) \cdot B_2$
$B_2 = dec_{sk_B}(ENC_{pk_B}(A, R_A)) \cdot B_3$
$B_3 = s_{C_{BT}}(A, B, ENC_{pk_T}(R_A)) \cdot B_4$
$B_4 = r_{C_{TB}}(SIGN_{sk_T}(pk_A), ENC_{pk_B}(SIGN_{sk_T}(R_A, k_{AB}, A, B))) \cdot B_5$
$B_5 = de\text{-}sign_{pk_T}(SIGN_{sk_T}(pk_A)) \cdot B_6$
$B_6 = dec_{sk_B}(ENC_{pk_B}(SIGN_{sk_T}(R_A, k_{AB}, A, B))) \cdot B_7$
$B_7 = rsg_{R_B} \cdot B_8$
$B_8 = enc_{pk_A}(SIGN_{sk_T}(R_A, k_{AB}, A, B), R_B) \cdot B_9$
$B_9 = s_{C_{BA}}(ENC_{pk_A}(SIGN_{sk_T}(R_A, k_{AB}, A, B), R_B)) \cdot B_{10}$
$B_{10} = r_{C_{AB}}(ENC_{k_{AB}}(d_{AB})) \cdot B_{11}$
$B_{11} = dec_{k_{AB}}(ENC_{k_{AB}}(d_{AB})) \cdot B_{12}$
$B_{12} = \{d_{AB} = \perp\} \cdot s_{C_{BO}}(\perp) \cdot B + \{d_{AB} \neq \perp\} \cdot B_{13}$
$B_{13} = \{d_{R_B} \neq R_B\} \cdot s_{C_{BO}}(\perp)B + \{d_{R_B} = R_B\} \cdot B_{14}$
$B_{14} = s_{C_{BO}}(D) \cdot B$

Trent's state transitions described by $APTC_G$ are as follows.

$T = Loc_T :: r_{C_{AT}}(A, B) \cdot T_2$
$T_2 = sign_{sk_T}(pk_B) \cdot T_3$
$T_3 = s_{C_{TA}}(SIGN_{sk_T}(pk_B)) \cdot T_4$
$T_4 = r_{C_{BT}}(A, B, ENC_{pk_T}(R_A)) \cdot T_5$
$T_5 = dec_{sk_T}(ENC_{pk_T}(R_A)) \cdot T_6$
$T_6 = sign_{sk_T}(pk_A) \cdot T_7$
$T_7 = rsg_{k_{AB}} \cdot T_8$
$T_8 = sign_{sk_T}(R_A, k_{AB}, A, B) \cdot T_9$
$T_9 = enc_{pk_B}(SIGN_{sk_T}(R_A, k_{AB}, A, B)) \cdot T_{10}$
$T_{10} = s_{C_{TB}}(SIGN_{sk_T}(pk_A), ENC_{pk_B}(SIGN_{sk_T}(R_A, k_{AB}, A, B))) \cdot T$

The sending action and the reading action of the same type data through the same channel can communicate with each other, otherwise, will cause a deadlock δ. We define the following communication functions.

$\gamma(r_{C_{AT}}(A, B), s_{C_{AT}}(A, B)) \triangleq c_{C_{AT}}(A, B)$
$\gamma(r_{C_{BT}}(A, B, ENC_{pk_T}(R_A)), s_{C_{AT}}(A, B, ENC_{pk_T}(R_A))) \triangleq c_{C_{AT}}(A, B, ENC_{pk_T}(R_A))$
$\gamma(r_{C_{TA}}(SIGN_{sk_T}(pk_B)), s_{C_{TA}}(SIGN_{sk_T}(pk_B)))$
$\triangleq c_{C_{TA}}(SIGN_{sk_T}(pk_B))$
$\gamma(r_{C_{TB}}(SIGN_{sk_T}(pk_A), ENC_{pk_B}(SIGN_{sk_T}(R_A, k_{AB}, A, B))),$
$s_{C_{TB}}(SIGN_{sk_T}(pk_A), ENC_{pk_B}(SIGN_{sk_T}(R_A, k_{AB}, A, B))))$
$\triangleq c_{C_{TB}}(SIGN_{sk_T}(A, pk_A))$
$\gamma(r_{C_{AB}}(ENC_{sk_P}(A, R_A)), s_{C_{AB}}(ENC_{sk_P}(A, R_A)))$
$\triangleq c_{C_{AB}}(ENC_{sk_P}(A, R_A))$

$$\gamma(r_{C_{BA}}(ENC_{pk_A}(SIGN_{sk_T}(d_{R_A}, k_{AB}, A, B), R_B)),$$
$$s_{C_{BA}}(ENC_{pk_A}(SIGN_{sk_T}(d_{R_A}, k_{AB}, A, B), R_B)))$$
$$\triangleq c_{C_{BA}}(ENC_{pk_A}(SIGN_{sk_T}(d_{R_A}, k_{AB}, A, B), R_B))$$
$$\gamma(r_{C_{AB}}(ENC_{k_{AB}}(R_B, D)), s_{C_{AB}}(ENC_{k_{AB}}(R_B, D))) \triangleq c_{C_{AB}}(ENC_{k_{AB}}(R_B, D))$$

Let all modules be in parallel, then the protocol $A \quad B \quad T$ can be presented by the following process term.

$$\tau_I(\partial_H(\Theta(A \between B \between T))) = \tau_I(\partial_H(A \between B \between T))$$

where $H = \{r_{C_{AT}}(A, B), s_{C_{AT}}(A, B), r_{C_{BT}}(A, B, ENC_{pk_T}(R_A)), s_{C_{AT}}(A, B, ENC_{pk_T}(R_A)),$
$r_{C_{TA}}(SIGN_{sk_T}(pk_B)), s_{C_{TA}}(SIGN_{sk_T}(pk_B)),$
$r_{C_{TB}}(SIGN_{sk_T}(pk_A), ENC_{pk_B}(SIGN_{sk_T}(R_A, k_{AB}, A, B))),$
$s_{C_{TB}}(SIGN_{sk_T}(pk_A), ENC_{pk_B}(SIGN_{sk_T}(R_A, k_{AB}, A, B))),$
$r_{C_{AB}}(ENC_{sk_P}(A, R_A)), s_{C_{AB}}(ENC_{sk_P}(A, R_A)),$
$r_{C_{BA}}(ENC_{pk_A}(SIGN_{sk_T}(d_{R_A}, k_{AB}, A, B), R_B)),$
$s_{C_{BA}}(ENC_{pk_A}(SIGN_{sk_T}(d_{R_A}, k_{AB}, A, B), R_B)),$
$r_{C_{AB}}(ENC_{k_{AB}}(R_B, D)), s_{C_{AB}}(ENC_{k_{AB}}(R_B, D))|D \in \Delta\},$
$I = \{c_{C_{AT}}(A, B), c_{C_{AT}}(A, B, ENC_{pk_T}(R_A)), c_{C_{TA}}(SIGN_{sk_T}(pk_B)),$
$c_{C_{TB}}(SIGN_{sk_T}(A, pk_A)), c_{C_{AB}}(ENC_{sk_P}(A, R_A)),$
$c_{C_{BA}}(ENC_{pk_A}(SIGN_{sk_T}(d_{R_A}, k_{AB}, A, B), R_B)), c_{C_{AB}}(ENC_{k_{AB}}(R_B, D)),$
$\{k_{AB} = NULL\}, \{k_{AB} \neq NULL\}, de\text{-}sign_{pk_T}(SIGN_{sk_T}(pk_B)),$
$rsg_{R_A}, enc_{sk_P}(A, R_A), \{d_{R_A} = R_A\}, \{d_{R_A} \neq R_A\}, enc_{k_{AB}}(R_B, D),$
$dec_{sk_B}(ENC_{pk_B}(A, R_A)), dec_{sk_B}(ENC_{pk_B}(A, R_A)), de\text{-}sign_{pk_T}(SIGN_{sk_T}(pk_A)),$
$dec_{sk_B}(ENC_{pk_B}(SIGN_{sk_T}(R_A, k_{AB}, A, B))), rsg_{R_B}, enc_{pk_A}(SIGN_{sk_T}(R_A, k_{AB}, A, B), R_B),$
$dec_{k_{AB}}(ENC_{k_{AB}}(d_{AB})), \{d_{AB} = \bot\}, \{d_{AB} \neq \bot\},$
$\{d_{R_B} = R_B\}, \{d_{R_B} \neq R_B\}, sign_{sk_T}(pk_B), dec_{sk_T}(ENC_{pk_T}(R_A)),$
$sign_{sk_T}(pk_A), rsg_{k_{AB}}, sign_{sk_T}(R_A, k_{AB}, A, B), enc_{pk_B}(SIGN_{sk_T}(R_A, k_{AB}, A, B))|D \in \Delta\}.$

Then we get the following conclusion on the protocol.

Theorem 9.6. *The Woo-Lam protocol in Fig. 9.7 is secure.*

Proof. Based on the above state transitions of the above modules, by use of the algebraic laws of $APTC_G$, we can prove that

$\tau_I(\partial_H(A \between B \between T)) = \sum_{D\in\Delta}(Loc_A :: r_{C_{AI}}(D) \cdot (Loc_B :: s_{C_{BO}}(\bot) + Loc_B :: s_{C_{BO}}(D))) \cdot \tau_I(\partial_H(A \between B \between T)).$

For the details of proof, please refer to Section 3.10, and we omit it.

That is, the Woo-Lam protocol in Fig. 9.7 $\tau_I(\partial_H(A \between B \between T))$ can exhibit desired external behaviors:

1. For the man-in-the-middle attack, because pk_A and pk_B are signed by Trent, the protocol would be $\tau_I(\partial_H(A \between B \between T)) = \sum_{D\in\Delta}(r_{C_{AI}}(D) \cdot s_{C_{BO}}(\bot)) \cdot \tau_I(\partial_H(A \between B \between T))$, it is desired, the Woo-Lam protocol can be against the man-in-the-middle attack;

2. For replay attack, the using of the random number R_A, R_B, makes that $\tau_I(\partial_H(A \between B \between T)) = \sum_{D\in\Delta}(r_{C_{AI}}(D) \cdot s_{C_{BO}}(\perp)) \cdot \tau_I(\partial_H(A \between B \between T))$, it is desired;
3. Without man-in-the-middle and replay attack, the protocol would be $\tau_I(\partial_H(A \between B \between T)) = \sum_{D\in\Delta}(r_{C_{AI}}(D) \cdot s_{C_{BO}}(D)) \cdot \tau_I(\partial_H(A \between B \between T))$, it is desired;
4. For the unexpected and non-technical leaking of sk_A, sk_B, k_{AB}, or they being not strong enough, or Trent being dishonest, they are out of the scope of analyses of security protocols;
5. For malicious tampering and transmission errors, they are out of the scope of analyses of security protocols.

□

A

A parallel programming language

In this appendix, we design a detailed parallel programming language, abbreviated PPL. PPL includes the four basic structures: sequence, choice, iteration, and parallelism, and also non-determinism, communications (causalities between different parallel branches), and conflictions between different parallel branches. Note that, for the integrity, the semantics of traditional parts are also involved.

In Section A.1, we give the syntax of PPL. We give the operational semantics and denotational semantics in Sections A.2 and A.3, and the relation between them in Section A.4, we give the axiomatic semantics in Section A.5. We discuss non-determinism in Section A.6, communications in Section A.7, and conflictions in Section A.8, and the structuring algorithm in Section A.9.

A.1 Syntax

The syntactic sets of PPL are as follows.

- Numbers set **N**, with positive, negative integers, and zero, and $n, m \in \mathbf{N}$;
- Truth values set **T**, with values {**true**, **false**};
- Storage locations **Loc**, and $X, Y \in \mathbf{Loc}$;
- Arithmetic expressions **Aexp**, and $a \in \mathbf{Aexp}$;
- Boolean expressions **Bexp**, and $b \in \mathbf{Bexp}$;
- Commands **Com**, and $c \in \mathbf{Com}$.

The formation rules of PPL are:

For **Aexp**:

$$a ::= n \mid X \mid a_0 + a_1 \mid a_0 - a_1 \mid a_0 \times a_1$$

For **Bexp**:

$$b ::= \mathbf{true} \mid \mathbf{false} \mid a_0 = a_1 \mid a_0 \leq a_1 \mid \neg b \mid b_0 \wedge b_1 \mid b_0 \vee b_1$$

For **Com**:

$$c ::= \mathbf{skip} \mid X := a \mid c_0; c_1 \mid \mathbf{if}\ b\ \mathbf{then}\ c_0\ \mathbf{else}\ c_1 \mid \mathbf{while}\ b\ \mathbf{do}\ c \mid c_0 \parallel c_1$$

We see that the syntax of PPL is almost same to traditional imperative language, except for the explicit parallel operator $\parallel$ in **Com**.

A.2 Operational semantics

The set of states Σ are composed of $\sigma : \mathbf{Loc} \to \mathbf{N}$, so, $\sigma(X)$ is the values of storage location X under the state σ. For more about operational semantics, please refer to Plotkin's book [20].

In this section, we give the operational semantics of PPL.

A.2.1 Operational rules of Aexp

$\langle a, \sigma \rangle$ is called the configuration of arithmetic expression a, while $\langle a, \sigma \rangle \to n$ denotes that the value of a is n under the state σ.

The evaluation rule of integer n:

$$\langle n, \sigma \rangle \to n$$

The evaluation rule of storage location X:

$$\langle X, \sigma \rangle \to \sigma(X)$$

The evaluation rule of sums:

$$\frac{\langle a_0, \sigma \rangle \to n_0 \quad \langle a_1, \sigma \rangle \to n_1}{\langle a_0 + a_1, \sigma \rangle \to n}, n = n_0 + n_1$$

The evaluation rule of subtractions:

$$\frac{\langle a_0, \sigma \rangle \to n_0 \quad \langle a_1, \sigma \rangle \to n_1}{\langle a_0 - a_1, \sigma \rangle \to n}, n = n_0 - n_1$$

The evaluation rule of products:

$$\frac{\langle a_0, \sigma \rangle \to n_0 \quad \langle a_1, \sigma \rangle \to n_1}{\langle a_0 \times a_1, \sigma \rangle \to n}, n = n_0 \times n_1$$

Then we can define the following equivalence $\sim$ as follows.

Definition A.1 (Equivalence of operational semantics for arithmetic expressions). $a_0 \sim a_1$ iff $\forall n \in \mathbf{N}, \forall \sigma \in \Sigma. \langle a_0, \sigma \rangle \to n \Leftrightarrow \langle a_1, \sigma \rangle \to n$.

A.2.2 Operational rules of Bexp

The evaluation rule of **true**:

$$\langle \mathbf{true}, \sigma \rangle \to \mathbf{true}$$

The evaluation rule of **false**:

$$\langle \mathbf{false}, \sigma \rangle \to \mathbf{false}$$

The evaluation rule of equality:

$$\frac{\langle a_0, \sigma\rangle \to n_0 \quad \langle a_1, \sigma\rangle \to n_1}{\langle a_0 = a_1, \sigma\rangle \to \mathbf{true}}, n_0 = n_1$$

$$\frac{\langle a_0, \sigma\rangle \to n_0 \quad \langle a_1, \sigma\rangle \to n_1}{\langle a_0 = a_1, \sigma\rangle \to \mathbf{false}}, n_0 \neq n_1$$

The evaluation rule of $\leq$:

$$\frac{\langle a_0, \sigma\rangle \to n_0 \quad \langle a_1, \sigma\rangle \to n_1}{\langle a_0 \leq a_1, \sigma\rangle \to \mathbf{true}}, n_0 \leq n_1$$

$$\frac{\langle a_0, \sigma\rangle \to n_0 \quad \langle a_1, \sigma\rangle \to n_1}{\langle a_0 \leq a_1, \sigma\rangle \to \mathbf{false}}, n_0 \geq n_1$$

The evaluation rule of $\neg$:

$$\frac{\langle b, \sigma\rangle \to \mathbf{true}}{\langle \neg b, \sigma\rangle \to \mathbf{false}}$$

$$\frac{\langle b, \sigma\rangle \to \mathbf{false}}{\langle \neg b, \sigma\rangle \to \mathbf{true}}$$

The evaluation rule of $\wedge$:

$$\frac{\langle b_0, \sigma\rangle \to t_0 \quad \langle b_1, \sigma\rangle \to t_1}{\langle b_0 \wedge b_1, \sigma\rangle \to t}, t = \mathbf{true}, t_0 \equiv \mathbf{true} \wedge t_1 \equiv \mathbf{true}; t = \mathbf{false}, \mathit{otherwise}$$

The evaluation rule of $\vee$:

$$\frac{\langle b_0, \sigma\rangle \to t_0 \quad \langle b_1, \sigma\rangle \to t_1}{\langle b_0 \vee b_1, \sigma\rangle \to t}, t = \mathbf{true}, t_0 \equiv \mathbf{true} \vee t_1 \equiv \mathbf{true}; t = \mathbf{false}, \mathit{otherwise}$$

Then we can define the following equivalence $\sim$ as follows.

Definition A.2 (Equivalence of operational semantics for boolean expressions). $b_0 \sim b_1$ iff $\forall t \in \mathbf{T}, \forall \sigma \in \Sigma.\langle b_0, \sigma\rangle \to t \Leftrightarrow \langle b_1, \sigma\rangle \to t$.

A.2.3 Operational rules for Com

$\langle c, \sigma\rangle$ denotes the configuration of the command c, which means that the command c executes under the state σ. And $\langle c\sigma\rangle \to \sigma'$ means that the command c executing under the state σ evolves to the state σ'. For $n \in \mathbf{N}$ and $X \in \mathbf{Loc}$, $\sigma[n/X]$ denotes using n to replace the contents of X under the state σ.

The execution rule of **skip**:

$$\langle \mathbf{skip}, \sigma\rangle \to \sigma$$

The execution rule of assignment:

$$\frac{\langle a, \sigma\rangle \to n}{\langle X := a, \sigma\rangle \to \sigma[n/X]}$$

The execution rule of sequence:

$$\frac{\langle c_0, \sigma \rangle \rightarrow \sigma'}{\langle c_0; c_1, \sigma \rangle \rightarrow \langle c_1, \sigma' \rangle}$$

The execution rule of choice:

$$\frac{\langle b, \sigma \rangle \rightarrow \textbf{true} \quad \langle c_0, \sigma \rangle \rightarrow \sigma'}{\langle \textbf{if } b \textbf{ then } c_0 \textbf{ else } c_1, \sigma \rangle \rightarrow \sigma'}$$
$$\frac{\langle b, \sigma \rangle \rightarrow \textbf{false} \quad \langle c_1, \sigma \rangle \rightarrow \sigma'}{\langle \textbf{if } b \textbf{ then } c_0 \textbf{ else } c_1, \sigma \rangle \rightarrow \sigma'}$$

The execution rule of iteration:

$$\frac{\langle b, \sigma \rangle \rightarrow \textbf{false}}{\langle \textbf{while } b \textbf{ do } c, \sigma \rangle \rightarrow \sigma}$$
$$\frac{\langle b, \sigma \rangle \rightarrow \textbf{true} \quad \langle c, \sigma \rangle \rightarrow \sigma'' \quad \langle \textbf{while } b \textbf{ do } c, \sigma'' \rangle \rightarrow \sigma'}{\langle \textbf{while } b \textbf{ do } c, \sigma \rangle \rightarrow \sigma'}$$

The execution rule of parallelism:

$$\frac{\langle c_1, \sigma \rangle \rightarrow \sigma' \quad \langle c_0, \sigma \rangle \rightarrow \sigma''}{\langle c_0 \parallel c_1, \sigma \rangle \rightarrow \sigma' \uplus \sigma''}$$

where $\sigma' \uplus \sigma''$ are the final states after c_0 and c_1 execute simultaneously.

Note that, for true concurrency, there are still three other properties should be processed: communications, conflictions, and race conditions (we leave them to the next section).

1. Communication is occurring between two atomic communicating commands, which can be defined by a communication function $\gamma(c_0, c_1) \triangleq c(c_0, c_1)$. Communications can be implemented by several ways: share storage locations, invocation of functions by values, or network communications. For a pure imperative programming language, we only consider the case of share storage locations, so, there is no need to define new communicating commands. So, two commands in communication are with a relation $\gamma(c_0, c_1) \triangleq c(c_0, c_1)$, but rules of $c_0 \parallel c_1$ are still the same to the above ones. We will discuss the general communications in Section A.7;
2. Confliction may have two forms: one exists as the condition rules define; the other may exist among the parallel branches, which must be eliminated. But the elimination of confliction existing in parallel branches may lead to non-deterministic results (refer to [8] for details). For simplicity, we assume that the programs written by PPL at this time have no conflictions, because a program with the conflictions existing among parallel branches has an equal program without conflicts. That is, the conflictions can be eliminated and structured, and we will discuss the elimination of conflictions between parallel branches in Section A.8;

3. Race condition may exist in two parallel commands, for example, they are all executing assignment to a same storage location. Two parallel commands in race condition must be executed serially. We should define new rules for race condition, but, these rules also lead to non-deterministic results. So, we also assume that the programs written by PPL deal with this situation and the non-deterministic execution is eliminated. In fact, we can write $c_0 \parallel (\textbf{skip}; c_1)$ or $(\textbf{skip}; c_0) \parallel c_1$, or put c_0, c_1 in a condition, where c_0 and c_1 are in race condition. But, indeed, the above parallelism is still can be used widely in non-sharing memory computation (distributed computing), or non-racing of sharing memory computation. For the general form of non-determinism, we will discuss in Sections A.6 and A.7.

We can get the following propositions. Where $\sim$ is an equivalence relation on commands by the definition, and Σ is the set of states:

Definition A.3 (Equivalence of operational semantics for commands). $c_0 \sim c_1$ iff $\forall \sigma, \sigma' \in \Sigma, \langle c_0, \sigma \rangle \to \sigma' \Leftrightarrow \langle c_1, \sigma \rangle \to \sigma'$

Proposition A.4. $c_0 \parallel c_1 \sim c_1 \parallel c_0$, *for* $c_0, c_1 \in \textbf{Com}$.

Proof. By use of the transition rules of $\parallel$, we can get the following derivations of $c_0 \parallel c_1$ for $\forall \sigma \in \Sigma$:

$$\frac{\langle c_1, \sigma \rangle \to \sigma' \quad \langle c_0, \sigma \rangle \to \sigma''}{\langle c_0 \parallel c_1, \sigma \rangle \to \sigma' \uplus \sigma''}$$

And we can get the following derivations of $c_1 \parallel c_0$ for $\forall \sigma \in \Sigma$:

$$\frac{\langle c_0, \sigma \rangle \to \sigma' \quad \langle c_1, \sigma \rangle \to \sigma''}{\langle c_1 \parallel c_0, \sigma \rangle \to \sigma' \uplus \sigma''}$$

So, it is obvious that $c_0 \parallel c_1 \sim c_1 \parallel c_0$, for $c_0, c_1 \in \textbf{Com}$, as desired. □

Proposition A.5. $(c_0 \parallel c_1) \parallel c_2 \sim c_0 \parallel (c_1 \parallel c_2)$, *for* $c_0, c_1, c_2 \in \textbf{Com}$.

Proof. By use of the transition rules of $\parallel$, we can get the following derivations of $(c_0 \parallel c_1) \parallel c_2$ for $\forall \sigma \in \Sigma$:

$$\frac{\langle c_0, \sigma \rangle \to \sigma' \quad \langle c_1, \sigma \rangle \to \sigma'' \quad \langle c_2, \sigma \rangle \to \sigma'''}{\langle (c_0 \parallel c_1) \parallel c_2, \sigma \rangle \to \sigma' \uplus \sigma'' \uplus \sigma'''}$$

And we can get the following derivations of $c_0 \parallel (c_1 \parallel c_2)$ for $\forall \sigma \in \Sigma$:

$$\frac{\langle c_0, \sigma \rangle \to \sigma' \quad \langle c_1, \sigma \rangle \to \sigma'' \quad \langle c_2, \sigma \rangle \to \sigma'''}{\langle c_0 \parallel (c_1 \parallel c_2), \sigma \rangle \to \sigma' \uplus \sigma'' \uplus \sigma'''}$$

So, it is obvious that $(c_0 \parallel c_1) \parallel c_2 \sim c_0 \parallel (c_1 \parallel c_2)$, for $c_0, c_1, c_2 \in \textbf{Com}$, as desired. □

Proposition A.6. $(\textbf{\textit{if}}\ b\ \textbf{\textit{then}}\ c_0\ \textbf{\textit{else}}\ c_1) \parallel c_2 \sim \textbf{\textit{if}}\ b\ \textbf{\textit{then}}\ c_0 \parallel c_2\ \textbf{\textit{else}}\ c_1 \parallel c_2$, *for* $c_0, c_1, c_2 \in \textbf{Com}$.

Proof. By use of the transition rules of choice and $\|$, we can get the following derivations of $(\textbf{if } b \textbf{ then } c_0 \textbf{ else } c_1) \parallel c_2$:

$$\frac{\langle b,\sigma\rangle \to \textbf{true} \quad \langle c_0,\sigma\rangle \to \sigma' \quad \langle c_2,\sigma\rangle \to \sigma''}{\langle(\textbf{if } b \textbf{ then } c_0 \textbf{ else } c_1) \parallel c_2,\sigma\rangle \to \sigma' \uplus \sigma''}$$

$$\frac{\langle b,\sigma\rangle \to \textbf{false} \quad \langle c_1,\sigma\rangle \to \sigma' \quad \langle c_2,\sigma\rangle \to \sigma''}{\langle(\textbf{if } b \textbf{ then } c_0 \textbf{ else } c_1) \parallel c_2,\sigma\rangle \to \sigma' \uplus \sigma''}$$

And we can get the following derivations of $\textbf{if } b \textbf{ then } c_0 \parallel c_2 \textbf{ else } c_1 \parallel c_2$:

$$\frac{\langle b,\sigma\rangle \to \textbf{true} \quad \langle c_0,\sigma\rangle \to \sigma' \quad \langle c_2,\sigma\rangle \to \sigma''}{\langle(\textbf{if } b \textbf{ then } c_0 \parallel c_2 \textbf{ else } c_1 \parallel c_2,\sigma\rangle \to \sigma' \uplus \sigma''}$$

$$\frac{\langle b,\sigma\rangle \to \textbf{false} \quad \langle c_1,\sigma\rangle \to \sigma' \quad \langle c_2,\sigma\rangle \to \sigma''}{\langle(\textbf{if } b \textbf{ then } c_0 \parallel c_2 \textbf{ else } c_1 \parallel c_2,\sigma\rangle \to \sigma' \uplus \sigma''}$$

So, it is obvious that $(\textbf{if } b \textbf{ then } c_0 \textbf{ else } c_1) \parallel c_2 \sim \textbf{if } b \textbf{ then } c_0 \parallel c_2 \textbf{ else } c_1 \parallel c_2$, for $c_0, c_1, c_2 \in$ **Com**, as desired. □

Proposition A.7. *For* $c_0, c_1, c_2, c_3 \in$ **Com**,

1. $(c_0; c_1) \parallel c_2 \sim (c_0 \parallel c_2); c_1$;
2. $(c_0; c_1) \parallel (c_2; c_3) \sim (c_0 \parallel c_2); (c_1 \parallel c_3)$.

Proof. (1) By use of the transition rules of sequence and $\|$, we can get the following derivations of $(c_0; c_1) \parallel c_2$:

$$\frac{\langle c_0,\sigma\rangle \to \sigma' \quad \langle c_2,\sigma\rangle \to \sigma''}{\langle(c_0; c_1) \parallel c_2,\sigma\rangle \to \langle c_1,\sigma' \uplus \sigma''\rangle}$$

And we can get the following derivations of $(c_0 \parallel c_2); c_1$:

$$\frac{\langle c_0,\sigma\rangle \to \sigma' \quad \langle c_2,\sigma\rangle \to \sigma''}{\langle(c_0 \parallel c_2); c_1,\sigma\rangle \to \langle c_1,\sigma' \uplus \sigma''\rangle}$$

So, it is obvious that $(c_0; c_1) \parallel c_2 \sim (c_0 \parallel c_2); c_1$, for $c_0, c_1, c_2 \in$ **Com**, as desired.

(2) By use of the transition rules of sequence and $\|$, we can get the following derivations of $(c_0; c_1) \parallel (c_2; c_3)$:

$$\frac{\langle c_0,\sigma\rangle \to \sigma' \quad \langle c_2,\sigma\rangle \to \sigma''}{\langle(c_0; c_1) \parallel (c_2; c_3),\sigma\rangle \to \langle c_1 \parallel c_3,\sigma' \uplus \sigma''\rangle}$$

And we can get the following derivations of $(c_0 \parallel c_2); (c_1 \parallel c_3)$:

$$\frac{\langle c_0,\sigma\rangle \to \sigma' \quad \langle c_2,\sigma\rangle \to \sigma''}{\langle(c_0 \parallel c_2); (c_1 \parallel c_3),\sigma\rangle \to \langle c_1 \parallel c_3,\sigma' \uplus \sigma''\rangle}$$

So, it is obvious that $(c_0; c_1) \parallel (c_2; c_3) \sim (c_0 \parallel c_2); (c_1 \parallel c_3)$, for $c_0, c_1, c_2, c_3 \in$ **Com**, as desired. □

Proposition A.8. *$c \parallel$ **skip** $\sim c$, for $c \in$* **Com**.

Proof. By use of the transition rules of **skip** and $\parallel$, we can get the following derivations of $c \parallel$ **skip**:

$$\frac{\langle c, \sigma\rangle \to \sigma' \quad \langle \textbf{skip}, \sigma\rangle \to \sigma}{c \parallel \textbf{skip}, \sigma\rangle \to \sigma' \uplus \sigma}$$

And it is obvious that:

$$\frac{\langle c, \sigma\rangle \to \sigma'}{c, \sigma\rangle \to \sigma'}$$

For $\sigma' \uplus \sigma = \sigma'$, it is obvious that $c \parallel$ **skip** $\sim c$, for $c \in$ **Com**, as desired. □

Lemma A.9. *For $c_0, c_1 \in$* **Com**,

1. $c_0 \parallel c_1 \sim c_0 \parallel (\textbf{skip}; c_1) \sim c_0; c_1;$
2. $c_0 \parallel c_1 \sim (\textbf{skip}; c_0) \parallel c_1 \sim c_1; c_0.$

Proof. It is obvious by Proposition A.7 and A.8. □

From Lemma A.9, we can see that the execution orders of $c_0 \parallel c_1$ cause non-determinism, they can be executed in any sequential order or in parallel simultaneously. But, without race condition, the final states after the execution of $c_0 \parallel c_1$ are deterministic.

A.3 Denotational semantics

Denotational semantics can be used to describe the semantics of PPL. For more about denotational semantics, please refer to Mosses's book [21].

In this section, we give the denotational semantics for PPL.

A.3.1 Denotational semantics of Aexp

We define the denotational semantics of **Aexp** as $\mathcal{A}$: **Aexp** $\to (\Sigma \to \mathbf{N})$. The concrete denotational semantics of **Aexp** are following.

$\mathcal{A}[\![n]\!] = \{(\sigma, n) | \sigma \in \Sigma\}$
$\mathcal{A}[\![X]\!] = \{(\sigma, \sigma(X)) | \sigma \in \Sigma\}$
$\mathcal{A}[\![a_0 + a_1]\!] = \{(\sigma, n_0 + n_1) | (\sigma, n_0) \in \mathcal{A}[\![a_0]\!] \& (\sigma, n_1) \in \mathcal{A}[\![a_1]\!]\}$
$\mathcal{A}[\![a_0 - a_1]\!] = \{(\sigma, n_0 - n_1) | (\sigma, n_0) \in \mathcal{A}[\![a_0]\!] \& (\sigma, n_1) \in \mathcal{A}[\![a_1]\!]\}$
$\mathcal{A}[\![a_0 \times a_1]\!] = \{(\sigma, n_0 \times n_1) | (\sigma, n_0) \in \mathcal{A}[\![a_0]\!] \& (\sigma, n_1) \in \mathcal{A}[\![a_1]\!]\}$

A.3.2 Denotational semantics of Bexp

We define the denotational semantics of **Bexp** as $\mathcal{B}$: **Bexp** $\to (\Sigma \to \mathbf{T})$. The concrete denotational semantics of **Bexp** are following.

$\mathcal{B}[\![\mathbf{true}]\!] = \{(\sigma, \mathbf{true})|\sigma \in \Sigma\}$
$\mathcal{B}[\![\mathbf{false}]\!] = \{(\sigma, \mathbf{false})|\sigma \in \Sigma\}$
$\mathcal{B}[\![a_0 = a_1]\!] = \{(\sigma, \mathbf{true})|\sigma \in \Sigma \& \mathcal{A}[\![a_0]\!]\sigma = \mathcal{A}[\![a_1]\!]\sigma\} \cup \{(\sigma, \mathbf{false})|\sigma \in \Sigma \& \mathcal{A}[\![a_0]\!]\sigma \neq \mathcal{A}[\![a_1]\!]\sigma\}$
$\mathcal{B}[\![a_0 \leq a_1]\!] = \{(\sigma, \mathbf{true})|\sigma \in \Sigma \& \mathcal{A}[\![a_0]\!]\sigma \leq \mathcal{A}[\![a_1]\!]\sigma\} \cup \{(\sigma, \mathbf{false})|\sigma \in \Sigma \& \mathcal{A}[\![a_0]\!]\sigma \nleq \mathcal{A}[\![a_1]\!]\sigma\}$
$\mathcal{B}[\![\neg b]\!] = \{(\sigma, \neg_T t)|\sigma \in \Sigma \& (\sigma, t) \in \mathcal{B}[\![b]\!]\}$
$\mathcal{B}[\![b_0 \wedge b_1]\!] = \{(\sigma, t_0 \wedge_T t_1)|\sigma \in \Sigma \& (\sigma, t_0) \in \mathcal{B}[\![b_0]\!] \& (\sigma, t_1) \in \mathcal{B}[\![b_1]\!]\}$
$\mathcal{B}[\![b_0 \vee b_1]\!] = \{(\sigma, t_0 \vee_T t_1)|\sigma \in \Sigma \& (\sigma, t_0) \in \mathcal{B}[\![b_0]\!] \& (\sigma, t_1) \in \mathcal{B}[\![b_1]\!]\}$

A.3.3 Denotational semantics of Com

We define the denotational semantics of **Com** as $\mathcal{C} : \mathbf{Com} \to (\Sigma \to \Sigma)$. The denotational semantics of **Com** are following.

$\mathcal{C}[\![\mathbf{skip}]\!] = \{(\sigma, \sigma)|\sigma \in \Sigma\}$
$\mathcal{C}[\![X := a]\!] = \{(\sigma, \sigma[n/X])|\sigma \in \Sigma \& n = \mathcal{A}[\![a]\!]\sigma\}$
$\mathcal{C}[\![c_0; c_1]\!] = \mathcal{C}[\![c_1]\!] \circ \mathcal{C}[\![c_0]\!]$
$\mathcal{C}[\![\text{if } b \text{ then } c_0 \text{ else } c_1]\!] = \{(\sigma, \sigma')|\mathcal{B}[\![b]\!]\sigma = \mathbf{true} \& (\sigma, \sigma') \in \mathcal{C}[\![c_0]\!]\} \cup$
$\{(\sigma, \sigma')|\mathcal{B}[\![b]\!]\sigma = \mathbf{false} \& (\sigma, \sigma') \in \mathcal{C}[\![c_1]\!]\}$
$\mathcal{C}[\![\text{while } b \text{ do } c]\!] = fix(\Gamma)$

with $\Gamma(\phi) = \{(\sigma, \sigma')|\mathcal{B}[\![b]\!]\sigma = \mathbf{true} \& (\sigma, \sigma') \in \phi \circ \mathcal{C}[\![c]\!]\} \cup \{(\sigma, \sigma')|\mathcal{B}[\![b]\!]\sigma = \mathbf{false}\}$
$\mathcal{C}[\![c_0 \parallel c_1]\!] = \mathcal{C}[\![c_0]\!]\} \cup \{\mathcal{C}[\![c_1]\!]$

We can get the following propositions.

Proposition A.10. $\mathcal{C}[\![c_0 \parallel c_1]\!] = \mathcal{C}[\![c_1 \parallel c_0]\!]$, *for* $c_0, c_1 \in \mathbf{Com}$.

Proof. By the definition of the denotation of $\parallel$, we can get:

$\mathcal{C}[\![c_0 \parallel c_1]\!] = \mathcal{C}[\![c_0]\!] \cup \mathcal{C}[\![c_1]\!]$
$\mathcal{C}[\![c_1 \parallel c_0]\!] = \mathcal{C}[\![c_1]\!] \cup \mathcal{C}[\![c_0]\!]$

So, $\mathcal{C}[\![c_0 \parallel c_1]\!] = \mathcal{C}[\![c_1 \parallel c_0]\!]$, for $c_0, c_1 \in \mathbf{Com}$, as desired. □

Proposition A.11. $\mathcal{C}[\![(c_0 \parallel c_1) \parallel c_2]\!] = \mathcal{C}[\![c_0 \parallel (c_1 \parallel c_2)]\!]$, *for* $c_0, c_1, c_2 \in \mathbf{Com}$.

Proof. By the definition of the denotation of $\parallel$, we can get:

$\mathcal{C}[\![(c_0 \parallel c_1) \parallel c_2]\!] = (\mathcal{C}[\![c_0]\!] \cup \mathcal{C}[\![c_1]\!]) \cup \mathcal{C}[\![c_2]\!]$
$\mathcal{C}[\![c_0 \parallel (c_1 \parallel c_2)]\!] = \mathcal{C}[\![c_0]\!] \cup (\mathcal{C}[\![c_1]\!] \cup \mathcal{C}[\![c_2]\!])$
$\mathcal{C}[\![(c_0 \parallel c_1) \parallel c_2]\!] = \mathcal{C}[\![c_0 \parallel (c_1 \parallel c_2)]\!]$, for $c_0, c_1, c_2 \in \mathbf{Com}$, as desired. □

Proposition A.12. $\mathcal{C}[\![(\textit{\textbf{if}}\ b\ \textit{\textbf{then}}\ c_0\ \textit{\textbf{else}}\ c_1) \parallel c_2]\!] = \mathcal{C}[\![\textit{\textbf{if}}\ b\ \textit{\textbf{then}}\ c_0 \parallel c_2\ \textit{\textbf{else}}\ c_1 \parallel c_2]\!]$, *for* $c_0, c_1, c_2 \in$ **Com**.

Proof. By the definition of the denotation of choice and $\|$, we can get:

$\mathcal{C}[\![(\textbf{if } b \textbf{ then } c_0 \textbf{ else } c_1) \parallel c_2]\!] = \{(\sigma,\sigma')|\mathcal{B}[\![b]\!]\sigma = \textbf{true}\&(\sigma,\sigma') \in \mathcal{C}[\![c_0]\!]\} \cup \{(\sigma,\sigma')|\mathcal{B}[\![b]\!]\sigma = \textbf{false}\&(\sigma,\sigma') \in \mathcal{C}[\![c_1]\!]\} \cup \mathcal{C}[\![c_2]\!]$

$\mathcal{C}[\![\textbf{if } b \textbf{ then } c_0 \parallel c_2 \textbf{ else } c_1 \parallel c_2]\!] = \{(\sigma,\sigma')|\mathcal{B}[\![b]\!]\sigma = \textbf{true}\&(\sigma,\sigma') \in \mathcal{C}[\![c_0]\!] \cup \mathcal{C}[\![c_2]\!]\} \cup \{(\sigma,\sigma')|\mathcal{B}[\![b]\!]\sigma = \textbf{false}\&(\sigma,\sigma') \in \mathcal{C}[\![c_1]\!] \cup \mathcal{C}[\![c_2]\!]\}$

So, $\mathcal{C}[\![(\textbf{if } b \textbf{ then } c_0 \textbf{ else } c_1) \parallel c_2]\!] = \mathcal{C}[\![\textbf{if } b \textbf{ then } c_0 \parallel c_2 \textbf{ else } c_1 \parallel c_2]\!]$, for $c_0, c_1, c_2 \in \textbf{Com}$, as desired. □

Proposition A.13. *For* $c_0, c_1, c_2, c_3 \in \textbf{Com}$,

1. $\mathcal{C}[\![(c_0; c_1) \parallel c_2]\!] = \mathcal{C}[\![(c_0 \parallel c_2); c_1]\!]$;
2. $\mathcal{C}[\![(c_0; c_1) \parallel (c_2; c_3)]\!] = \mathcal{C}[\![(c_0 \parallel c_2); (c_1 \parallel c_3)]\!]$.

Proof. (1) By the definition of the denotation of sequence and $\|$, we can get:

$\mathcal{C}[\![(c_0; c_1) \parallel c_2]\!] = (\mathcal{C}[\![c_1]\!] \circ \mathcal{C}[\![c_0]\!]) \cup \mathcal{C}[\![c_2]\!]$
$\mathcal{C}[\![(c_0 \parallel c_2); c_1]\!] = \mathcal{C}[\![c_1]\!] \circ (\mathcal{C}[\![c_0]\!] \cup \mathcal{C}[\![c_2]\!])$

So, $\mathcal{C}[\![(c_0; c_1) \parallel c_2]\!] = \mathcal{C}[\![(c_0 \parallel c_2); c_1]\!]$, as desired.

(2) By the definition of the denotation of sequence and $\|$, we can get:

$\mathcal{C}[\![(c_0; c_1) \parallel (c_2; c_3)]\!] = (\mathcal{C}[\![c_1]\!] \circ \mathcal{C}[\![c_0]\!]) \cup (\mathcal{C}[\![c_3]\!] \circ \mathcal{C}[\![c_2]\!]$
$\mathcal{C}[\![(c_0 \parallel c_2); (c_1 \parallel c_3)]\!] = (\mathcal{C}[\![c_1]\!] \cup \mathcal{C}[\![c_3]\!]) \circ (\mathcal{C}[\![c_2]\!] \cup \mathcal{C}[\![c_0]\!]$

So, $\mathcal{C}[\![(c_0; c_1) \parallel (c_2; c_3)]\!] = \mathcal{C}[\![(c_0 \parallel c_2); (c_1 \parallel c_3)]\!]$, as desired. □

Proposition A.14. $\mathcal{C}[\![c \parallel \textbf{skip}]\!] = \mathcal{C}[\![c]\!]$, *for* $c \in \textbf{Com}$.

Proof. By the definition of the denotation of **skip** and $\|$, we can get:

$\mathcal{C}[\![c \parallel \textbf{skip}]\!] = \mathcal{C}[\![c]\!] \cup \mathcal{C}[\![\textbf{skip}]\!]$

So, $\mathcal{C}[\![c \parallel \textbf{skip}]\!] = \mathcal{C}[\![c]\!]$, for $c \in \textbf{Com}$, as desired. □

Lemma A.15. *For* $c_0, c_1 \in \textbf{Com}$,

1. $c_0 \parallel c_1 \sim c_0 \parallel (\textbf{skip}; c_1) \sim c_0; c_1$;
2. $c_0 \parallel c_1 \sim (\textbf{skip}; c_0) \parallel c_1 \sim c_1; c_0$.

Proof. It is obvious by Proposition A.13 and A.14. □

A.4 Relations between operational and denotational semantics

The operational and denotational semantics still agree on the evaluation of **Aexp** and **Bexp**, we do not repeat any more, please refer to [22] for details. We will prove the agreement of the case **Com** as follows.

Lemma A.16. *For all commands c and states σ, σ',*

$$\langle c, \sigma\rangle \to \sigma' \Rightarrow (\sigma, \sigma') \in \mathcal{C}[\![c]\!]$$

Proof. We will use rule-induction on the operational semantics of commands. For $c \in \mathbf{Com}$ and $\sigma, \sigma' \in \Sigma$, define

$$P(c, \sigma, \sigma') \Leftrightarrow_{def} (\sigma, \sigma') \in \mathcal{C}[\![c]\!]$$

We will show P is closed under the rules for the execution of commands, and we will only prove the new case of $\|$, other commands please refer to [22] for details.

Recall the transition rules of $\|$ are:

$$\frac{\langle c_1, \sigma\rangle \to \sigma' \quad \langle c_0, \sigma\rangle \to \sigma''}{\langle c_0 \parallel c_1, \sigma\rangle \to \sigma' \uplus \sigma''}$$

Assume that

$$\langle c_0, \sigma\rangle \to \sigma' \& P(c_0, \sigma, \sigma') \& \langle c_1, \sigma\rangle \to \sigma'' \& P(c_1, \sigma, \sigma'')$$

From the meaning of P, we can get that

$$\mathcal{C}[\![c_0]\!]\sigma = \sigma' \text{ and } \mathcal{C}[\![c_1]\!]\sigma = \sigma''$$

We can get

$$\mathcal{C}[\![c_0 \parallel c_1]\!]\sigma = \sigma' \uplus \sigma''$$

which means that $P(c_0 \parallel c_1, \sigma, \sigma' \uplus \sigma'')$ holds for the consequence of the rule, and is closed under this rule. □

Theorem A.17. *For all commands c and states σ, σ',*

$$\mathcal{C}[\![c]\!] = \{(\sigma, \sigma') | \langle c, \sigma\rangle \to \sigma'\}$$

Proof. Lemma A.16 gives the $\Leftarrow$ direction of proof, we only need to prove

$$(\sigma, \sigma') \in \mathcal{C}[\![c]\!] \Rightarrow \langle c, \sigma\rangle \to \sigma'$$

It is sufficient to induct on the structure of command c, we only prove the new case of $c \equiv c_0 \parallel c_1$, other cases please refer to [22] for details.

Suppose $(\sigma, \sigma' \uplus \sigma'') \in \mathcal{C}[\![c]\!]$. Then there are some states, such that $(\sigma, \sigma') \in \mathcal{C}[\![c_0]\!]$, $(\sigma, \sigma'') \in \mathcal{C}[\![c_1]\!]$. By the hypothesis of c_0, c_1, we get

$$\langle c_0, \sigma\rangle \to \sigma' \text{ and } \langle c_1, \sigma\rangle \to \sigma''$$

So, $\langle c_0 \parallel c_1, \sigma\rangle \to \sigma' \uplus \sigma''$, as desired. □

A.5 Axiomatic semantics

In this section, we give an axiomatic semantics for PPL by extending the Hoare rules with parallelism.

A.5.1 Extended Hoare rules for parallelism

PPL should be extended to support assertion.

For **Aexp**, it should be extended to:

$$a ::= n \mid X \mid i \mid a_0 + a_1 \mid a_0 - a_1 \mid a_0 \times a_1$$

where i ranges over integer variables, **Intvar**.

For **Bexp**, it should be extended to support boolean assertion:

$$A ::= \mathbf{true} | \mathbf{false} | a_0 = a_1 | a_0 \leq a_1 | \neg A | A_0 \wedge A_1 | A_0 \vee A_1 | A_0 \Rightarrow A_1 | \forall i.A | \exists i.A$$

And the formation rule of **Com** is maintained:

$$c ::= \mathbf{skip} \mid X := a \mid c_0; c_1 \mid \mathbf{if}\ b\ \mathbf{then}\ c_0\ \mathbf{else}\ c_1 \mid \mathbf{while}\ b\ \mathbf{do}\ c \mid c_0 \parallel c_1$$

Note that, **Com** contains a parallel composition $\parallel$.

The denotational semantics should also contain an interpretation I.

The full extended Hoare rules are as follows.

Rule for **skip**:

$$\{A\}\mathbf{skip}\{A\}$$

Rule for assignments:

$$\{B[a/X]\}X := a\{B\}$$

Rule for sequencing:

$$\frac{\{A\}c_0\{C\} \quad \{C\}c_1\{B\}}{\{A\}c_0; c_1\{B\}}$$

Rule for conditionals:

$$\frac{\{A \wedge b\}c_0\{B\} \quad \{A \wedge \neg b\}c_1\{B\}}{\{A\}\mathbf{if}\ b\ \mathbf{then}\ c_0\ \mathbf{else}\ c_1\{B\}}$$

Rule for while loops:

$$\frac{\{A \wedge b\}c\{A\}}{\{A\}\mathbf{while}\ b\ \mathbf{do}\ c\{A \wedge \neg b\}}$$

Rule for consequence:

$$\frac{\models (A \Rightarrow A') \quad \{A'\}c\{B'\} \quad \models (B' \Rightarrow B)}{\{A\}c\{B\}}$$

Rule for parallelism:

$$\frac{\{A\}c_0\{C\} \quad \{C\}c_1\{B\} \quad \{A\}c_1\{D\} \quad \{D\}c_0\{B\}}{\{A\}c_0 \parallel c_1\{B\}}$$

A.5.2 Soundness of the extended Hoare rules

We can prove that each rule is sound by the following soundness theorem.

Theorem A.18. *Let* $\{A\}c\{B\}$ *be a partial correctness assertion, if* $\vdash \{A\}c\{B\}$, *then* $\models \{A\}c\{B\}$.

Proof. It is sufficient to induct on the rule to prove each rule is valid. We only prove the new case of $\parallel$ rule, other cases please refer to [22] for details.

Assume that $\models \{A\}c_0\{C\}$ and $\models \{C\}c_1\{B\}$, and $\models \{A\}c_1\{D\}$ and $\models \{D\}c_0\{B\}$. Let I be an interpretation. Suppose $\sigma \models^I A$. Then $\mathcal{C}[\![c_0]\!]\sigma \models^I C$ and $\mathcal{C}[\![c_1]\!](\mathcal{C}[\![c_0]\!]\sigma) \models^I B$, and $\mathcal{C}[\![c_1]\!]\sigma \models^I D$ and $\mathcal{C}[\![c_0]\!](\mathcal{C}[\![c_1]\!]\sigma) \models^I B$. Hence, $\models \{A\}c_0 \parallel c_1\{B\}$, as desired. □

A.5.3 Completeness of the extended Hoare rules

Gödel's Incompleteness Theorem implies that the extended Hoare rules are incomplete. We prove the relative completeness in the sense of Cook.

Theorem A.19. *PPL extended with assertion is expressive.*

Proof. It is sufficient to induct on the structure of command c, such that for all assertions B there is an assertion $w[\![c, B]\!]$, for all interpretations I

$$wp^I[\![c, B]\!] = w[\![c, B]\!]^I$$

We only prove the new case of parallelism $c \equiv c_0 \parallel c_1$, other cases please refer to [22] for details.

Inductively define $w[\![c_0 \parallel c_1, B]\!] \equiv w[\![c_0, w[\![c_1, B]\!]]\!]$ and $w[\![c_0 \parallel c_1, B]\!] \equiv w[\![c_1, w[\![c_0, B]\!]]\!]$. Then, for $\sigma \in \Sigma$ and any interpretation I,

$\sigma \in wp^I[\![c_0 \parallel c_1, B]\!]$ iff $\mathcal{C}[\![c_0 \parallel c_1]\!]\sigma \models^I B$
iff $\mathcal{C}[\![c_1]\!](\mathcal{C}[\![c_0]\!]\sigma) \models^I B$ and $\mathcal{C}[\![c_0]\!](\mathcal{C}[\![c_1]\!]\sigma) \models^I B$
iff $\mathcal{C}[\![c_0]\!]\sigma \models^I w[\![c_1, B]\!]$ and $\mathcal{C}[\![c_1]\!]\sigma \models^I w[\![c_0, B]\!]$
iff $\sigma \models^I w[\![c_0, w[\![c_1, B]\!]]\!]$ and $\sigma \models^I w[\![c_1, w[\![c_0, B]\!]]\!]$
iff $\sigma \models^I w[\![c_0 \parallel c_1, B]\!]$. □

Lemma A.20. *For* $c \in$ **Com** *and* B *is an assertion, let* $w[\![c, B]\!]$ *be an assertion expressing the weakest precondition with* $w[\![c, B]\!]^I = wp^I[\![c, B]\!]$. *Then*

$$\vdash \{w[\![c, B]\!]\}c\{B\}$$

Proof. It suffices to induct on the structure of commands c, we only prove the new case of parallelism $c \equiv c_0 \parallel c_1$, other cases please refer to [22] for details.

For $\sigma \in \Sigma$ and any interpretation I,

$\sigma \models^I w[\![c_0 \parallel c_1, B]\!]$ iff $\mathcal{C}[\![c_0 \parallel c_1]\!]\sigma \models^I B$
iff $\mathcal{C}[\![c_1]\!](\mathcal{C}[\![c_0]\!]\sigma) \models^I B$ and $\mathcal{C}[\![c_0]\!](\mathcal{C}[\![c_1]\!]\sigma) \models^I B$
iff $\mathcal{C}[\![c_0]\!]\sigma \models^I w[\![c_1, B]\!]$ and $\mathcal{C}[\![c_1]\!]\sigma \models^I w[\![c_0, B]\!]$
iff $\sigma \models^I w[\![c_0, w[\![c_1, B]\!]]\!]$ and $\sigma \models^I w[\![c_1, w[\![c_0, B]\!]]\!]$.

We get $\vdash \{w[\![c_0, w[\![c_1, B]\!]]\!]\}c_0 \parallel c_1\{B\}$ and $\vdash \{w[\![c_1, w[\![c_0, B]\!]]\!]\}c_0 \parallel c_1\{B\}$.
Hence, by the consequence rule, we obtain

$$\vdash \{w[\![c_0 \parallel c_1, B]\!]\}c_0 \parallel c_1\{B\}$$ □

Theorem A.21. *For any partial correctness assertion* $\{A\}c\{B\}$, *if* $\models \{A\}c\{B\}$, *then* $\vdash \{A\}c\{B\}$.

Proof. Suppose $\models \{A\}c\{B\}$, then $\vdash \{w[\![c, B]\!]\}c\{B\}$ where $w[\![c, B]\!]^I = wp^I[\![c, B]\!]$ for any interpretation I (by the above Lemma). Hence, $\models (A \Rightarrow w[\![c, B]\!])$, we obtain $\vdash \{A\}c\{B\}$. □

A.6 Non-determinism

The guarded commands can make the use of non-determinism more rigorous. To provide each command with a conditional guard, it is useful to eliminate the uncontrolled non-determinism.

The syntax of guarded commands is also composed of **Aexp**, **Bexp**, and **Com**, and the syntax of **Aexp** and **Bexp** are the same as those of PPL in Section A.1. And the formation rules for the command c and guarded commands gc are as follows.

$$c ::= \mathbf{skip} \;\mid\; \mathbf{abort} \;\mid\; X := a \;\mid\; c_0; c_1 \;\mid\; \mathbf{if}\ gc\ \mathbf{fi} \;\mid\; \mathbf{do}\ gc\ \mathbf{od}$$
$$gc ::= b \to c \;\mid\; gc_0 \Box gc_1$$

where $gc_0 \Box gc_1$ is the alternative construct of gc_0 and gc_1.

The operational rules of commands:

$$\langle \mathbf{skip}, \sigma\rangle \to \sigma$$

$$\frac{\langle a, \sigma\rangle \to n}{\langle X := a, \sigma\rangle \to \sigma[n/X]}$$

$$\frac{\langle c_0, \sigma\rangle \to \sigma'}{\langle c_0; c_1, \sigma\rangle \to \langle c_1, \sigma'\rangle} \qquad \frac{\langle c_0, \sigma\rangle \to \langle c_0', \sigma'\rangle}{\langle c_0; c_1, \sigma\rangle \to \langle c_0'; c_1, \sigma'\rangle}$$

$$\frac{\langle gc, \sigma\rangle \to \langle c, \sigma'\rangle}{\langle \mathrm{if}\ gc\ \mathrm{fi}, \sigma\rangle \to \langle c, \sigma'\rangle}$$

$$\frac{\langle gc, \sigma\rangle \to \mathbf{fail}}{\langle \mathrm{do}\ gc\ \mathrm{od}, \sigma\rangle \to \sigma} \qquad \frac{\langle gc, \sigma\rangle \to \langle c, \sigma'\rangle}{\langle \mathrm{do}\ gc\ \mathrm{od}, \sigma\rangle \to \langle c; \mathrm{do}\ gc\ \mathrm{od}, \sigma'\rangle}$$

The operational rules of guarded commands:

$$\frac{\langle b, \sigma\rangle \to \mathbf{true}}{\langle b \to c, \sigma\rangle \to \langle c, \sigma\rangle}$$

$$\frac{\langle gc_0, \sigma\rangle \to \langle c, \sigma'\rangle}{\langle gc_0 \Box gc_1, \sigma\rangle \to \langle c, \sigma'\rangle} \quad \frac{\langle gc_1, \sigma\rangle \to \langle c, \sigma'\rangle}{\langle gc_0 \Box gc_1, \sigma\rangle \to \langle c, \sigma'\rangle}$$

$$\frac{\langle b, \sigma\rangle \to \mathbf{false}}{\langle b \to c, \sigma\rangle \to \mathbf{fail}} \quad \frac{\langle gc_0, \sigma\rangle \to \mathbf{false} \quad \langle gc_1, \sigma\rangle \to \mathbf{false}}{\langle gc_0 \Box gc_1, \sigma\rangle \to \mathbf{fail}}$$

A.7 Communications

In this section, we extend communicating processes with the support for true concurrency.

The syntax of PPL is also composed of **Aexp**, **Bexp**, the names of communication channels $\alpha, \beta, \gamma \in$ **Chan**, and **Com**, and the syntax of **Aexp** and **Bexp** are the same as those of PPL in Section A.1. And the formation rules for the command c and guarded commands gc are as follows.

$$c ::= \mathbf{skip}|\mathbf{abort}|X := a \quad |\alpha?X|\alpha!a|c_0; c_1|\mathbf{if}\ gc\ \mathbf{fi}|\mathbf{do}\ gc\ \mathbf{od}|c_0 \parallel c_1|c \setminus \alpha$$

$$gc ::= b \to c \quad | \quad b \wedge \alpha?X \to c \quad | \quad b \wedge \alpha!a \quad | \quad gc_0 \Box gc_1$$

where $gc_0 \Box gc_1$ is the alternative construct of gc_0 and gc_1.

The operational rules of commands:

$$\langle \mathbf{skip}, \sigma\rangle \to \sigma$$

$$\frac{\langle a, \sigma\rangle \to n}{\langle X := a, \sigma\rangle \to \sigma[n/X]}$$

$$\langle \alpha?X, \sigma\rangle \xrightarrow{\alpha?n} \sigma[n/X]$$

$$\frac{\langle a, \sigma\rangle \to n}{\langle \alpha!a, \sigma\rangle \xrightarrow{\alpha!n} \sigma}$$

$$\frac{\langle c_0, \sigma\rangle \to \sigma'}{\langle c_0; c_1, \sigma\rangle \to \langle c_1, \sigma'\rangle} \quad \frac{\langle c_0, \sigma\rangle \to \langle c_0', \sigma'\rangle}{\langle c_0; c_1, \sigma\rangle \to \langle c_0'; c_1, \sigma'\rangle}$$

$$\frac{\langle gc, \sigma\rangle \to \langle c, \sigma'\rangle}{\langle \mathbf{if}\ gc\ \mathbf{fi}, \sigma\rangle \to \langle c, \sigma'\rangle}$$

$$\frac{\langle gc, \sigma\rangle \to \mathbf{fail}}{\langle \mathbf{do}\ gc\ \mathbf{od}, \sigma\rangle \to \sigma} \quad \frac{\langle gc, \sigma\rangle \to \langle c, \sigma'\rangle}{\langle \mathbf{do}\ gc\ \mathbf{od}, \sigma\rangle \to \langle c; \mathbf{do}\ gc\ \mathbf{od}, \sigma'\rangle}$$

$$\frac{\langle c_0, \sigma\rangle \xrightarrow{\lambda} \langle c_0', \sigma'\rangle \quad c_0 \% c_1}{\langle c_0 \parallel c_1, \sigma\rangle \xrightarrow{\lambda} \langle c_0' \parallel c_1, \sigma'\rangle}$$

$$\frac{\langle c_1, \sigma\rangle \xrightarrow{\lambda} \langle c_1', \sigma'\rangle \quad c_0 \% c_1}{\langle c_0 \parallel c_1, \sigma\rangle \xrightarrow{\lambda} \langle c_0 \parallel c_1', \sigma'\rangle}$$

$$\frac{\langle c_0, \sigma\rangle \xrightarrow{\lambda_1} \langle c_0', \sigma'\rangle \quad \langle c_1, \sigma\rangle \xrightarrow{\lambda_2} \langle c_1', \sigma''\rangle}{\langle c_0 \parallel c_1, \sigma\rangle \xrightarrow{\{\lambda_1, \lambda_2\}} \langle c_0' \parallel c_1', \sigma' \uplus \sigma''\rangle}$$

$$\frac{\langle c_0,\sigma\rangle \xrightarrow{\alpha!n} \langle c_0',\sigma\rangle \quad \langle c_1,\sigma\rangle \xrightarrow{\alpha?n} \langle c_1',\sigma'\rangle}{\langle c_0 \parallel c_1,\sigma\rangle \xrightarrow{\gamma_\alpha(n)} \langle c_0' \parallel c_1',\sigma'\rangle}$$

$$\frac{\langle c_0,\sigma\rangle \xrightarrow{\alpha?n} \langle c_0',\sigma'\rangle \quad \langle c_1,\sigma\rangle \xrightarrow{\alpha!n} \langle c_1',\sigma\rangle}{\langle c_0 \parallel c_1,\sigma\rangle \xrightarrow{\gamma_\alpha(n)} \langle c_0' \parallel c_1',\sigma'\rangle}$$

$$\frac{\langle c,\sigma\rangle \xrightarrow{\lambda} \langle c',\sigma'\rangle}{\langle c\setminus\alpha,\sigma\rangle \xrightarrow{\lambda} \langle c'\setminus\alpha,\sigma'\rangle} \text{ if } \lambda \equiv \alpha?n \text{ and } \lambda \equiv \alpha!n \text{ do not hold.}$$

Here $c_0\%c_1$ denotes that c_0 and c_1 are in race condition.
The operational rules of guarded commands:

$$\frac{\langle b,\sigma\rangle \to \mathbf{true}}{\langle b\to c,\sigma\rangle \to \langle c,\sigma\rangle}$$

$$\frac{\langle gc_0,\sigma\rangle \to \langle c,\sigma'\rangle}{\langle gc_0 \square gc_1,\sigma\rangle \to \langle c,\sigma'\rangle} \quad \frac{\langle gc_1,\sigma\rangle \to \langle c,\sigma'\rangle}{\langle gc_0 \square gc_1,\sigma\rangle \to \langle c,\sigma'\rangle}$$

$$\frac{\langle b,\sigma\rangle \to \mathbf{false}}{\langle b\to c,\sigma\rangle \to \mathbf{fail}} \quad \frac{\langle gc_0,\sigma\rangle \to \mathbf{false} \quad \langle gc_1,\sigma\rangle \to \mathbf{false}}{\langle gc_0 \square gc_1,\sigma\rangle \to \mathbf{fail}}$$

$$\frac{\langle b,\sigma\rangle \to \mathbf{false}}{\langle b\wedge\alpha?X\to c,\sigma\rangle \to \mathbf{fail}}$$

$$\frac{\langle b,\sigma\rangle \to \mathbf{false}}{\langle b\wedge\alpha!X\to c,\sigma\rangle \to \mathbf{fail}}$$

$$\frac{\langle b,\sigma\rangle \to \mathbf{true}}{\langle b\wedge\alpha?X\to c,\sigma\rangle \xrightarrow{\alpha?n} \langle c,\sigma[n/X]\rangle}$$

$$\frac{\langle b,\sigma\rangle \to \mathbf{true} \quad \langle a,\sigma\rangle \to n}{\langle b\wedge\alpha!a\to c,\sigma\rangle \xrightarrow{\alpha!n} \langle c,\sigma\rangle}$$

Note that, for true concurrency, we can see that communications, conflictions, and race conditions are solved as follows.

1. Communication is explicitly supported in PPL, the two communicating commands $\alpha?X$ and $\alpha!X$ will merge to one communication command $\gamma_\alpha(X)$, and the unstructured communication will be eliminated;
2. Since each command is with a guard, the conflictions among actions can be achieved by set the commands with exclusive guards;
3. As the operational rules state, the actions in parallel in race condition must be executed sequentially and will cause the non-deterministic execution order. Though the execution order is non-deterministic, by setting appropriate guards to the parallel commands, the final execution configuration can be deterministic.

We can get the following propositions. Where $\sim$ is an equivalence relation on commands by the definition, where Σ is the set of states:

Definition A.22 (Equivalence of operational semantics for commands). $c_0 \sim c_1$ iff $\forall \sigma, \sigma' \in \Sigma, \langle c_0, \sigma\rangle \rightarrow \sigma' \Leftrightarrow \langle c_1, \sigma\rangle \rightarrow \sigma'$

Proposition A.23. $c_0 \parallel c_1 \sim c_1 \parallel c_0$, *for* $c_0, c_1 \in \mathbf{Com}$.

Proof. By use of the transition rules of $\parallel$, we can get the following derivations of $c_0 \parallel c_1$ for $\forall \sigma \in \Sigma$:

$$\frac{\langle c_0, \sigma\rangle \xrightarrow{c_0} \sigma'' \quad \langle c_1, \sigma''\rangle \xrightarrow{c_1} \sigma'}{\langle c_0 \parallel c_1, \sigma\rangle \xrightarrow{c_0;c_1} \sigma'}$$

$$\frac{\langle c_1, \sigma\rangle \xrightarrow{c_1} \sigma''' \quad \langle c_0, \sigma'''\rangle \xrightarrow{(} c_0)\sigma'}{\langle c_0 \parallel c_1, \sigma\rangle \xrightarrow{(} c_1; c_0)\sigma'}$$

$$\frac{\langle c_1, \sigma\rangle \xrightarrow{c_1} \sigma' \quad \langle c_0, \sigma\rangle \xrightarrow{c_0} \sigma''}{\langle c_0 \parallel c_1, \sigma\rangle \xrightarrow{\{c_0,c_1\}} \sigma' \uplus \sigma''}$$

And we can get the following derivations of $c_1 \parallel c_0$ for $\forall \sigma \in \Sigma$:

$$\frac{\langle c_1, \sigma\rangle \xrightarrow{c_1} \sigma''' \quad \langle c_0, \sigma'''\rangle \xrightarrow{c_0} \sigma'}{\langle c_1 \parallel c_0, \sigma\rangle \xrightarrow{c_1;c_0} \sigma'}$$

$$\frac{\langle c_0, \sigma\rangle \xrightarrow{c_0} \sigma'' \quad \langle c_1, \sigma''\rangle \xrightarrow{c_1} \sigma'}{\langle c_1 \parallel c_0, \sigma\rangle \xrightarrow{c_0;c_1} \sigma'}$$

$$\frac{\langle c_0, \sigma\rangle \xrightarrow{c_0} \sigma' \quad \langle c_1, \sigma\rangle \xrightarrow{c_1} \sigma''}{\langle c_1 \parallel c_0, \sigma\rangle \xrightarrow{\{c_0,c_1\}} \sigma' \uplus \sigma''}$$

So, it is obvious that $c_0 \parallel c_1 \sim c_1 \parallel c_0$, for $c_0, c_1 \in \mathbf{Com}$, as desired. □

Proposition A.24. $(c_0 \parallel c_1) \parallel c_2 \sim c_0 \parallel (c_1 \parallel c_2)$, *for* $c_0, c_1, c_2 \in \mathbf{Com}$.

Proof. By use of the transition rules of $\parallel$, we can get the following derivations of $(c_0 \parallel c_1) \parallel c_2$ for $\forall \sigma \in \Sigma$:

$$\frac{\langle c_0, \sigma\rangle \xrightarrow{c_0} \sigma' \quad \langle c_1, \sigma\rangle \xrightarrow{c_1} \sigma'' \quad \langle c_2, \sigma\rangle \xrightarrow{c_2} \sigma'''}{\langle (c_0 \parallel c_1) \parallel c_2, \sigma\rangle \xrightarrow{\{c_0,c_1,c_2\}} \sigma' \uplus \sigma'' \uplus \sigma'''}$$

And we can get the following derivations of $c_0 \parallel (c_1 \parallel c_2)$ for $\forall \sigma \in \Sigma$:

$$\frac{\langle c_0, \sigma\rangle \xrightarrow{c_0} \sigma' \quad \langle c_1, \sigma\rangle \xrightarrow{c_1} \sigma'' \quad \langle c_2, \sigma\rangle \xrightarrow{c_2} \sigma'''}{\langle c_0 \parallel (c_1 \parallel c_2), \sigma\rangle \xrightarrow{\{c_0,c_1,c_2\}} \sigma' \uplus \sigma'' \uplus \sigma'''}$$

So, it is obvious that $(c_0 \parallel c_1) \parallel c_2 \sim c_0 \parallel (c_1 \parallel c_2)$, for $c_0, c_1, c_2 \in \mathbf{Com}$, as desired.
For the case of the parallel commands in race condition, we omit it. □

Proposition A.25. *For* $c_0, c_1, c_2, c_3 \in \mathbf{Com}$,

1. $(c_0; c_1) \parallel c_2 \sim (c_0 \parallel c_2); c_1$;
2. $(c_0; c_1) \parallel (c_2; c_3) \sim (c_0 \parallel c_2); (c_1 \parallel c_3)$.

Proof. (1) By use of the transition rules of sequence and $\parallel$, we can get the following derivations of $(c_0; c_1) \parallel c_2$:

$$\frac{\langle c_0, \sigma\rangle \xrightarrow{c_0} \sigma' \quad \langle c_2, \sigma\rangle \xrightarrow{c_2} \sigma''}{\langle (c_0; c_1) \parallel c_2, \sigma\rangle \xrightarrow{\{c_0, c_2\}} \langle c_1, \sigma' \uplus \sigma''\rangle}$$

And we can get the following derivations of $(c_0 \parallel c_2); c_1$:

$$\frac{\langle c_0, \sigma\rangle \xrightarrow{c_0} \sigma' \quad \langle c_2, \sigma\rangle \xrightarrow{c_2} \sigma''}{\langle (c_0 \parallel c_2); c_1, \sigma\rangle \xrightarrow{\{c_0, c_2\}} \langle c_1, \sigma' \uplus \sigma''\rangle}$$

So, it is obvious that $(c_0; c_1) \parallel c_2 \sim (c_0 \parallel c_2); c_1$, for $c_0, c_1, c_2 \in \mathbf{Com}$, as desired.

(2) By use of the transition rules of sequence and $\parallel$, we can get the following derivations of $(c_0; c_1) \parallel (c_2; c_3)$:

$$\frac{\langle c_0, \sigma\rangle \xrightarrow{c_0} \sigma' \quad \langle c_2, \sigma\rangle \xrightarrow{c_2} \sigma''}{\langle (c_0; c_1) \parallel (c_2; c_3), \sigma\rangle \xrightarrow{\{c_0, c_2\}} \langle c_1 \parallel c_3, \sigma' \uplus \sigma''\rangle}$$

And we can get the following derivations of $(c_0 \parallel c_2); (c_1 \parallel c_3)$:

$$\frac{\langle c_0, \sigma\rangle \xrightarrow{c_0} \sigma' \quad \langle c_2, \sigma\rangle \xrightarrow{c_2} \sigma''}{\langle (c_0 \parallel c_2); (c_1 \parallel c_3), \sigma\rangle \xrightarrow{\{c_0, c_2\}} \langle c_1 \parallel c_3, \sigma' \uplus \sigma''\rangle}$$

So, it is obvious that $(c_0; c_1) \parallel (c_2; c_3) \sim (c_0 \parallel c_2); (c_1 \parallel c_3)$, for $c_0, c_1, c_2, c_3 \in \mathbf{Com}$, as desired. □

Proposition A.26. $c \parallel \mathbf{skip} \sim c$, *for* $c \in \mathbf{Com}$.

Proof. By use of the transition rules of **skip** and $\parallel$, we can get the following derivations of $c \parallel \mathbf{skip}$:

$$\frac{\langle c, \sigma\rangle \xrightarrow{c} \sigma' \quad \langle \mathbf{skip}, \sigma\rangle \rightarrow \sigma}{c \parallel \mathbf{skip}, \sigma\rangle \xrightarrow{c} \sigma' \uplus \sigma}$$

And it is obvious that:

$$\frac{\langle c, \sigma\rangle \xrightarrow{c} \sigma'}{c, \sigma\rangle \xrightarrow{c} \sigma'}$$

For $\sigma' \uplus \sigma = \sigma'$, it is obvious that $c \parallel \mathbf{skip} \sim c$, for $c \in \mathbf{Com}$, as desired. □

Lemma A.27. *For* $c_0, c_1 \in \mathbf{Com}$,

1. $c_0 \parallel c_1 \sim c_0 \parallel (\mathbf{skip}; c_1) \sim c_0; c_1$;
2. $c_0 \parallel c_1 \sim (\mathbf{skip}; c_0) \parallel c_1 \sim c_1; c_0$.

Proof. It is obvious by Proposition A.25 and A.26. □

From Lemma A.27, we can see that the execution orders of $c_0 \parallel c_1$ cause non-determinism, they can be executed in any sequential order or in parallel simultaneously. But, with the assistance of guards, the final states after the execution of $c_0 \parallel c_1$ can be deterministic.

Proposition A.28. *For* $c, c_0, c_1 \in \mathbf{Com}$,

1. $\alpha!n \parallel \alpha?n \sim \gamma_\alpha(n)$;
2. $(c; \alpha!n) \parallel \alpha?n \sim c; \gamma_\alpha(n)$;
3. $(c; \alpha?n) \parallel \alpha!n \sim c; \gamma_\alpha(n)$;
4. $(c_0; \alpha!n) \parallel (c_1; \alpha?n) \sim c_0 \parallel c_1; \gamma_\alpha(n)$;
5. $(c_0; \alpha?n) \parallel (c_1; \alpha!n) \sim c_0 \parallel c_1; \gamma_\alpha(n)$.

Proof. By use of the transition rules of $\parallel$, we can prove the above equations. □

From Proposition A.28, we can see that communications among parallel branches are eliminated and the parallelism is structured.

A.8 Conflictions

Corresponding to Fig. 2.2, the program is:

(1; (if (b) then (2; 3))) ∥ (4; (if (¬ b) then (5; 6)))

Corresponding to Fig. 2.8, the program is:

if (b) then (1; 2; 3) ∥ 4 else 1 ∥ (4; 5; 6)

We can prove that the above two programs are equivalent, and the confliction between parallel branches is eliminated and the parallelism is structured.

A.9 Structuring algorithm

By PPL, we know that the truly concurrent graph can be structured. As an implementation-independent language, the structuring algorithm of PPL can be designed as follows:

1. Input the unstructured truly concurrent graph;
2. By use of PPL, implement the graph as a program;
3. By use of the laws of PPL, structure the program.

References

[1] M. Danelutto, M. Torquati, P. Kilpatrick, A green perspective on structured parallel programming, in: Euromicro International Conference on Parallel, Distributed and Network-Based Processing IEEE, 2015, pp. 430–437.
[2] M. Mccool, J. Reinders, A. Robison, Structured parallel programming: patterns for efficient computation, in: Structured Parallel Programming, 2012, pp. 614–627.
[3] G. Winskel, M. Nielsen, Models for concurrency, in: Samson Abramsky, Dov M. Gabbay, Thomas S.E. Maibaum (Eds.), Handbook of Logic in Computer Science, vol. 4, Clarendon Press, Oxford, UK, 1995.
[4] M. Nielsen, G.D. Plotkin, G. Winskel, Petri nets, event structures and domains, part I, Theoretical Computer Science 13 (1981) 85–108.
[5] G. Winskel, Event structures, in: Wilfried Brauer, Wolfgang Reisig, Grzegorz Rozenberg (Eds.), Petri Nets: Applications and Relationships to Other Models of Concurrency, in: Lecture Notes in Computer Science, vol. 255, Springer, Berlin, 1985, pp. 325–392.
[6] T. Elrad, N. Francez, Decomposition of distributed programs into communication-closed layers, Science of Computer Programming 2 (3) (1982) 155–173.
[7] W. Yuan, Y. Sun, "SEQ OF PAR" structured parallel programming, Chinese Journal of Computers 20 (1997) 230–237.
[8] Y. Wang, Algebraic laws for true concurrency, Manuscript, arXiv:1611.09035, 2016.
[9] E.W. Dijkstra, Go to statement considered harmful, Communications of the ACM 11 (3) (1968) 147–148.
[10] O.J. Dahl, E.W. Dijkstra, C.A.R. Hoare, Structured programming, Programming and Computer Software 18 (7) (1972) 179–185.
[11] M. Cole, Why structured parallel programming matters, in: European Conference on Parallel Processing, Springer, Berlin, Heidelberg, 2004.
[12] L.V. Kale, N. Chrisochoides, J. Kohl, K. Yelick, Concurrency-based approaches to parallel programming, Office of scientific and technical information technical reports, 1995.
[13] R.D. Cosmo, Z. Li, V. Martin, Parallel programming with the OcamlP3l system, with applications to coupling numerical codes, https://www.dicosmo.org/Articles/2004-ClementDiCosmoMartinVodickaWeisZheng.pdf, 2003.
[14] J. Darlington, Y. Guo, H.W. To, J. Yang, Parallel skeletons for structured composition, ACM SIGPLAN Notices 30 (8) (1995) 19–28.
[15] M. McCool, A.D. Robison, J. Reinders, Structured Parallel Programming: Patterns for Efficient Computation, Elsevier, 2012.
[16] A.D. Kshemkalyani, M. Singhal, Distributed Computing: Principles, Algorithms, and Systems, Cambridge University Press, 2011.
[17] J. Wiedermann, Parallel Turing machines. TR: RUU-CS-84-11, 1984.
[18] S.A. Cook, Towards a complexity theory of synchronous parallel computation, L'enseignement Mathématique XXVII 27 (2) (1980) 75–100.
[19] R.E. Prather, Structured Turing machines, Information and Control 35 (1977) 159–171.
[20] G.D. Plotkin, A structural approach to operational semantics, Journal of Logic and Algebraic Programming 60–61 (2004) 17–139.
[21] P.D. Mosses, Denotational semantics, in: Handbook of Theoretical Computer Science, vol. B, MIT Press, 1991.
[22] G. Winskel, The Formal Semantics of Programming Languages, MIT Press, 1993.
[23] F. Moller, The importance of the left merge operator in process algebras, in: M.S. Paterson (Ed.), Proceedings 17th Colloquium on Automata, Languages and Programming (ICALP'90), Warwick, in: LNCS, vol. 443, Springer, 1990, pp. 752–764.

[24] K.A. Bartlett, R.A. Scantlebury, P.T. Wilkinson, A note on reliable full-duplex transmission over half-duplex links, Communications of the ACM 12 (5) (1969) 260–261.
[25] F.W. Vaandrager, Verification of two communication protocols by means of process algebra, Report CS-R8608, CWI, Amsterdam, 1986.

Index

Printed in the United States
by Baker & Taylor Publisher Services